STUDY GUIDE WITH READINGS

TO ACCOMPANY PAPALIA/OLDS

HUMAN DEVELOPMENT

SIXTH EDITION

THOMAS L. CRANDELL

Broome Community College

GEORGE R. BIEGER

Indiana University of Pennsylvania

MCGRAW-HILL, INC.

New York St. Louis San Francisco Auckland Bogota
Caracas Lisbon London Madrid Mexico Milan
Montreal New Delhi Paris San Juan
Singapore Sydney Tokyo Toronto

Study Guide with Readings
to Accompany
Papalia/Olds:
HUMAN DEVELOPMENT

Copyright © 1995, 1992, 1989, 1986 by McGraw-Hill, Inc. All rights reserved. Previously published under the title of *Study Guide to Accompany Papalia/Olds: Human Development.* Copyright © 1981 by McGraw-Hill, Inc. All rights reserved. Printed in the United States of America. Except as permitted under the United States Copyright Act of 1976, no part of this publication may be reproduced or distributed in any form or by any means, or stored in a data base or retrieval system, without the prior written permission of the publisher.

This book is printed on recycled paper
containig 10% postconsumer waste.

2 3 4 5 6 7 8 9 0 SEM SEM 9 0 9 8 7 6 5

ISBN 0-07-048761-8

The editors were Jane Vaicunas and Beth Kaufman;
the production supervisor was Leroy Young.
Semline, Inc., was printer and binder.

CONTENTS

PERMISSIONS AND CREDITS

Jane Adams, "Whose Life Is It, Anyway?" *Good Housekeeping*, Copyright © February 1994, by Jane Adams from *I'm Still Your Mother: How to Get Along with your Grown Up Children for the Rest of Your Life*. Delacorte Press. Reprinted by permission.

Gerald W. Bracey, "Culture, Science, and the Concept of Child," *Phi Delta Kappan*, May 1990. Copyright © 1990, Phi Delta Kappan, Inc. Reprinted by permission.

Diane Brad, "Good Touch, Bad Touch, How to Guard Against Sex Abuse," *MacLean's Magazine*, Copyright © March 1, 1993, Maclean Hunter Ltd. Reprinted by permission.

Diane Cole, "When a Child Dies," *Parents*, Copyright © March 1994, Gruner + Jahr USA Publishing. Reprinted by permission.

Paula Dranov, "New Hope for Couples Who Can't Conceive," *Redbook*, Copyright © August 1993, The Hearst Corporation. All rights reserved. Reprinted by permission of the author.

Robert N. Emde, "The Horror! The Horror! Reflections on our Culture of Violence and Its Implications for Early Development and Morality," *Psychiatry*, Vol. 56. Copyright © February 1993. Reprinted by permission.

Ellen Goodman, "There Will Never Be Another You...We Think," *Boston Globe*, Copyright © November 3, 1993, The Boston Globe Company. Reprinted by permission.

Bill Hewitt, "Turning Back the Clock," *People*, Copyright © January 24, 1994, Time, Inc. All rights reserved. Reprinted by permission.

Betty Holcomb, "What Your Baby Really Knows," *Working Mother*, Copyright © March 1992, WORKING MOTHER Magazine. Reprinted by permission.

Kenneth Labich, "The New Unemployed," *Fortune*, Copyright © March 8, 1993. Time, Inc. All rights reserved. Reprinted by permission.

J. Ronald Lally, "What NO Really Means," *Parents*, Copyright © March 1994, Gruner + Jahr USA Publishing. Reprinted by permission.

Richard M. Lerner and Cheryl K. Olson, "The Imaginary Audience: Why Every Preteen Sees Herself as the Center of the World," *Parents*, Copyright © February 1994, Gruner + Jahr USA Publishing. Reprinted by permission.

Connie Leslie with Nina Biddle, Debra Rosenberg, and Joe Wayne, "Girls Will Be Girls," *Newsweek*, © August 2, 1993. Newsweek, Inc. All rights reserved. Reprinted by permission.

Michael Lipson, "What Do You Say to a Child with AIDS?" *Hastings Center Report 23*, No. 2, Copyright © 1993. Reprinted by permission.

Julia Martin, "Health Risks and Heredity," *Child*, Copyright © February 1994. Reprinted by permission.

Nancy Samalin and Patricia McCormick, "Who, Me? Honesty Comes Easy When It's Safe for Kids to Tell the Truth," *Parents*, Copyright © April 1994, Gruner + Jahr USA Publishing. Reprinted by permission.

Brian Steinberg, "Me and My Work Ethic," *USA Weekend*, Copyright © March 11, 1994. Reprinted by permission of the author.

Susan Champlin Taylor, "The End of Retirement," *Modern Maturity*, Copyright © Oct.-Nov. 1993. American Association of Retired Persons. Reprinted by permission.

PREFACE

TO THE STUDENT

This *Study Guide with Readings*, which accompanies *Human Development*, Sixth Edition, by Papalia and Olds, is designed to help you master the material presented in the textbook.

As educational psychologists, we recognize that people differ with respect to their learning styles and preferences. Consequently, we encourage you to continue using the study methods and techniques which you have found successful. At the same time, however, you should recognize that each new learning experience brings with it a unique set of objectives, vocabulary, and applications. We have written and organized the *Study Guide* with the express purpose of making the important facts, terms, and concepts discussed in the textbook easier for you to identify, learn, and recall.

Also, we believe that if you follow our suggestions for using the *Study Guide* and for studying and taking tests, you will improve your performance on classroom quizzes and avoid--or at least reduce--the anxiety which often debilitates students at exam time.

While the *Study Guide* is designed to help you organize and learn information more effectively, remember that there is no "fast track" to learning. Learning is the result of motivation, organization, and hard work. The student who wants high grades and has the diligence to study for them should find this *Study Guide* especially helpful. In addition, the student who has been away from formal schooling for some time will find that the *Study Guide* provides an easy-to-use framework for identifying and learning important material in the text, organizing study time, and preparing for tests and examinations with more confidence.

Enjoy your course in human development!

ORGANIZATION OF THE STUDY GUIDE

Each chapter in the *Study Guide* corresponds to the same chapter in the textbook. The chapters are all organized according to the following scheme.

Introduction

The first section--the introduction--provides you with a brief overview of the main topics discussed in the textbook chapter.

Use the introduction to familiarize yourself with some of the important issues in the chapter and to organize your thinking in preparation for learning the major facts and concepts that will be presented.

Chapter Outline

The chapter outline gives all the headings and subheadings within the text chapter and thus shows you the complete structure, or framework, of the text material. Enough space is left between entries for you to make brief notes.

The chapter outlines will help you preview each chapter, will clarify the relationship among topics and subtopics, and will later be useful for reviewing.

Key Terms

This section of key terms provides you with a list of the basic vocabulary that you should learn in each chapter. It is designed to help you focus on the most important terminology--which reflects the most important information and concepts.

The key terms are listed in alphabetical order, and space is provided for you to make short notes of definitions or examples. Note that for each key term, a page number in the text is cited; this is where the definition or explanation is located. Once you have made notes of definitions, examples, or both, the key terms sections will be an excellent reference to review for examinations.

Note that when key terms are used in the "learning objectives" (the next section of each *Study Guide* chapter), they are set in *italic* at their first appearance.

Learning Objectives

Each learning objective corresponds to a major principle or concept discussed in the main text. The learning objectives let you know in advance what will be required of you; you should also find that, by making new words and concepts seem familiar, they will make the material easier to grasp.

We have left some space between objectives so that you can take notes as you read the textbook chapter.

Some of the objectives require rote learning of the text material (examples are those which ask you to define, list, describe, or explain). Other objectives focus on higher-level comprehension of abstract conceptual material (examples are those that ask you to compare and contrast or to analyze). You should read all the objectives before you read the text chapter. By doing so, you will give yourself an organizational framework for integrating and understanding the material in the text.

The learning objectives also serve as a yardstick to measure your understanding of the text and will indicate if you need to spend more time studying certain material.

Furthermore, the objectives can be particularly beneficial if your instructor gives essay-type questions or examinations, since essay questions may often resemble these objectives. Writing out "answers" to some of the objectives will give you practice in dealing with essay exams.

Supplemental Readings

For each chapter in the textbook, we have selected an interesting current article which complements or expands on one or more important concepts. The readings are intended to "bring to life" some of the issues which are presented more theoretically in the text.

Collectively, the readings should have something for everyone, and each reading is a provocative and insightful analysis of an issue reflecting one of the developmental tasks of life.

Two or three general questions follow each reading, to help you assess your understanding of the issues in the article and how they relate to the material in the text.

Self-Tests

The section of self-tests is a carefully selected group of objective questions--multiple-choice and completion items--that test your understanding of facts and concepts in the textbook chapter. Working out answers to these questions will help you to integrate the chapter material and prepare for questions you might encounter on examinations.

Answer Key

Answers are provided for each item in the self-tests. It is a good idea to check off or highlight any questions you missed and spend additional time on that material, referring back to the textbook. To help you restudy the material you find troublesome, we have provided a text page reference for each answer.

Note also that the multiple-choice items are coded *factual* or *conceptual* to indicate the type of learning being measured by the test item.

STUDYING, TAKING TESTS, AND YOU

Let's face it--if you are using this *Study Guide* as part of a course, one of your personal objectives is passing examinations. You want to know how to do well on exams and, in particular, how the *Study Guide* can help you.

There are several different ways to learn anything, and how you study for a test--that is, how you go about learning--can affect your ability to answer test questions. To take a very simple example, you may be able to recognize the names of the two authors of your textbook if you are presented with four pairs of names and asked to choose the correct answer (a multiple-choice question):

1. The authors of your textbook are
   a. Crandell and Bieger
   b. McGraw and Hill
   c. Papalia and Olds
   d. Watson and Skinner

However, you may not be able to recall the authors' names if you are asked to produce them without being given any choices (a completion question):

2. The authors of your textbook are __________ and __________ .

This difference between recognition and recall (a topic discussed in some detail in the text) is only one aspect of studying and learning.

Research shows that there are at least four main obstacles which prevent students from doing as well as they should on tests.

Obstacle 1: Some students have difficulty seeing relationships between new concepts and what they already know. Consequently, they do not know how to study effectively.

Obstacle 2: Some students do not know how to use supplemental instructional materials (such as this *Study Guide*) effectively.

Obstacle 3: Many students have never developed a successful strategy for preparing for and taking tests, especially objective tests: multiple-choice, matching, completion, and true-false items. (You might say that they are not "test smart.")

Obstacle 4: Many students develop test anxiety.

On the following pages, we offer specific strategies that will help you overcome these obstacles.

USING THE STUDY GUIDE TO LEARN MORE EFFECTIVELY

To improve your overall understanding of the material in the textbook and to help yourself recall that material on tests, follow these steps in the sequence described.

Step 1:
Previewing the Chapter

Before reading each chapter in the textbook, read the introduction to the chapter in the *Study Guide* and preview the key terms.

Next, read and familiarize yourself with the chapter outline and the learning objectives in the *Study Guide*. This will help you see the scope and direction of the material in the text. The *Study Guide* serves as an advance organizer (a bridge between old and new learning), enabling you to anticipate important issues, facts, and concepts in the textbook.

This preview should take only a few minutes.

Step 2:
Reading the Chapter

Creating study units. Read the textbook chapter, but *don't* try to read the entire chapter at one sitting. Research has demonstrated that the capacity for long-term retention increases if we do not try to overload our short-term memory with too much new information at one time.

Therefore, break the chapter into smaller "chunks" or units for study. You can use the chapter outlines in the *Study Guide* to establish your "chunks" or study units. Preferably, each unit, and thus each learning session, should cover only about 7 to 9 pages of the text.

Using the key terms and learning objectives. As you read the textbook chapter, use the space provided in the *Study Guide* to define each key term briefly and to jot down short notes for each of the learning objectives. The purpose of this approach is to involve you directly with the material during and following your reading of the textbook.

Using the key terms and objectives in this way will make you actively involved in reading, and being an active reader will increase your learning and comprehension of the material.

Merely reading a chapter passively does not mean that you have mastered it. Everything may seem to make sense as you read it; however, if you try to recall the material or summarize the main points, you will frequently find that terms, concepts, and names are not retrievable. On the other hand, by defining key terms and responding to the learning objectives, you will make the information in the chapter more significant and hence easier to recall on a test (or, for that matter, in appropriate situations in "real life").

Step 3:
Reviewing the Chapter and Testing Your Mastery

After you have read the chapter--being sure to follow the procedure described in Step 2--you should review what you have learned. (Remember to use the chapter outline, key terms, and learning objectives for reviewing.)

Then take the self-tests in the *Study Guide*. The purpose of the self-tests is to evaluate your understanding and recall of the material and to reinforce what you have learned.

As we've already noted, an answer key is provided at the end of each chapter in the *Study Guide*, so that you can check your answers to the self-tests.

Take the self-tests seriously. If you could not answer a question, do not merely look up the correct answer in the key. For each answer in the key, a text page reference is given; use this reference to find the textbook passage that answers the question, and reread that passage. Then reanswer the question. In this way, you will shore up any areas that need additional review and help store the information in long-term memory.

Step 4:
Rereading the Chapter

Reread the textbook chapter, and then go through the self-tests again.

As you go through Step 4, you should find that the chapter material is more "connected"--and therefore much easier to remember.

Summary: The Four Steps

In summary, these are the steps we recommend that you follow.

Step 1: Preview. Read the introduction to the chapter in the *Study Guide*, and examine the key terms.

Step 2: Read. Break the textbook chapter down into small study units, and read it one unit at a time. As you read, write down in the *Study Guide* brief definitions of the key terms and brief notes on each of the learning objectives.

Step 3: Review and test yourself. Review what you have learned; then take the self-tests in the *Study Guide*. Check your answers against the answer key and correct your mistakes.

Step 4: Reread. Read the textbook chapter again, and then take the self-tests again.

A Note on Learning and the Senses

Keep in mind that not everyone learns in the same way. For example, some students understand information better when they see it in written form--they learn best from the textbook, the *Study Guide*, lecture notes and handouts, etc. Other students prefer to hear information; they learn best from listening to lectures, making and listening to tape recordings of lectures, making and listening to recordings of their own notes on the learning objectives and their own definitions of terms, and studying with other student groups where answers can be discussed.

If you need oral assistance in learning, you should be aware that many textbooks have been recorded on tape; check with your library to see if *Human Development* by Papalia and Olds is available. You may also be able to work directly with a tutor on your campus. Some colleges provide "note-takers" for students who need this extra assistance.

Of course, many people learn best by combining seeing and hearing. By simultaneously using the senses which are most helpful to you, you will make the material more memorable and more retrievable at test time.

PREPARING FOR AND TAKING TESTS

As we noted above, there are at least four factors that can prevent you from doing your best on tests and examinations: (1) ineffective studying, (2) ineffective use of supplemental materials, (3) lack of strategies for taking tests, and (4) inability to overcome test anxiety. Our step-by-step procedure for using the *Human Development* textbook and this *Study Guide*--a procedure which can also be adapted for use with other textbooks and other supplements--will help you overcome the first two of these barriers. Strategies for taking tests and dealing with test anxiety are beyond the scope of this *Study Guide*, but we can give you some useful, if brief, advice.

Overcoming Test Anxiety

Test anxiety can be defined as a feeling of helplessness before or during a test.

It is important to realize that examinations cause many people to become anxious and that this is normal. Complete freedom from test anxiety is unattainable; and even if it were attainable, it would probably not be desirable. Low to moderate anxiety before a test actually tends to have a positive effect on test performance.

However, if your test anxiety is so high that it prevents you from demonstrating what you have learned, then it becomes a problem and should be addressed. Unfortunately, such anxiety is usually a complex problem, which often cannot be traced to any single cause. Personality traits (such as a tendency to take risks), emotional states (such as a negative outlook and fear of failure), and personal needs and priorities (such as overemphasis on grades) can sabotage your performance on tests.

If you consistently experience test anxiety, we recommend that you make an appointment with someone in the college or university counseling center to discuss the problem and work out a procedure for dealing with it. College counselors are trained to help you assess the cause or causes of your test anxiety and to provide you with strategies for reducing it and for improving your performance on tests.

Becoming "Test Smart"

Students who are "test smart" are able to prepare for tests efficiently and to take advantage of the characteristics of tests.

For example, different tests (such as multiple-choice tests and essay tests) have different properties, which students can be taught to recognize. In fact, your college library or bookstore should be able to provide materials dealing with the nature of tests and "test smarts"; and we can recommend one such reference: a practical, pocket-sized book by Jason Millman, entitled *How to Take Tests* (Cornell Publishing, Cornell University, Ithaca, New York). Some colleges also offer workshops or study sessions on how to take different kinds of tests. Remember that instructors want your test scores to reflect what you have learned. If you do poorly because you do not understand the nature of the test, then the test becomes an obstacle to accurate assessment rather than a tool for assessment. Familiarizing yourself with various kinds of tests will help ensure that your grade will be determined by your learning.

Below, we suggest some strategies that will help you prepare for and take tests, so that an examination will become a genuine opportunity for you to demonstrate what you have learned.

Intellectual preparation

Preparing for a test has intellectual, emotional, and physical aspects. Let's look first at some strategies for intellectual preparation.

- Attend classes.
- Follow our step-by-step procedure for using *Human Development* and the *Study Guide*. Remember that this procedure can be adapted for use with other textbooks and supplements.
- Schedule regular study sessions in a specific, quiet place; and set small, reachable goals for each study session.
- Study relevant quizzes and tests that you have already taken.
- Become familiar, in advance, with the purpose and format of the test. Ask your instructor what types of questions will appear.
- See yourself--realistically--as succeeding on the test.

Emotional and physical preparation

Now let's look at some strategies for preparing yourself emotionally and physically.

- Appreciate the usefulness of the test.
- Relax.
- Concentrate.
- Get a good night's sleep before the test.
- Eat a good meal before the test. Avoid sugars before the test, and consume no caffeine.
- Arrive early for the test, and come prepared with all necessary supplies (such as #2 pencil, pens, paper).

Taking the test: general strategies

Use time wisely. Since the time allowable for taking the test is limited, it's important to use that time efficiently.

- Find out how long you have to complete the test.
- Look over the entire test briefly before you start to answer any questions. Find out which items yield the most points.
- Begin to work as rapidly as is possible with some reasonable assurance of accuracy.
- At the outset, omit items that stump you, or just take a guess. If you have enough time when you've completed the rest of the test, remember to return to these items.
- Work immediately, and quickly, on the items which will yield the most points.
- If you become too nervous to work, stop briefly and use some relaxation techniques to calm yourself.
- If you have any time left when you've finished the test (including any difficult items you skipped at the beginning), use it to reconsider and improve your answers. As a rule, however, don't change an answer unless you are absolutely certain that you misread the question initially or that you missed some important aspect of it. Your first answer is often the correct one.

Read all directions and questions carefully. Students often lose points simply because they haven't followed directions or because they have misinterpreted questions.

- Before you start writing, become familiar with the test directions.

- Pay particular attention to the directions that most influence how you will take the test.
- Ask the examiner for clarification when necessary.
- Keep the test directions in mind while you are answering the questions.
- Be careful to read each question "as is"--not as you might like it to be.
- Pay attention to any vocabulary terms that appear in the questions. If you are allowed to make your own notes on your exam paper, sometimes it helps to circle or highlight vocabulary terms in a question; this can help you pinpoint what the question is asking for.
- If you can write your own notes on the exam paper, it may be helpful in multiple-choice to cross out answers that you have eliminated as incorrect and in matching sections to cross off items you've already paired up.

Taking the test:
Strategies for specific types of questions

Multiple-choice items. The typical multiple-choice format consists of an incomplete sentence with several options for completing it or a question with several possible answers. (You may have to circle the correct choice, or write its identifying letter or number in an answer space.)

- Read the fragment or question carefully, anticipate the answer, and then look for your anticipated answer among the choices.
- If the choices do not include the answer you anticipated, consider all the alternatives using a process of elimination. It can be helpful to treat the item as a "completion" question, covering all the choices and then uncovering one at a time.
- If, in a four-choice format, you have eliminated two of the choices but are undecided about the remaining two, treat each of the remaining two as a "true-false" question.
- Relate each option to the question.

Matching items. The typical matching format consists of two sets of items to be paired off. They might be in side-by-side columns; or one set might be inside a box, or there may be some other setup. (Arrangements for indicating the answers vary.)

- As always, read the directions carefully.
- Count the number of items in each set.
- Determine the relationship between the two sets.
- Try the first item. If you can't find its "partner" in the second set, skip to the second item. Keep skipping until you find one matching pair, then go on until you find another pair, and so on.
- When you have matched all the items you know, use a process of elimination for the remaining items. If you are allowed to write your own notes on the exam paper, cross out the items you have already matched.

Completion items. The typical completion, or "fill-in" item is a sentence with one or more blanks; you are to make the sentence read correctly by supplying whatever is needed in each blank. (You may be asked to write your answer in the blank itself or in a separate answer space.)

- Give a general answer if you don't know the specific answer.
- Examine the sentence for grammatical clues. (For example, *a* or *an* preceding a blank tells you that the answer is singular; *these* or *those* tells you that the answer is plural.)

True-false items. The typical true-or-false item is a statement which you are to identify as correct or incorrect. (You may have to write *T or true* or *F or false* in an answer space; or check off or circle a *T* or an *F*.

- Remember the odds (50-50).
- As always, read each item carefully.
- Look for qualifiers (*not, new, recent,* etc.).
- Watch for absolute terms (*always, never, all, none, every*). Items using absolute terms are usually false.
- Watch for conditional terms (*some, few, occasionally, sometimes*). Items using conditional terms are usually true.

Essay items. An essay item may be phrased as a question ("Why did Freud believe that ... ?" or as an imperative ("Explain why Freud believed that ..."). You are to write a full answer. Often, your answer will be graded not only for content but also for grammar and for the logic of your presentation. (Space may be provided for each answer; or all the essay items may be on a printed sheet, with answers to be written in an examination booklet or on your paper.)

- When a test has more than one essay item, read each one carefully.
- If you are allowed to make notes on the exam paper, jot down beside each essay item the relevant points that occur to you.
- If you can make notes on the exam paper, you may also want to highlight or circle parts of the question that indicate exactly what you are being asked to write about.
- Analyze the verbs in the item: *contrast, compare, describe, list, explain,* etc. Circle them for emphasis if that is permitted.
- Organize your answer before you start writing.
- If you are not sure of the best answer, quickly write down all your ideas.
- Follow a format: introduction, body, conclusion.
- If you do not have enough time to write a full essay answer, give your answer in outline form.
- When you have finished an essay item, read it over. Check to be sure that you have followed each of the direction verbs you identified (you may have circled these, as noted above).
- WRITE LEGIBLY.

"Bubble sheets" and optical scanner sheets. These are not, of course, types of questions; nevertheless, they are formats that you should know how to deal with. Three hints:

- Before turning in your exam, make sure that you have filled in all the spaces.
- If you skip any items on the test, be sure to complete the remaining items in the correct order.
- Check to make sure you did not fill in two answers for the same question.

IN CONCLUSION

As we mentioned earlier, there are no shortcuts to learning; and there are no shortcuts to good grades. Good grades are the result of hard work. But for serious students who want their grades to reflect the amount of effort they have spent studying, these study tips and guidelines for test-taking should be very helpful.

This *Study Guide* was designed as an educational tool to help you learn the material in *Human Development*. Therefore, you should plan to use it as a working document. Mark up the pages: make notes on the chapter outlines, make notes of definitions and examples of the key terms, jot down your thoughts about the learning objectives, and write in your answers to the self-tests.

Doing all this, and following our suggestions, will help you improve your overall memory of the material you are learning.

ACKNOWLEDGMENTS

Several people have contributed to the development of this *Study Guide*, and their help is gratefully acknowledged here. Corinne Crandell, Colleen Crandell, and Karen Bieger generously contributed their time and talents in helping us with the important but tedious work necessary to write valid and reliable test questions. We express special thanks to our gracious editors at McGraw Hill: to Beth Kaufman and Jane Vaicunas for their guidance and continued support of our work.

Thomas L. Crandell
George R. Bieger

CHAPTER 1

About Human Development

INTRODUCTION

Chapter 1 provides an overview of the field of human development from both theoretical and research perspectives. Several important issues are discussed, including:

- A historical presentation of the study of human development leading to the current life-span view.
- The influences on human development, ranging from those which are purely individual to those common to specific (cross-cultural) groups.
- Correlation, nonexperimental methods, experimental methods, and data-collection techniques used to discover more about human nature, as well as the framework of ethical considerations for conducting research on human subjects.
- The four dominant theories of development: psychoanalytic, learning, cognitive, and humanistic--and the role they play in helping to explain, interpret, and predict and modify human behavior and guide future research.

The authors' intent in this textbook is to provide the reader with practical information based on research with human subjects, as much as is currently available--and to portray people as unique individuals with the capacity to change and to influence their own development.

CHAPTER OUTLINE

I. Human Development: The Subject and the Text

A. What is Human Development?
B. How This Book Approaches Human Development
  1. We Celebrate the Human Being
  2. We Respect All Periods of the Life Span
  3. We Believe in Human Resilience
  4. We Recognize that People Help Shape Their Own Development
  5. We Believe that Knowledge is Useful

II. Human Development: The Study and Its History

A. Aspects of Development
  1. Physical Development
  2. Intellectual (Cognitive) Development
  3. Personality and Social Development
B. Periods of the Life Span
C. Individual Differences in Development
D. Influences on Development
  1. Types of Influences: Sources and Effects
    a. Internal and external influences
    b. Normative and nonnormative influences
  2. Contexts of Influences: An Ecological Approach
  3. Timing of Influences: Critical Periods
E. How the Study of Human Development Has Evolved
  1. Studies of Childhood
  2. Studies of Adolescence, Adulthood, and Aging
  3. Life-Span Studies

III. Human Development: Research Methods

A. Correlation
B. Nonexperimental Methods
  1. Case Studies
  2. Observation
    a. Naturalistic observation
    b. Laboratory observation
    c. Evaluation of observational studies
  3. Interviews
C. Experimental Methods
  1. Variables and Groups
  2. Sampling and Assignment
  3. Types of Experiments
    a. Laboratory experiments
    b. Field experiments
    c. Natural experiments
  4. Comparing Experimentation with Other Methods

D. Data Collection Designs for Studying Development
    1. Cross-Sectional and Longitudinal Studies
    2. Sequential Studies
E. Ethics of Research
    1. Ethical Issues
        a. Informed consent
        b. Deception
        c. Self-esteem
        d. Privacy
    2. Ethical Standards

IV. Human Development: Theoretical Perspectives

A. Theories and Hypotheses
B. Psychoanalytic Perspective
    1. Sigmund Freud: Psychosexual Theory
        a. Id, ego, and superego
        b. Defense mechanisms
        c. Stages of psychosexual development
    2. Erik Erikson: Psychosocial Theory
        a. Erikson's approach
        b. Erikson's eight crises
    3. Jean Baker Miller: Relational Theory
    4. Psychoanalytic Perspective
C. Learning Perspective: Behaviorism and Social-Learning Theory
    1. Behaviorism
        a. Classical conditioning
        b. Operant conditioning
    2. Social-Learning Theory
    3. Evaluation of Learning Perspective
D. Cognitive Perspective
    1. The Cognitive-Stage Theory of Jean Piaget
        a. Cognitive structures
        b. Principles of cognitive development
    2. Evaluation of Piaget's Theory
    3. Information-Processing Approach
E. Humanistic Perspective
    1. Abraham Maslow: Self-Actualization and the Hierarchy of Needs
    2. Evaluation of Humanistic Theory

V. A Word to Students

KEY TERMS

accommodation (page 36)

adaptation (36)

assimilation (36)

behaviorism (30)

case studies (14)

classical conditioning (31)

cognitive development (34)

cognitive perspective (34)

cohort (9)

control group (19)

correlation (14)

critical period (10)

cross-sectional study (21)

cross-sequential study (22)

data (23)

defense mechanisms (25)

dependent variable (19)

ecological approach (9)

ego (25)

environmental influences (8)

equilibration (36)

experiment (17)

experimental group (19)

extinction (33)

heredity (8)

human development (3)

humanistic perspective (37)

hypothesis (23)

id (25)

independent variable (19)

interview (17)

laboratory observation (16)

learning perspective (30)

longitudinal study (21)

naturalistic observation (16)

operant conditioning (32)

organization (36)

psychoanalytic perspective (24)

psychosexual development (25)

psychosocial development (29)

punishment (32)

qualitative change (3)

quantitative change (3)

random sample (19)

reinforcement (32)

relational theory (29)

sample (19)

scheme (35)

scientific method (14)

shaping (33)

social-learning theory (33)

superego (25)

theory (23)

LEARNING OBJECTIVES

After finishing Chapter 1, you should be able to:

1. Explain what is meant by the study of *human development*. (p. 3)

2. Differentiate between *quantitative* and *qualitative* changes in development. (p. 3)

    a. Give an example of a *quantitative* change.

    b. Give an example of a *qualitative* change.

3. List four major steps applied in the study of *human development* and give an illustration of each. (p. 5)

    a.

    b.

    c.

    d.

4. Recall the four major aspects of the self in which growth and change occur and describe an example of each. (p. 6)

    a.

    b.

    c.

    d.

5. Name and briefly describe eight periods of development within the life span. (pp. 7-8, Table 1-1)

   a.

   b.

   c.

   d.

   e.

   f.

   g.

   h.

6. Distinguish between internal and external influences on development and cite an example of each. (p. 8)

   a. internal

   b. external

7. Differentiate between normative and nonnormative influences on development. (pp. 8-9)

   a. Give an example of a normative age-graded influence.

   b. Give an example of a normative history-graded influence.

   c. Give an example of a nonnormative influence.

8. On the basis of the *ecological approach* to development, briefly describe the four different levels of *environmental influence*. (p. 9)

   a.

   b.

   c.

   d.

9. State how cross-cultural research is applied in the study of human development. (p. 10)

10. Define the concept of *critical period* and how this concept relates to human development. (p. 10)

11. Explain how societal and medical progress in the 19th century caused adults to take a new view of childhood. (pp. 11-12)

12. Explain the life-span approach to understanding human development. (p. 12)

13. Define the term *scientific method* and explain its application to psychological research. (p. 14)

14. Describe *correlation*, the research technique that examines the statistical relationship between variables. (p. 14)

15. Name and describe the three categories of nonexperimental methods for collecting data: (pp. 14-17)

    a.

    b.

    c.

16. Define the following terms as they relate to *experimental* research: (pp. 17-19)

    a. *independent variable*

    b. *dependent variable*

    c. *experimental group*

    d. *control group*

    e. *random sample*

17. List the three types of *experiments*, give an example of each, and cite advantages and disadvantages of each. (pp. 19-20)

    a.

    b.

    c.

18. Critique the *experimental* method over the *nonexperimental* methods. (p. 20)

19. Compare and contrast the three methods of *data* collection design: (pp. 21-22)

    a. *cross-sectional* studies

    b. *longitudinal* studies

    c. sequential studies

20. In your own words, summarize each of the following issues as it relates to the ethics of human research: (pp. 22-23)

    a. informed consent

    b. deception

    c. self-esteem

    d. privacy

    e. ethical standards

21. Define the following research terms: (p. 23)

    a. *theory*

    b. *data*

    c. *hypothesis*

22. Briefly describe the goals of the *psychoanalytic perspective*, and name the physician who is attributed with having originated it. (p. 24)

23. Summarize what Freud meant by each of these terms: (p. 25)

    a. *id*

    b. *ego*

    c. *superego*

24. List and define Freud's five stages of *psychosexual development*. (pp. 25-28)

    a.

    b.

    c.

    d.

    e.

25. Explain in your own words each of Erik Erikson's eight *psychosocial development* crises of development and indicate approximately at what ages these occur: (pp. 27-30 and Table 1-6)

    a. trust vs. mistrust

    b. autonomy versus shame

    c. initiative versus guilt

    d. industry versus inferiority

    e. identity versus identity confusion

    f. intimacy versus isolation

    g. generativity versus stagnation

    h. integrity versus shame

26. Summarize the *relational theory* and identify its founder. (p. 29)

27. Critique the *psychoanalytic perspective.* (p. 30)

28. Explain the two major theories comprised by the *learning perspective.* (pp. 30-33)

    a. *behaviorism*

    b. *social-learning theory*

29. Briefly describe the *cognitive* perspective of development and name its major proponent. (p. 34)

30. Identify and describe Piaget's four stages of *cognitive development* and indicate at approximately what age each occurs. (p. 34 and Table 1-6)

    a.

    b.

    c.

    d.

31. Critique Piaget's cognitive-stage theory. (p. 36)

32. Define what is meant by the information-processing approach to *cognitive development.* (p. 37)

33. Explain the major beliefs of the *humanistic perspective*, and name the person who is credited with its development. (p. 37)

34. Briefly describe Maslow's hierarchy of needs that motivate human behavior. (p. 38 and Figure 1-4)

35. Critique the *humanistic perspective* to human development. (p. 38)

SUPPLEMENTAL READING

Gerald W. Bracey is a research psychologist and policy analyst for the National Education Association. This article is reprinted with permission from *Phi Delta Kappan*, Inc., © May 1990.

Culture, Science, and the Concept of Child

by Gerald W. Bracey

Not too long ago I told a friend that I was thinking about writing an article charging that all educational research is a lie. This article would not fault the academic obsession with "knowledge production," though that is dreadful enough. Nor would it harp on the limitations of the methods of quantitative research, though they are severe enough. No, the thrust of this article would be that educational research is largely unguided by anything other than implicit ideas of child development or of what it means to be human. Much research seems to be a combination of naive realism and unthinking behaviorism. Certainly if you tried to reconstruct a human being from the features described in the literature of educational research, your construction would be a peculiar-looking creature.

The field of developmental psychology attends, in part, to such concepts as "child." It turns out that the concept of a child, which is influenced by the prevailing ideology of development, is now in flux and has been for some time. At least, those are some of the conclusions I draw from an article by Kathryn Young of Yale University in the February 1990 issue of Child Development.

Young notes that women's magazines began to publish articles about child care near the end of the 19th century and that such publications "evolved into a sustained alliance between experts and parents in which pediatricians, psychologists, educators, and child developmentalists have assumed the role of counsel to parents." Two publications, Parents Magazine and Infant Care Manual, have long histories of communicating information from professionals to parents. Young set out to see what these publications were telling parents between 1955 and 1984.

She analyzed the articles in both publications for topical content (how often certain topics appeared) and thematic content (what was said about certain themes, such as breast-feeding or the role of the mother in development). The 443 articles on infants that were published between 1955 and 1984 fell about evenly into two categories: information from research and theory and information about practical concerns and infant care.

Young also looked at the frequency data on the percentage of articles appearing in each of the three decades covered, 1955-64, 1965-74, and 1975-84. Different topics showed different patterns. Articles on the mother/child relationship accounted for about 10% of the articles in the first two decades, then rose to 20% in the third decade. Articles on feeding, on the other hand, accounted for 25% of all articles between 1955 and 1964, then fell to about 15% for the next two decades.

Articles about working mothers were virtually nonexistent in the first two decades, then rose to about 8% of the articles in the third. Similarly, pieces about infant cognition rose from about 7% in the first two decades to about 15% in the third.

When one looks at what the articles actually said, other trends emerge. Although mother/child interaction continued to be important throughout the three decades, the overarching power and centrality of the maternal role declined. Similarly, articles in the first two decades emphasized the role of the mother as full-time caretaker. An article that appeared in Parents Magazine in 1960 said that "a baby needs his mother as vitally as he needs food and air." Only in the Eighties did Parents Magazine begin to reassure mothers that out-of-home care for infants is okay and to provide advice about child-care centers. So marked has this trend become that some articles have appeared that reassure mothers that it is also okay to stay at home with the children.

Although the coverage of fathers by Parents Magazine did not change much in terms of frequency, the emphasis shifted from the father as someone the mother should include but not expect a lot out of to the view that the father has an integral and unique role to play.

The topic of feeding cycled with the times, emphasizing breast-feeding in the Fifties, advising either method in the Sixties and Seventies, and shifting back to breast-feeding in the Eighties. This shift occurred in spite of what Young calls "attempts of both publications to present a balanced perspective" and in spite of the lack of solid research evidence about the benefits of breast feeding.

Shifting away from themes about child-rearing practice, Parents Magazine maintained a notion of infants as active and thinking, presenting Piaget's concepts when they became popular in the late Fifties and early Sixties. Infant Care, on the other hand, was slower in shifting from the view of infants as passive receptacles to the view of infants as active learners.

Discussions about communication and temperament also followed the research findings of the periods. Young writes:

"Two trends are noted in what experts tell parents. The first trend is research-driven, as experts have used psychological research of the last 30 years as the basis for the information and advice they present to parents. Equally powerful is a second trend that in certain areas expert advice is more based on the broader social context and changing demographics."

Clearly, our conceptions of children change. The cry, "Women and children first," is of recent origin, even for sinking ships. Our conception is clearly not that of the English in the early stages of the Industrial Revolution, when children worked in factories for 14 hours a day, seven days a week. It has even been argued that, until the 17th century, the concept of childhood did not exist at all. Children were given no special clothes, toys, or attention. They were generally ignored until they were about 7 years old. Then, when it looked as if they might actually live to adulthood, they were treated as adults. As recently as 1979, another Yale psychologist, William Kessen, referred to both children and child psychology as "cultural inventions."

Although it may be disconcerting to people trained to perceive science as the objective pursuit of truth, all socially meaningful constructs, such as the concept of the child, will always be affected by culture, and, yes, by a degree of expediency. I think, though, that those of us in education would do better if our concepts were made more explicit and comprehensive than they currently are. (From Young's article, I don't think that 30 years of Parents Magazine painted a comprehensive picture either.)

Tips for Readers of Research

Some tips bear repeating. So, in the spirit that there are "lies, damned lies, and statistics," I repeat some advice about looking at statistics in ways other than the ways they are presented to you by various authors and reports.

For example, a recent survey concluded that the two most dangerous cars in America were two Chevrolet creations, the Corvette and the Camaro. This conclusion was drawn from a statistic showing number of deaths per accident. Well, to begin with, one can ask whether this is the best measure of "dangerousness." How about accidents per thousand miles driven? Or the number of recalls by the manufacturer? Clearly, there are other statistics that could be used.

More important, though, does it strike you as reasonable that these full-sized cars would be inherently more dangerous than the tiny Subaru Justy, Ford Festiva, or Toyota Tercel? Me either. The Corvette, of course, is a pure power machine, and one might wish to inquire about the average speed of those Corvettes at the time of all those accidents. A Camaro, on the other hand, is a lot like acne; it affects males more often than females, and most people grow out of it when they reach adulthood. Since it is sadly the case that young males have more accidents than other people, one might want to know the sex and the average age of the drivers in Camaro accidents.

When identifying trends in reporting about infant development, the subject discussed above, the choice of statistical measures may affect our perception of importance. Kathryn Young used percentage of articles appearing in publications over a 30-year period. Seems a reasonable choice. But I note that most of the topical magazines that I subscribe to have grown thicker in recent years. The use of a percentage lets us see the importance of certain topics relative to other topics. The role of fathers, for example, may have gotten significantly more important in terms of the number of articles published, but this would be obscured if numbers were rising in other categories as well.

On the other hand, the length of articles in many publications has diminished as we have become a more factoid-oriented society with an apparently declining attention span for print. As a result, we could be having more articles that say a lot less. Without analyses in addition to the one Young offered, reasonable though it was, we simply cannot tell.

Questions:

Referring to Chapter 1 in your text, is Young's research experimental or nonexperimental?

What do you think is the hypothesis behind behind Young's research?

After reading this article, do you think that studying trends is a valid method for identifying changes in development across the life-span?

SELF-TESTS

Multiple-Choice

Circle the letter of the response which best completes or answers each of the following statements and questions.

1. A change in height or weight is referred to as what kind of change?
   a. qualitative
   b. psychological
   c. quantitative
   d. social

2. What kind of developmental change is illustrated by Alzheimer's disease, which affects memory and other cognitive abilities?
   a. qualitative
   b. process
   c. quantitative
   d. social

3. The authors have presented the research in this text with which philosophy in mind?
   a. People actively shape and influence their own lives.
   b. Research can be cited only on work with animal subjects.
   c. Research cannot be presented with practical applications.
   d. People do not seem to have the potential for change.

4. Research conducted by observing and recording children's behavior after they watch certain television programs is called what kind of research?
   a. implied
   b. cross-sectional
   c. developmental
   d. applied

5. The unique way each person views the world and expresses emotions is considered the result of what kind of development?
   a. physical
   b. personality and social
   c. intellectual
   d. none of the above

6. Which of the following statements is false concerning individual differences in human development?
   a. There is a wide range of individual differences in the timing and expression of developmental change.
   b. The range of individual differences is greatest when children are young.
   c. When deviation from the norm is extreme, there is cause to consider a person's development exceptionally advanced or exceptionally delayed.
   d. Results of development can vary considerably, especially as people grow older.

7. The inborn biological endowment that people inherit from their parents is an internal influence known as
   a. cultural influence
   b. inherited response
   c. heredity
   d. external influence

8. Noninherited influences upon development attributed to a person's experiences are called
   a. original influences
   b. environmental influences
   c. genetic influences
   d. genetic responses

9. Most individuals in the U.S. retire from paid employment between 55 and 70 years old. Which of the following terms is used for an event such as retirement that influences development?
   a. common
   b. normative
   c. similar
   d. nonnormative

10. In January 1994 a major earthquake occurred northwest of Los Angeles, California. The Southern Californians who lived through this traumatic event shared what kind of event?
    a. external event
    b. normative age-graded event
    c. normative history-graded event
    d. nonnormative life event

11. Studying people who are unemployed because of a depressed economy comes directly from which approach to understanding development?
    a. psychosocial
    b. learning
    c. ecological
    d. psychoanalytic

12. Jane was exposed to the illness chicken pox when she was in her second month of pregnancy. There is cause for some concern for the developing fetus because
    a. the concept of mesosystem may apply
    b. the concept of exosystem may apply
    c. the concept of macrosystem may apply
    d. the concept of critical periods may apply

13. Which of the following statements is <u>true</u> concerning the study of human development?
    a. Philippe Aries discovered in his search through historical sources that children have always been regarded as different from adults.
    b. Linda Pollock found in her studies that children were viewed as miniature adults and were treated like other adults.
    c. The controversy about the influences of heredity and environment began as early as the 1500s.
    d. Adults began to feel more responsible for their children, passed laws against child labor, and encouraged spending time in school by the end of the 19th century.

14. Careful observation, recording of data, testing of alternative hypotheses, and public dissemination of findings and conclusions are phases of which method?
    a. humanistic
    b. correlational
    c. open-ended
    d. scientific

15. A researcher is examining statistically the relationship between the number of hours children watch television per week and their grades in school. Which research technique is being applied?
    a. naturalistic observation method
    b. correlation method
    c. case study method
    d. experimental method

16. Which of the following research techniques is/are considered nonexperimental?
    a. case studies
    b. interviews
    c. naturalistic observation
    d. all of the above

17. Which of the following research techniques is/are considered experimental?
    a. case studies
    b. interviews
    c. clinical studies
    d. a research design using a treatment and a control group and controlling for many variables

18. Louis is a participant in a research group to study if a certain vitamin will lower bad cholesterol. He's unaware that he is being given the real vitamin and not a sugar pill. Which of the following statements is true?
    a. The vitamin is the dependent variable.
    b. The vitamin is the independent variable.
    c. Louis is in the control group.
    d. Louis is participating in a natural experiment.

19. Which of the following is stated by your authors to be a disadvantage in conducting laboratory-based experiments?
    a. Lab experiments allow for the greatest amount of control.
    b. Lab experiments are set up to be replicated by other researchers.
    c. Only experiments can tell us about cause-and-effect relationships.
    d. We cannot be sure that conclusions found in the lab apply to real life.

20. Data can be collected about development through
    a. cross-sectional studies
    b. longitudinal studies
    c. sequential studies
    d. all of the above

21. It has recently been publicized that a small sample of U.S. citizens who were institutionalized 30 years ago had been administered a radioactive substance in an experiment. They were unaware that they were subjects and uninformed that they had been given doses of radioactive medicine during the course of this experiment. What ethical guideline(s) established by the American Psychological Association was/were violated?
    a. informed consent
    b. deception
    c. protection from harm
    d. all of the above

22. The psychoanalytic perspective differs from other theoretical perspectives because it is concerned with
    a. animal rather than human subjects
    b. how the environment controls behavior
    c. how thinking affects behavior
    d. how the unconscious affects behavior

23. When there is an arrest in a person's development as a result of too little or too much gratification at a given stage, Freudians would call the person
    a. unhealthy
    b. fixated
    c. deprived of pleasure
    d. lacking goals

24. Jacque's parents have recently divorced. He has become increasingly dependent on them to make his decisions. Freud called this defense
    a. repression
    b. regression
    c. projection
    d. fixation

25. In the psychosocial-development theory formulated by Erik Erikson
    a. behaviors are measured and recorded
    b. study of the id, ego, and superego are paramount
    c. the systems of home, society, religion, etc., are considered the strongest influences on development
    d. personality development is viewed across the lifespan in terms of successful or unsuccessful resolution of a "conflict" at each of eight stages of development

26. Julia has been encouraged to be kind to others, to help all her family members, and to be a peace maker in her family. However, her brother Grant has been encouraged to get high grades in school and to excel in athletic competition. The effect of this split in female and male development is at the heart of which theory?
    a. relational
    b. psychoanalytic
    c. behavioral
    d. cognitive

27. The study of behavior that tries to identify and isolate environmental factors that make people behave in certain ways without regard to their own will is related to which perspective?
    a. learning
    b. cognitive
    c. psychoanalytic
    d. humanistic

28. A baby girl begins to suck when she sees her mother preparing her bottle before a feeding. This sucking response is an example of a/an
    a. unconditioned stimulus
    b. conditioned stimulus
    c. conditioned response
    d. unconditioned response

29. Whenever Carlo's mother raises her voice, he knows he is about to be sent to his room for misbehaving. Carlo learns to recoil whenever his mother raises her voice. This learning is an example of
    a. operant conditioning
    b. negative reinforcement
    c. classical conditioning
    d. shaping

30. A stimulus which follows a desired behavior and increases the likelihood that the behavior will be repeated is called
    a. a conditioned response
    b. negative conditioning
    c. punishment
    d. reinforcement

31. When a particular response is sometimes reinforced and sometimes not (intermittent reinforcement), the result is usually
    a. extinction
    b. more durable behavior
    c. punishment
    d. shaping

32. Reinforcement in the form of praise from the mother when a child learns to speak sounds that are progressively more like words is identified as
    a. extinction
    b. durable behavior
    c. punishment
    d. shaping

33. Behavioral theory is to ____________ as social-learning theory is to ____________.
    a. environmental experience; observation and imitation of models
    b. unconscious urges; environmental experience
    c. historical influences; observation and imitation of models
    d. biological factors; environmental experience

34. Regina, a 3-year-old, spends a great deal of time watching television. Social-learning theorists predict that
    a. her behavior will be molded by her environment
    b. she will develop role models from characters on the screen
    c. she will stop playing with her peers
    d. her own characteristics will not influence which TV characters she chooses as role models

35. The theoretician who formulated a theory of cognitive development as occurring in a series of stages with accompanying qualitative changes is
    a. Piaget
    b. Freud
    c. Maslow
    d. Skinner

36. A young boy has been successful in getting a toy by reaching for it with his hands. When it is moved out of his reach, he gets it by climbing onto a nearby step stool. What is the term for this action?
    a. equilibration
    b. assimilation
    c. shaping
    d. accommodation

37. From a more recent perspective on understanding development, a psychologist who is researching how people learn (through sensory input, attention, memory, and problem-solving) sees people as
    a. being controlled by their environment
    b. active participants in their development
    c. motivated to learn because they are modeling their behavior after others
    d. being motivated by unconscious drives

38. Which recent perspective, identified by Maslow, suggests that people have a progression of needs to be met?
    a. cognitive
    b. behavioristic
    c. humanistic
    d. psychoanalytic

39. A person who reaches the highest levels of Maslow's hierarchy of needs is considered
    a. self-actualized
    b. externally influenced
    c. more human
    d. self-aware

40. While taking a major test, a college student suddenly realizes that he is very thirsty. Before long, he realizes that he can no longer concentrate on completing the exam because he must get a drink of water. This student's actions seem to confirm which theory?
    a. relational
    b. psychoanalytic
    c. cognitive
    d. humanistic

Completion

Supply the term or terms needed to complete each of the following statements.

1. Changes in body, brain, sensory capacities, and motor skills are all part of ____________________ development.

2. Changes in a variety of mental abilities, such as learning, memory, reasoning, thinking, and use of language, are aspects of __________ development.

3. The range of individual differences _____________ as people grow older.

4. Influences on development which originate with heredity are called _____________ influences.

5. Noninherited influences on development attributed to a person's experiences with the world outside the self are called _____________ influences.

6. Life events occurring in a similar way for most people in a given group are referred to as _________________ events.

7. According to Bronfenbrenner's ecological approach, to understand individual human development, we must understand each person within the context of multiple _______________.

8. A specific time during development when a given event will have its greatest impact is called a _______________ period.

9. Whether or not the capacity for learning language is inborn has been examined through _____________ research.

10. A pioneer in the child study movement, G. Stanley Hall, was the first psychologist to formulate a theory of __________, published in 1904.

11. In the 1950s, Neugarten and her associates had begun studying and formulating theories about ____________ age.

12. The prevalent idea today is that human development is a _________ process.

13. Investigating the relationship between variables or events by applying a mathematical formula is the ____________________ method.

14. _________________ studies consider a person's life or a single case, recording behavior but not explaining it.

15. In _______________ observation, researchers observe and record people's behavior in real-life settings without manipulating the environment.

16. With the _____________ method, people are surveyed and asked to state their attitudes or opinions or relate aspects of their life histories.

17. In a controlled experiment, the variable over which the experimenter has direct control is the _______________ variable.

18. The _____________ group of subjects will be exposed to the experimental manipulation, also known as the treatment, but the ___________________ group will not receive the treatment.

19. A ____________ is a set of related statements about data, the information that is obtained through research.

20. Although young children at first seek immediate gratification, they eventually develop a ___________ which incorporates values and thinking into their personality.

21. Freud said that people unconsciously combat anxiety (over aggressive and sexual conflicts) by distorting reality using _______________ mechanisms, such as regression.

22. Erikson's approach, called psychosocial theory, emphasizes the quest for _______________ as a major theme in life and traces personality development across the life span.

23. The ____________ perspective views all personality growth as occurring within emotional connections beginning in infancy.

24. The American behaviorist credited with applying stimulus-response theories of learning to the study of child development is ___________.

25. Positive reinforcement, negative reinforcement, and punishment are the basis for _________________ conditioning.

26. Reinforcement is most effective when it is ____________________.

27. Albert Bandura is a proponent of social-learning theory, which states that children learn by ______________ and ___________________ models (e.g., their parents).

28. Proponents of the cognitive perspective argue that although internal and external influences interact, the source of change is ___________, and development occurs in qualitative stages.

29. According to the ______________ perspective, people are able to take control of their own lives and influence their own development.

30. Maslow identified a hierarchy of needs; a person who attains the highest level on this hierarchy is described as ____________________________.

ANSWERS FOR SELF-TESTS — CHAPTER 1

Multiple-Choice

		Page				Page	
1.	c	3	factual	21.	d	23	factual
2.	a	3	factual	22.	d	24	factual
3.	a	4	conceptual	23.	b	25	factual
4.	d	5	conceptual	24.	b	26	conceptual
5.	b	6	factual	25.	d	29	factual
6.	b	6	conceptual	26.	a	30	conceptual
7.	c	8	factual	27.	a	30	conceptual
8.	b	8	factual	28.	c	31	conceptual
9.	b	8	factual	29.	c	31	factual
10.	d	9	conceptual	30.	d	32	factual
11.	c	9	conceptual	31.	b	33	conceptual
12.	d	10	conceptual	32.	d	33	conceptual
13.	d	12	conceptual	33.	a	31-33	conceptual
14.	d	14	factual	34.	b	34	conceptual
15.	b	14	conceptual	35.	a	34	factual
16.	d	14-15	factual	36.	d	36	conceptual
17.	d	17	factual	37.	b	37	conceptual
18.	b	19	conceptual	38.	c	37	factual
19.	d	20	conceptual	39.	a	37	factual
20.	d	21-22	factual	40.	d	37	conceptual

Completion

		Page			Page
1.	physical	6	16.	interview/survey questionnaire	17
2.	intellectual	6	17.	independent	19
3.	increases	8	18.	experimental; control	19
4.	internal/biological/ genetic	8	19.	theory	23
5.	external or environmental	8	20.	superego	25
6.	normative	8	21.	defense	25
7.	environments or systems	9	22.	identity	29
8.	critical	10	23.	relational	29
9.	cross-cultural	10	24.	John Watson	32
10.	adolescence	12	25.	operant/instrumental	32
11.	middle	12	26.	immediate	33
12.	life-span or life-long	12	27.	observing/imitating	33
13.	correlation	14	28.	internal	34
14.	case	14	29.	humanistic	37
15.	naturalistic	16	30.	self-actualized	37

CHAPTER 2

Conception Through Birth

INTRODUCTION

Chapter 1 examined the subject of human development and discussed several research methods and theoretical perspectives that are used in the study of various aspects of human development. Chapter 2 discusses what the most current research has found about the beginning of human development, the period from conception until birth. Several issues are covered, including:

- Fertilization and the basic genetic principles that describe the mechanisms of heredity.
- One of the most perplexing questions in the study of human development: whether human nature is primarily inherited or learned.
- Stages of prenatal birth, including germinal, embryonic, and fetal.
- Methods of assessing development before birth, such as amniocentesis, chorionic villus sampling, blood sampling, and umbilical cord sampling.
- Various influences in the prenatal environment which can affect the developing fetus.
- The benefits and dangers associated with genetic testing.
- The stages of the birth process and various settings for childbirth available today.

The chapter also discusses the interaction between heredity and environmental influences on the developing organism.

CHAPTER OUTLINE

I. Fertilization

A. How Does Fertilization Take Place?
B. What Causes Multiple Births?
C. What Determines Sex?

II. Heredity and Environment

A. What is the Role of Heredity?
   1. Mechanisms of Heredity: Genes and Chromosomes
   2. Patterns of Genetic Transmission
      a. Mendel's Laws
      b. Dominant and Recessive Inheritance
      c. Sex-linked Inheritance and Other Forms
   3. Genetic and Chromosomal Abnormalities
      a. Defects Transmitted by Dominant Inheritance
      b. Defects Transmitted by Recessive Inheritance
      c. Defects Transmitted by Sex-Linked Inheritance
      d. Chromosomal Abnormalities
   4. Genetic Counseling
B. How Do Heredity and Environment Interact?
   1. "Nature versus Nurture": Hereditary and Environmental Factors
      a. Hereditary and Environmental Influences on Traits
      b. Maturation
   2. Ways to Study the Relative Effects of Heredity and Environment
   3. Some Characteristics Influenced by Heredity and Environment
      a. Intelligence
      b. Personality
   4. Some Disorders Influenced by Heredity and Environment
      a. Alcoholism
      b. Schizophrenia
      c. Infantile Autism
      d. Depression
   5. The Importance of the Environment

III. Prenatal Development

A. Stages of Prenatal Development
   1. Germinal Stage (Fertilization to about 2 Weeks)
   2. Embryonic Stage (2 to 8-12 Weeks)
   3. Fetal Stage (8-12 Weeks to Birth)
B. The Prenatal Environment
   1. Maternal Factors
   2. Prenatal Nourishment
   3. Maternal Drug Intake
   4. Other Maternal Factors
   5. Paternal Factors: Environmental Influences Transmitted by the Father

IV. Birth

A. Stages of Childbirth
B. Methods of Childbirth
   1. Medicated Delivery
   2. Natural and Prepared Childbirth
   3. Cesarean Delivery
   4. Medical Monitoring
C. Settings for Childbirth

KEY TERMS

---

alleles (page 51)

amniocentesis (61, Box 2-1)

autosomes (49)

cesarean delivery (83)

chorionic villus sampling (61, Box 2-1)

chromosomes (50)

concordant (65)

depression (69)

dizygotic twins (47)

DNA (deoxyribonucleic acid) (50)

dominant inheritance (50)

Down syndrome (58)

electronic fetal monitoring (84-85)

embryonic stage (70)

fertilization (46)

fetal alcohol syndrome (FAS) (76)

fetal stage (72)

gametes (46)

gene (50)

genetic counseling (59)

genetics (49)

genotype (51)

germinal stage (70)

heredity (49)

heterozygous (51)

homozygous (51)

independent segregation (51)

infantile autism (67)

karyotype (59)

maternal blood test (61, Box 2-1)

maturation (63)

medicated delivery (82)

monozygotic twins (47)

multifactorial inheritance (52)

multiple alleles (52)

natural childbirth (83)

ovulation (46)

personality (66)

phenotype (51)

prepared childbirth (83)

recessive inheritance (51)

schizophrenia (67)

sex chromosomes (49)

sex-linked inheritance (52)

spontaneous abortion (70)

temperament (66)

teratogenic (73)

ultrasound (62, Box 2-1)

zygote (46)

LEARNING OBJECTIVES

After finishing Chapter 2, you should be able to:

1. Describe the processes leading to conception: (page 46)

   a. *ovulation*

   b. *fertilization*

2. Identify and explain the two mechanisms which produce multiple births. (pp. 47-48)

   a.

   b.

3. Name and describe the mechanism that determines a baby's sex. (p. 49)

4. Explain how *heredity* is determined at *fertilization*. (pp. 49-50)

5. Explain briefly how hereditary traits are transmitted--as separate units or as a group. Name the scientist responsible for this finding. (50)

6. Recall the principles that govern the transmission of inherited traits. (pp. 50-52)

7. Differentiate between what is meant by *dominant, recessive*, and *sex-linked inheritance*. (pp. 51-52, 57)

   a. *dominant*

   b. *recessive*

   c. *sex-linked*

8. Distinguish between *phenotype* and *genotype*. (p. 51)

9. List some of the birth defects which are caused by *genetic* and *chromosomal* abnormalities. (p. 52)

10. Explain how hereditary and environmental factors interact to influence human nature. (pp. 52, 56-65)

11. Describe the methods for prenatal diagnosis of birth defects. (pp. 61-62, Box 2-1)

   a. d.

   b. e.

   c. f.

12. Define *maturation* and explain how it can be affected by environmental forces. (p. 63)

13. List some of the benefits and dangers of genetic testing. (p. 64, Box 2-2)

14. Describe the various methods for studying the relative effects of *heredity* and environment. (pp. 65-67)

15. Explain how certain characteristics and disorders are influenced by both *heredity* and environment. (pp. 67-69)

16. List and describe the three stages of prenatal development. (pp. 70-73)

    a.

    b.

    c.

17. Identify and explain some of the maternal factors that influence prenatal development. (pp. 73-80)

18. Describe and explain some of the paternal factors that influence prenatal development. (pp. 80-81)

19. List and describe the three stages of childbirth. (p. 81)

    a.

    b.

    c.

20. Name and explain the various methods of childbirth. (pp. 82-84)

21. List some alternative settings for childbirth. (p. 85)

22. Compare and contrast some of the differences in maternity care in Western Europe and the United States. (p. 86, Box 2-5)

SUPPLEMENTAL READING

Ellen Goodman is a *Boston Globe* columnist. This article is reprinted with permission and first appeared on November 11, 1993 © The Boston Globe Company.

There Will Never Be Another You . . . We Think

Ellen Goodman

Boston--At some point all parents, except those with too much confidence and too little imagination, have lain awake at night thinking about how we would do it--childraising--differently if we had a second chance. We would be braver or more cautious, more permissive or more authoritarian, more understanding or more judgemental.

One of the givens of life, however, is that children are unique, or as Mr. Rogers would put it, special. We know that we can't raise a son or daughter one way, then start all over again with the same exact genetic matter.

Or can we?

Just a week ago, Dr. Jerry Hall announced to all the world that his team at George Washington University Medical Center had successfully split human embryos and made identical copies of them. None of these embryos was actually implanted in a womb. The researchers purposely chose genetically abnormal embryos that could not have been brought to term and were in fact discarded six days after fertilization.

But since then, the spectres raised by this research have been multiplying faster than any reproductive cell. There is the spectre of a freezer full of identically genetic "twins" all waiting for wombs. There is the spectre of bioscientists running amok in the gene pool.

Normally I don't belong to the Jurassic Park school of the scientifically anxious. I don't worry about mad scientists creating human monsters in their labs. When I think of biogenetic research, I don't conjure up the image of Frankenstein. What I do see is an ethical Jack-in-the-Box.

Wind up the science box and Surprise: Baby Louise pops out of the Petri dish! Surprise: Embryos in the Freezer section of your bio-market! Surprise: You too can copy an embryo at the bio-Xerox center! The research comes flying out of the lab and into the public consciousness with little warning. We learn what we can do before we figure out what we want to do.

This element of surprise is especially disturbing when we are talking about the act(s) of creation. The new reproductive choices of the past decade have forced an endless series of hard ethical decisions. We've seen one couple wrangle over custody of frozen pre-embryos. We've learned about the misuse of genetic testing to abort female fetuses. We've met parents who conceived a baby as a bone marrow donor for their daughter. We've read about a man who committed suicide, leaving behind 15 vials of frozen sperm as a legacy for his lover.

This time, the cloning of the human embryos was devised to help infertile couples. It would increase the supply of embryos in fertility clinics. But the idea of copying two, six or 10 other identical embryos raises questions that have little to do with infertility.

Is it all right to give birth to two or three genetically identical children over a period of years? If one child comes out "just right," should parents have the option of picking another such "winner"? Should adults be allowed to store away a "spare" in case they need one as a donor for a sick child?

What if a child who was cloned grows up and wants to give birth to her own pre-frozen twin? And while we are conjuring up fantasies, could a couple sell spare embryos the way they can now sell sperm or eggs?

My own answers to these questions are: No and Whoa. This biotechnology comes out of the marketplace of ideas which is too often literally a marketplace. This time the market is responding to the demand for a people product.

"Our goal," said Dr. Jerry Hall, "is to help parents achieve pregnancy." But it's fair to ask when these technologies put too much importance on pregnancy and not enough on parenting, even on children.

The concept of cloning embryos both overemphasizes and undermines individuality. On the one hand, cloning is part of a reproductive technology dedicated to the importance of passing along our own unique parental genes. On the other hand, the mass reproduction of one child inevitably devalues the uniqueness of that child.

Yes, we are products of our environment as well as our genes. Even two clones raised by the same parents would have some different experiences--just as identical twins do. But you don't have to believe in Frankenstein to worry about the effect of having a clone of your own in the freezer.

For the moment, the mass reproducing of people is still in its embryonic stage. But this latest scientific surprise reminds me of the line from an old song: "There will never be another you."

Don't be too sure.

Questions:

After having read Chapter 2, what would you say are some of the reasons for supporting the research by Dr. Hall and others?

After having read Chapter 2, what would you say are some of the reasons for legally limiting the research by Dr. Hall and others?

SELF-TESTS

Multiple-Choice

Circle the letter of the response which best completes or answers each of the following statements and questions.

1. After ejaculation, sperm maintain their ability to fertilize an ovum for approximately how long?
   a. 12 hours
   b. 48 hours
   c. 7 days
   d. 14 days

2. The term "dizygotic twins" identifies
   a. twins who develop from one-cell division
   b. identical twins
   c. twins created by different ova and different sperm and may be same sex or different sexes
   d. twins who are always of the same sex

3. Male is to __________; as female is to __________.
   a. XX; XY
   b. YY; XX
   c. XY; XX
   d. YY; XY

4. Rhonda and her husband Troy are the proud parents of a newborn baby boy. We can infer that the sperm cell which impregnated Rhonda
   a. carried a Y sex chromosome
   b. carried an X sex chromosome
   c. carried an XY sex chromosome
   d. carried an incomplete sex chromosome

5. Which of the following processes best accounts for the differences in genetic makeup of children of the same parents?
   a. mitosis
   b. multifactorial inheritance
   c. fertilization
   d. meiosis

6. Judith observes that the flowers growing outside her window are yellow. She has just examined the flowers'
   a. genotype
   b. alleles
   c. DNA
   d. phenotype

7. According to Mendel's laws, a homozygous green-seeded plant
   a. has 2 alleles for green seeds
   b. has 1 allele for green seeds and 1 allele for yellow seeds
   c. has only 1 allele for green seeds
   d. has 1 allele for yellow-green seeds

8. Christine is a normal female. Her husband, Dwayne, is an unaffected carrier of Tay-Sachs disease (a disease transmitted by recessive genes). Genetic counseling would reveal to Christine and Dwayne that
   a. they have a 50 percent chance of having a child with Tay-Sachs disease
   b. they have a 50 percent chance of having an unaffected child who is a carrier of Tay-Sachs disease
   c. they have a 100 percent chance of having a child with Tay-Sachs disease
   d. they have a 100 percent chance of having an unaffected child who is a carrier of Tay-Sachs disease

9. A 40-year-old woman expresses concern to her obstetrician regarding the health of her developing fetus; she fears the baby may have Down syndrome. The obstetrician would probably suggest testing by using
   a. maternal blood tests
   b. umbilical cord assessment
   c. ultrasound
   d. amniocentesis

10. Which of the following statements about chromosomal defects is the most accurate?
    a. All chromosomal defects are inherited.
    b. Accidental chromosomal abnormalities are not likely to recur in the same family.
    c. Down syndrome is the least common chromosomal disorder.
    d. All people with chromosomal abnormalities are severely retarded.

11. Which of the following factors is not associated with Down syndrome?
    a. maternal age
    b. paternal age
    c. heredity
    d. an extra chromosome

12. A couple might seek genetic counseling if
    a. one handicapped child has already been born
    b. there is a family history of hereditary illness
    c. one partner has a condition suspected to be inherited
    d. all of the above

13. Yan is 10 weeks pregnant and has decided to have the development of her 10-week old fetus assessed. Her physician, however, warns her that she should wait another 4 weeks to undergo a safer, more accurate procedure. The doctor is most likely trying to convince Yan not to undergo which of the following prenatal diagnostic techniques?
    a. chorionic villus sampling
    b. electronic fetal monitoring
    c. maternal blood tests
    d. preimplantation genetic diagnosis

14. The prenatal diagnostic technique which creates a picture of the uterus, the developing fetus, and placenta used to detect multiple pregnancies and major abnormalities is
    a. chorionic villus sampling
    b. umbilical cord assessment
    c. ultrasound
    d. amniocentesis

15. Umbilical cord assessment can allow a doctor to
    a. test for metabolic disorders and immunodeficiencies
    b. take samples of the fetus's blood
    c. examine liver function and heart failure
    d. all of the above

16. Which of the following situations best reflects the belief that environment seems to play a large part in the development of intellect and personality?
    a. An infant, raised in an overcrowded orphanage and receiving very little attention, learns to walk far earlier than usual.
    b. A baby whose parents encourage vocalization by acknowledging their child's first sounds starts to speak earlier than if his parents had ignored his early sounds.
    c. A group of infants whose parents encourage vocalization by acknowledging their children's first sounds, start to speak at exactly the same time.
    d. An infant who has regular exercise and lots of parental attention does not learn to walk until quite late.

17. Genetic testing may violate an individual's privacy. Which of the following scenarios most accurately reflects this statement?
    a. A woman who learns she has a genetic tendency for breast cancer is told to undergo frequent mammograms.
    b. A man who learns of a genetic predisposition to lung cancer is advised to stop smoking.
    c. An airline pilot afflicted with Alzheimer's disease is forced to stop flying planes.
    d. A healthy woman, with no prior automobile accidents or traffic tickets, has her auto insurance canceled because she carries a gene for a rare neurological condition.

18. The method which allows researchers to see only the influence of heredity is
    a. adoption studies
    b. intelligence testing
    c. family studies
    d. maturation

19. Juan is an obese child who was adopted shortly after birth. Juan's adoptive family, however, is not overweight. An adoption study would most likely reveal that
    a. Juan's biological parents are thin individuals.
    b. Environment has had a greater influence than heredity on Juan's obesity.
    c. Juan's biological parents are overweight individuals.
    d. Diet plays no role in obesity.

20. Sarah and Elise are identical twins. Linda and Louise are fraternal twins. Research shows us that Sarah and Elise will be more concordant than Linda and Louise in which of the following traits?
    a. senescence
    b. weight
    c. blood pressure
    d. all of the above

21. Brett was adopted as an infant. During adolescence, his I.Q. score was found to be extremely high. Which factor is most closely correlated with Brett's intelligence?
    a. his adoptive parents' I.Q.s
    b. his biological mother's I.Q.
    c. his adoptive sibling's I.Q.
    d. none of the above is associated with his intelligence

22. Kate's parents are both alcoholics. Research leads us to believe that
    a. Kate's brother has a greater risk of becoming an alcoholic than she does
    b. Having two alcoholic parents does nothing to increase Kate's chances of developing the disease
    c. Kate is four times as likely to develop alcoholism as is a daughter of non-alcoholic parents
    d. There is a 100 percent chance that Kate will become an alcoholic

23. Which of the following statements concerning schizophrenia is least accurate?
    a. Many studies suggest that schizophrenia has a strong genetic element.
    b. An individual whose father has schizophrenia is more likely to develop the disorder than is an individual whose cousin is affected by it.
    c. All identical twins are concordant for schizophrenia.
    d. An individual growing up in a city is more likely to develop schizophrenia than is an individual growing up in a rural area.

24. Billy is a 5-year-old afflicted with infantile autism. Billy's parents are told by their physician that
    a. Billy will begin experiencing hallucinations and delusions, common symptoms of autism.
    b. Billy's 2-year-old sister Charlene is 3 times more likely to develop infantile autism than is his 6-month-old brother Jason.
    c. It is not likely that Billy will show signs of retardation due to the disease; his I.Q., in fact, should be that of a normal child.
    d. Billy's autism is probably an inherited disorder, and the environment will have minimal affect on his development.

25. Research on the subject of shyness tells us that
    a. environmental factors do not affect shyness
    b. both heredity and environment influence shyness
    c. shy children tend to feel less anxious in stressful situations than other youngsters
    d. the more active a parents' social life, the greater the tendency for their child to be shy

26. Brian suffers from chronic unhappiness, insomnia, and has trouble concentrating. A physician would conclude that Brian is suffering from
    a. a disorder unaffected by life stress
    b. depression
    c. infantile autism
    d. normal temporary sadness

27. Recent efforts to acknowledge the role of genetics have shown that the heritability of a trait generally
    a. does not exceed 50 percent
    b. is often as great as 90 percent
    c. accounts for why siblings tend to be more alike than different
    d. is so high that the environmental influence on most traits is minimal

28. The term for the stage of prenatal development during which the organism is implanted in the wall of the uterus is
    a. germinal
    b. embryonic
    c. fetal
    d. gamete

29. The stage of prenatal development during which the organism develops the major body systems (respiratory, alimentary, nervous) is
    a. germinal
    b. embryonic
    c. fetal
    d. gamete

30. Veronica is concerned about her risks of undergoing a spontaneous abortion (miscarriage). Literature on prenatal development informs her that her chances of miscarrying are greatest during which stage?
    a. germinal
    b. embryonic
    c. fetal
    d. gamete

31. Sirena is a pregnant woman who eats a well-balanced diet and takes dietary supplements. Joanna, who is also pregnant, is a malnourished woman suffering from poor nutrition. We can reasonably infer that
    a. Joanna's baby will be bigger, healthier, and more alert if she receives dietary supplements during her pregnancy
    b. Joanna's baby is more likely to be born prematurely than Sirena's baby
    c. Joanna's baby is more likely to develop brain defects than Sirena's baby
    d. all of the above

32. Which of the following statements about the placenta is most accurate?
    a. The placenta is a barrier between mother and fetus.
    b. The placenta shields the fetus from the toxins in the mother's body.
    c. The placenta filters out most hazards, including hazardous drugs, while allowing oxygen, carbon dioxide, and water to reach the fetus.
    d. Virtually everything the mother takes in is passed to the fetus through the placenta.

33. Jeremy is a 5-year-old boy who exhibits a variety of central nervous system disorders. These include short attention span, restlessness, learning disabilities, and motor impairments. In addition, his I.Q. is lower than most children his age. From this information, we can reasonably assume that Jeremy suffers from
    a. DES exposure
    b. fetal alcohol syndrome
    c. acquired immune deficiency syndrome (AIDS)
    d. schizophrenia

34. A great deal of recent research has been performed on infants who were exposed to cocaine prenatally. These studies have found that
    a. The majority of babies whose mothers stopped using cocaine early in pregnancy still grew abnormally; exposure to the drug for a short time is just as damaging as exposure throughout the entire pregnancy.
    b. Most babies whose mothers used cocaine during pregnancy were of normal birthweight; very few were born prematurely.
    c. Given the proper environment, some cocaine-exposed infants can catch up in weight, length, and head circumference by one year of age.
    d. The development of cocaine-exposed infants tends to equal that of newborns not exposed to the drug prenatally.

35. Melanie is a pregnant woman who has the human immunodeficiency virus (HIV) in her blood. Her physician would probably inform Melanie that
    a. The virus has not yet caused the Acquired Immune Deficiency syndrome (AIDS) in her body; her fetus is not at risk.
    b. If her baby is born prematurely, it will be more susceptible to AIDS because the newborn will miss the protection of antibodies which may not appear until the last 3 months of gestation.
    c. Between 75-100 percent of HIV positive mothers transmit the virus to newborns.
    d. After her baby is born, it will take at least 2 years for the child to show symptoms of AIDS if infected.

36. Recent studies on the risks involved with delayed child-bearing indicate that
    a. 75 percent of women over 35 have a higher risk of delivering prematurely.
    b. As women age, they are no more likely to miscarry than younger women.
    c. Older mothers are twice as likely to experience complications of pregnancy such as diabetes and high blood pressure.
    d. A woman's fertility is not affected by aging.

37. Janette, a healthy physician, and Harriet, a healthy housewife, are both pregnant. Which of the following statements is most accurate concerning these two pregnant mothers?
    a. Janette has a greater risk of delivering prematurely because her occupation is much more stressful than Harriet's.
    b. Janette has a greater risk of delivering prematurely because her occupation is much more physically demanding than Harriet's.
    c. Both Janette and Harriet can continue to exercise in moderation without endangering their fetuses.
    d. If these women partake in any form of exercise, it is likely that their fetuses will show a serious decline in heart rate.

38. Which of the following paternal factors is least likely to have a harmful influence on the development of a fetus?
    a. a diet rich in Vitamin C
    b. cocaine
    c. nicotine
    d. paternal age

39. Recent studies on cesarean deliveries in the United States show that
    a. Women with lower incomes have cesarean deliveries at nearly twice the rate as women with more substantial incomes.
    b. There is some risk of the uterus rupturing when women having undergone a prior cesarean delivery later undergo vaginal delivery.
    c. Cesareans are performed more often by hospital residents than private physicians.
    d. Babies born through elective cesarean deliveries before labor has begun show levels of catecholamine almost as high as infants born vaginally.

40. Which of the following statements is most accurate?
    a. Proportionately more babies die at or soon after birth in the United States compared with a number of western European countries.
    b. It is now known that the father cannot transmit environmentally caused defects.
    c. It is best to do continuous, routine electronic fetal monitoring even when a pregnancy seems uncomplicated.
    d. The mortality rate in the United States has declined over the past several decades, in terms of world rankings.

Completion

Supply the term or terms needed to complete each of the following statements.

1. The release of an egg cell by the ovaries, about once a month, is called ____________________.

2. The unborn factors, inherited from our parents, that affect our development are called ________________.

3. Genes that govern alternative expressions of a characteristic are called __________.

4. An observable trait is called a ____________________; the underlying invisible genetic pattern that causes certain traits to be expressed is a ____________________.

5. ________________________ is usually prohibited by law to lower the risk of children's inheriting a disease passed on through recessive genes that both parents may have inherited from a common ancestor.

6. ________________________ is caused by an extra twenty-first chromosome or the translocation of part of the twenty-first chromosome onto another chromosome.

7. A ___________________ is a chart of enlarged photographs of one's chromosomes arranged according to size and structure to show any chromosomal abnormalities.

8. ________________________ is the unfolding of a biologically determined, age-related sequence of behavior patterns.

9. When adopted children are more like their biological parents and siblings on a particular trait, we see the influence of __________________; when they resemble their adoptive families more, we see the influence of __________________.

10. Longitudinal twin studies performed on 500 pairs of twins shows that ________________________ twins become more and more alike in I.Q. with age, while ________________________ twins become less alike.

11. ________________________ is a person's overall pattern of character, behavioral, temperamental, emotional, and mental traits, some of which are believed to be inherited.

12. While a tendency toward shyness may be inherited, the ________________ can either accentuate or modify this tendency.

13. The disorder of mood in which a person feels unhappy and often has trouble eating, sleeping, or concentrating is called ____________________.

14. During the germinal stage of development, the blastocyst is developing into the nurturing and protective organs called the ___________________, ___________________, and ____________________.

15. Environmental factors which are birth-defect producing are called ______________________________.

16. A combination of slowed prenatal and postnatal growth, disorders of the central nervous system, and body malformations attributable to maternal alcohol use during pregnancy are labeled ______________________________.

17. ___________________________ in pregnancy seems to have some of the same effects on school-age children as drinking in pregnancy, such as poor attention span, hyperactivity, learning problems, social maladjustment, and poor I.Q. scores.

18. "An apathetic, lethargic baby who in early childhood will have trouble loving his or her mother, making friends, and playing normally"--this describes a child whose mother probably used ____________________ during pregnancy.

19. When a fetus's blood contains a protein substance called the _______________, but the mother's blood does not, antibodies in the mother's blood may attack the fetus and possibly cause a miscarriage, stillbirth, jaundice, anemia, heart defects, mental retardation, or death.

20. An especially dangerous environmental hazard for pregnant women, which affected German infants after the spill out at the Chernobyl nuclear power plant is ________________________.

21. A man's use of cocaine can cause birth defects in his children since cocaine seems to attach itself to his __________________.

22. Alternative methods of childbirth seek to minimize the use of harmful ________________ while maximizing the parents' satisfaction as participants.

23. The _________________ method of childbirth instructs women in anatomy to remove fear of the unknown and trains them to vary their patterns of breathing to match the strength of contractions and to concentrate on sensations other than contractions.

24. ________________________ is an assessment technique that provides valuable information, especially in detecting a lack of oxygen, during high-risk pregnancies.

25. In many cultures, childbearing women are attended by a ________________, a woman who has had a baby herself and can give emotional support to the mother.

ANSWERS FOR SELF-TESTS — CHAPTER 2

Multiple-Choice

		Page	
1.	b	47	factual
2.	c	47	factual
3.	c	49	conceptual
4.	a	49	conceptual
5.	d	50	factual
6.	d	51	conceptual
7.	a	51	conceptual
8.	b	52	conceptual
9.	d	53	conceptual
10.	b	57-58	factual
11.	d	58-59	factual
12.	d	59	conceptual
13.	a	61	conceptual
14.	c	62	factual
15.	d	62	factual
16.	b	63	conceptual
17.	d	64	conceptual
18.	c	65	factual
19.	c	65	conceptual
20.	d	65	conceptual
21.	b	66	conceptual
22.	c	67	conceptual
23.	c	67	factual
24.	d	67	conceptual
25.	b	68	factual
26.	b	69	conceptual
27.	a	69	factual
28.	a	70	factual
29.	b	70	factual
30.	b	70	conceptual
31.	d	73-74	conceptual
32.	d	75	factual
33.	b	76	conceptual
34.	c	77-78	factual
35.	b	78	factual
36.	c	79	factual
37.	c	80	conceptual
38.	a	80	factual
39.	b	84	factual
40.	a	86	factual

Completion

		Page
1.	ovulation	46
2.	heredity	49
3.	alleles	51
4.	phenotype; genotype	51
5.	Inbreeding	57
6.	Down syndrome	58
7.	karyotype	59
8.	maturation	63
9.	heredity; environment	65
10.	identical; fraternal	66
11.	personality	66
12.	environment	68
13.	depression	69
14.	placenta, umbilical cord, amniotic sac	70
15.	teratogenic	73
16.	fetal alcohol syndrome (FAS)	76
17.	smoking	76
18.	cocaine	77
19.	Rh factor	79
20.	radiation	80
21.	sperm	80
22.	drugs (medicine)	82
23.	Lamaze (natural, prepared)	83
24.	electronic fetal monitoring	84
25.	midwife	87

CHAPTER 3

Physical Development In Infancy and Toddlerhood

INTRODUCTION

In Chapter 3 we learn that the first year of life is usually one of rapid physical growth, more so than at any other time in the child's life, with stabilized regulation of all major systems of the body.

- The first four weeks of life are the neonatal period. Physical characteristics, body systems, and brain and reflex behavior of the neonate are thoroughly discussed.
- At birth, immediate medical and behavioral assessment is crucial to predict a baby's health status. The Apgar Scale, various screening tests, and the Brazelton Scale are all used to examine the health of a newborn.
- Low-birthweight babies are at a higher risk of potential complications; several recommendations are made for preventing or overcoming the physiological and psychological problems of these babies. Also examined are the topics of postmaturity, infant mortality, sudden infant death syndrome (SIDS), and immunization.
- A neonate's initial reflex behaviors will disappear during the first year or so, being replaced by deliberate behaviors. More recent research examines the importance of early sensory stimulation for all newborns. Three principles of infant development are explained: head to toe, inner to outer, and simple to complex.
- Infant variations in daily cycles of nourishment, sleep, wakefulness, and activity are thoroughly described.
- Infants are able to make sense of their perceptions, and they can discriminate in the areas of sight, hearing, taste, smell, touch, and pain. Sensory systems of newborns are explained in detail.
- The developmental differences between boys and girls are briefly examined.
- The interaction of heredity and environment as it affects the timing of milestones of motor development is discussed, along with a multicultural view of motor development.

CHAPTER OUTLINE

I. **The Neonate**

- A. Physical Characteristics
- B. Body Systems
  - 1. Circulatory System
  - 2. Respiratory System
  - 3. Gastrointestinal System
  - 4. Temperature Regulation
- C. The Brain and Reflex Behavior
  - 1. Growth and Development of the Brain
  - 2. A Newborn's Reflexes
- D. The Newborn's Health
  - 1. Effects of Birth Trauma
  - 2. Medical and Behavioral Screening
    - a. Immediate Medical Assessment: The Apgar Scale
    - b. Neonatal Screening for Medical Conditions
    - c. Assessing Responses: The Brazelton Scale
  - 3. Low Birthweight
    - a. Who is likely to have a Low-Birthweight Baby?
    - b. Cross-cultural Aspects of Low Birthweight
    - c. Consequences of Low Birthweight
    - d. Treatment of Low-Birthweight Babies
  - 4. Postmaturity
  - 5. Infant Mortality
  - 6. Sudden Infant Death Syndrome
- E. Immunization for Better Health

II. **Development during the First 3 Years of Life**

- A. Principles of Development
  - 1. Top-to-Bottom Development
  - 2. Inner-to-Outer Development
  - 3. Simple-to-Complex Development
- B. States of Arousal: the Body's Cycles

III. **States of Arousal: The Body's Cycles**

- A. States of Arousal
- B. Growth and Nourishment
  - 1. Influences on Growth
  - 2. Breastfeeding
    - a. The Benefits of Breastfeeding
    - b. The Cultural Context of Breastfeeding
  - 3. Bottle Feeding
  - 4. Cow's Milk and Solid Foods

C. The Senses
   1. Sight
      a. Depth Perception
      b. Visual Preferences
   2. Hearing
   3. Smell
   4. Taste
   5. Touch and Pain
D. Motor Development
   1. Milestones of Motor Development
      a. Head Control
      b. Hand Control
      c. Locomotion
   2. Environmental Influences on Motor Development
   3. Can Motor Development be Speeded Up?
E. How Different are Boys and Girls?

KEY TERMS

---

anoxia (page 93)

Apgar scale (96-98)

birth trauma (96)

Brazelton Neonatal Behavioral Assessment Scale (98)

cephalocaudal principle (107)

cerebral cortex (95)

Denver Developmental Screening Test (117)

fontanels (93)

infant mortality rate (103)

lanugo (93)

low birthweight (100)

meconium (94)

neonatal period (92)

neonate (92)

physiologic jaundice (94)

preterm (premature) babies (100)

proximodistal principle (108)

reflex behaviors (96)

small-for-date babies (100)

states of arousal (108)

sudden infant death syndrome (SIDS) (104-105)

vernix caseosa (93)

visual cliff (114)

visual preferences (115)

LEARNING OBJECTIVES

After finishing Chapter 3, you should be able to:

1. Describe some common physical characteristics of the *neonate*. (pages 92-93)

2. Compare the demands on the major body systems before and after birth. (pp. 93-94)

3. Briefly describe the growth and development of the human brain. (pp. 94-96)

4. Describe the differences between the *Apgar Scale* and the *Brazelton Scale*. (pp. 96, 98-99)

5. Box 3-1 addresses a child's development of motor skills in various cultures. Comment briefly on the findings on this topic. (Box 3-1) (pp. 99-100)

6. The authors have given considerable information about the relationship between low birthweight and health complications. List several factors which can contribute to low birthweight, some of the consequences of low birthweight, and how it is treated. (pp. 100-103)

7. Explain postmaturity and its effect on newborns. (pp. 103)

8. Define *SIDS* and explain some findings about what may cause it. (pp. 104-105)

9. Compare rates of immunization in the U.S. and other countries and account for the discrepancies. (pp. 105-107)

10. Briefly describe the following three principles about babies' growth and development: (pp. 107-108)
    a. *top-to-bottom* development

    b. *inner-to-outer* development

    c. *simple-to-complex* development

11. List and briefly explain an infant's *states of arousal.* (pp. 108-110)

12. Discuss how heredity and environment interact in the process of physical growth. (p. 111)

13. Comment on the nourishment of newborns in the following areas: (pp. 111-112)
    a. breastfeeding

    b. bottle feeding

    c. cow's milk and solid foods

14. Describe what the normal infant's capacities seem to be in each of the following sensory systems: (pp. 113-117)
    a. sight

    b. hearing

    c. smell

    d. taste

    e. touch and pain

SUPPLEMENTAL READING

Julia Martin writes on health and parenting from Verona, New Jersey. This article is reprinted with permission from Child, ©February 1994.

Health Risks and Heredity

Julia Martin

When your child was born, you probably spotted certain uncanny family resemblances right away--your mother-in-law's ruddy skin, your oval face, your husband's deep-set eyes. But she may have also inherited a less obvious, but far more important family legacy: a genetic tendency toward certain diseases. Increasingly, scientists are discovering that the major illnesses that are killing people today--cancer, heart disease, and diabetes--are, to some extent, programmed by our genes.

But if your family tree has a few unhealthy limbs, there's no cause for alarm. Following a healthy lifestyle will significantly reduce your child's chances of getting these diseases, no matter what his genes say. So you need to teach your child to exercise regularly, watch fats, eat a diet high in fresh fruits and vegetables, and not drink or smoke.

Awareness of your family history is vital, however, to minimize your child's risk through early detection, prevention, and treatment. Thanks to rapid genetic advances, special therapies can help minimize or delay some hereditary diseases--even those without known cures.

Here's how to assess your child's risk of getting four common life-threatening diseases and how to increase her chances for lifelong good health.

Cancer

A small proportion of all cancers develop as a result of heredity, says Peter Greenwald, M.D., director of cancer prevention and control for the National Cancer Institute in Bethesda, Maryland.

To learn your child's cancer risk, find out if any of your "first-degree" relatives or in-laws (mother, father, siblings, or children) or "second-degree" relatives (aunts, uncles, grandparents) had cancer, the type, and at what age. Your child's doctor can tell you whether you need to consult a cancer specialist.

With many cancers, environmental influences (such as exposure to harmful chemicals), exercise, and eating habits make the real difference. "What you do as a child clearly affects your chances of developing cancer later in life," Dr. Greenwald says.

For example, a third of all cancers can be attributed to smoking, and children typically begin to feel pressured to smoke around sixth grade. A 1990 study by Weekly Reader, a newsmagazine for children, found that 24 percent of fourth-graders and 38 percent of sixth-graders thought that "many" of their peers had tried beer, wine, or liquor. These findings are particularly troublesome because drinking, especially when combined with smoking, can lead to cancers of the mouth and throat.

Skin cancer usually has its roots in excessive childhood exposure to ultraviolet radiation from the sun. And other types of cancer--including breast and colon--have been linked to a high-fat diet early in life.

To protect against cancer, kids over the age of 2 should be fed low-fat dairy products, lean meat, and a minimum of high-fat desserts. (Because they need fuel for their rapid growth, however, children under age 2 should not have fat or calories restricted.)

Encourage your child to eat at least five servings of fruits and vegetables a day, and be sure to do the same yourself. "What parents say is so important, but not as important as what they do," Dr. Greenwald says.

Heart Disease

About 50 percent of elementary school children have problems with elevated blood cholesterol, high blood pressure, or weight that may place them at risk for heart disease if the problems persist until later in life. In 1992, a national panel of experts that included based in Chicago, recommended cholesterol testing for children over age 2 who have a parent with a cholesterol level exceeding 250 milligrams per deciliter of blood or a parent or grandparent who had heart or blood vessel disease at age 55 or younger.

Not every doctor believes that testing is necessary for high-risk kids, however. Matthew Gillman, M.D., assistant professor of medicine, pediatrics, and public health at the Boston University School of Medicine, says all kids should follow the same prescription: that of maintaining an optimal weight, exercising, and eating a diet that derives 30 percent or less of its calories from fat, with less than 10 percent from saturated fat.

Hypertension

High blood pressure is an important risk factor for stroke and heart attack. It can also lead to kidney and eye disease. According to the American Heart Association in Dallas, 2.8 million children between the ages of 6 and 17 already have high blood pressure.

The National Task Force on Blood Pressure Control and Children recommends that pediatricians begin measuring a child's blood pressure yearly from age 3 or 4. If a child's pressure is higher than the 95th percentile for his age group, it is considered high.

The main way to keep your child's blood pressure at a healthy level is to watch his weight and increase his physical activity. Limiting salt, including high-sodium foods like chips, hot dogs, and canned foods, is also key. What children should eat are lots of potassium-rich fruits and vegetables, such as oranges, tomatoes, squash, and bananas.

Diabetes

Uncontrolled diabetes can lead to heart disease, stroke, eye and kidney damage, or numbness--and even amputation--of the limbs. But new research shows that with early detection, certain interventions may help delay the onset and severity of the disease.

Diabetes can be thought of as two different diseases. Type I (insulin-dependent) diabetes, once known as juvenile diabetes, usually strikes sometime before age 30. It is an autoimmune disease: The body's immune system attacks the insulin-producing cells of the pancreas. Symptoms may include increased appetite, thirst, and urination, as well as weight loss. Type II diabetes (non-insulin-dependent) accounts for 90 percent of diabetes cases. Patients are unable to manufacture insulin, or the pancreas makes it, but the body's cells fail to respond to it.

If you have a close relative or in-law with Type II diabetes, your family's diet should be low in saturated fat, total fat, and simple sugars (contained in table sugar, desserts, sodas, and some snacks), says James Gavin III, M.D., Ph.D., president of the American Diabetes Association in Alexandria, Virginia. It's also important to maintain a healthy weight, not smoke, and get lots of exercise. "Regular exercise can actually delay the onset of Type II diabetes," he says.

Because Type II diabetes generally strikes after age 40, testing isn't necessary for children. But if you have a strong family history of Type I diabetes, speak to your pediatrician about testing. A simple blood test can detect certain telltale proteins long before the disease appears. More complicated genetic tests are also available.

A controversial new study in Canada and Finland suggests that high-risk infants who are given cow's milk may be more likely to develop Type I diabetes. Researchers speculate that the immune system attacks a protein on the insulin-producing cells of the pancreas that is similar to a protein found in cow's milk. As a precaution, Dr. Gavin advises parents to consider nursing high-risk children under age 3 or feeding them a non-milk-based formula.

Questions:

Cite a few examples of what you believe to be hereditary influences on your own development.

Cite a few examples of what you believe to be environmental influences on your own development.

From your own personal experience, which do you believe has a greater impact on development--heredity or environment?

Charting Your Medical Family Tree

Make a copy of this medical family tree for each child. "This information is helpful to your child's pediatrician when choosing diagnostic tests or prescribing drugs," says Palma E. Formica, M.D., a family practitioner at St. Peter's Medical Center in New Brunswick, New Jersey, and an AMA trustee. It is important to note how old your relatives were when their health problems first occurred, since some illnesses may be attributed to old age rather than heredity.

	Child	Mother	Father	Sister(s)	Brother(s)	Grandmother	Grandfather	Grandmother	Grandfather	Aunt(s)	Uncle(s)
Alive											
Deceased											
Blood type											
Alcoholism											
Allergies											
Anemia											
Asthma											
Birth Complications											
Birth defects											
Cancer											
Diabetes											
Glaucoma											
Heart attack											
Heart disease											
Other											

SELF-TESTS

Multiple-Choice

Circle the letter of the response which best completes or answers each of the following statements and questions.

1. During the first 4 weeks of life after birth, which is a transition time from support from the mother's body to independent existence, an infant is called a/an
   a. gamete
   b. neonate
   c. zygote
   d. premature baby

2. Latoya's newborn son, Jose, is one day old. Latoya's obstetrician informs her that
   a. Jose may lose up to 10 percent of his baby weight over the next few days. This is a normal neonatal response, and Jose should be back to birthweight within two weeks.
   b. Jose should almost double his body weight over his first few days. This is due to an excess of body fluids.
   c. If Jose should develop secretion from his breasts over the next few days, this is reason for alarm. Such a fluid emission indicates a serious infection.
   d. Jose's skin color is likely to fade over the next few days. Most neonates have dark, thin skin at the time of birth.

3. Anoxia is to ________________ as physiologic jaundice is to ____________.
   a. lack of oxygen; immature liver function
   b. lack of oxygen; irregular heartbeat
   c. irregular heartbeat; lack of oxygen
   d. irregular bladder function; immature liver function

4. In a newborn infant, the subcortical structures are the most fully developed. As the baby matures, in what area of the brain do cells increase their complexity of connections the most?
   a. cerebellum
   b. hypothalamus
   c. cerebral cortex
   d. sensory layers

5. Becky is a newborn infant who has Down syndrome. Research by Rosenzweig and Bennett (1984, 1976) indicates that
   a. If Becky is exposed to an enriched environment at an early age, her developmental functioning can be enhanced.
   b. Whether Becky is exposed to an enriched or an isolated environment shortly after birth, her developmental abilities will not be affected.
   c. Because the brain does not have plasticity, Becky can never increase her ability to learn and store information.
   d. all of the above

6. Which of the following statements about motor development is most accurate?
   a. All infants respond with identical reflex behaviors to external stimuli.
   b. Cultural differences in motor development are completely independent of genetic differences among peoples.
   c. Regarding motor development, there is considerable difference between cultures.
   d. It is impossible to speed up or modify a child's motor development.

7. Raphael and Gregory were born on the same day. Gregory, though, learns to walk about 9 months before Raphael. Research on "normal motor development" allows us to reasonably infer that
   a. Since motor development is universal, Raphael must be handicapped to some degree.
   b. Gregory is an exceptional child; most babies learn to walk at precisely the same time.
   c. Raphael and Gregory are from different cultures. Thus, they have developed their motor skills quite differently.
   d. Because Raphael's mother has placed him in day care, he has grown very dependent to his caretakers. In turn, his motor development has been delayed.

8. Research by E. E. Werner (1985) on the effects of birth trauma, indicates that children are remarkably resilient. Which of the following scenarios best exemplifies this finding?
   a. Birth trauma never results in permanent brain damage, mental retardation or behavioral problems.
   b. A child who suffers a traumatic birth is later exposed to a favorable environment. However, his physical and psychological development remains impaired.
   c. A child who experiences a normal birth is later exposed to an inadequate, unstimulating environment. Because the child suffered no problems at birth, his physical and psychological development is still maximized.
   d. A child who suffers a traumatic birth is later exposed to a favorable environment. As a result, his physical and psychological development is greatly enhanced.

9. Which of the following factors is <u>not</u> assessed by the Apgar test?
   a. reflex irritability
   b. response to stress
   c. muscle tone
   d. heart rate

10. Which of the following women is statistically least likely to give birth to an underweight infant?
    a. Annette: she is black, 16 years old, and unmarried; this is her first child; she was underweight before pregnancy and has gained 14 pounds during the pregnancy.
    b. Brenda: she is black, 19 years old, and unmarried; this is her second child. She has gained 22 pounds during the pregnancy.
    c. Christine: she is white, 29 years old, and married; this is her second child; she has had two previous miscarriages.
    d. Dorothy: she is white, 41 years old, and married; this is her third child; she smokes.

11. Jarod is a 7-year-old boy who was born weighing only 3 pounds. A psychologist would likely inform Jarod's parents that
    a. He may need special education classes.
    b. He may overcome or avoid possible learning disabilities with an adequate environment.
    c. He may have reduced verbal ability.
    d. All of the above.

12. Low birthweight babies seem to recover more quickly and leave the hospital sooner if
    a. they are regularly visited by their parents, receiving lots of attention and stimulation.
    b. they are placed in an isolette while their parents remain unattached and isolated.
    c. they receive stimulation through regular massage.
    d. both a and c

13. A baby is considered ____________________ if it has not been delivered by 42 weeks after the mother's last menstrual period.
    a. postmature
    b. premature
    c. small-for-date
    d. brain damaged

14. The infant mortality rate for African-American babies is more than twice as high as for white ones. What factor largely accounts for this difference?
    a. poor nutrition
    b. teenage pregnancy
    c. low-birthweight babies
    d. lack of education

15. Which of the following infants has the greatest chance of dying from sudden infant death syndrome (SIDS)?
    a. a white, female baby of parents of low socioeconomic status
    b. a black, male baby whose parents are young, unmarried, and smoke
    c. a healthy baby whose parents put him to sleep on his back
    d. none of these infants possess risk factors related to SIDS

16. Which of the following statements about immunization is *least* accurate?
    a. Until the middle of the 19th century, contagious diseases such as measles, mumps, and diphtheria were often fatal.
    b. Between 1980 and 1985, the proportion of American children aged 1 to 4 who were immunized against major childhood illnesses increased.
    c. Currently, about 1 in 4 two-year-olds and 1 in 3 poor children are not protected against measles, rubella, polio, mumps, diphtheria, pertussis, and tetanus.
    d. Some parents have failed to immunize their children because they feared that the vaccines themselves might cause brain damage.

17. Shelnet is a 4-year-old African-American girl living in Chicago. Nicole is a 4-year-old French girl living in Paris. Studies on immunization would lead us to believe that
    a. Both of these children live in countries providing publicly subsidized health surveillance.
    b. Because Nicole resides in a European country, she is less likely than Shelnet to receive routine immunization.
    c. Shelnet resides in a country which maintained a national child health policy since the early 1900s.
    d. Because Shelnet resides in the U.S., she is less likely than Nicole to receive routine immunization.

18. The ________________ principle which dictates that development proceeds from the head to the lower parts of the body is called the
    a. cephalocaudal principle
    b. proximodistal principle
    c. reflex principle
    d. none of the above

19. Which of the following scenarios *best* exemplifies the simple-to-complex principle of development?
    a. Roberto and Suzette both learn to sit up before they learn to walk.
    b. At the time of her birth, Katrina's head is only one-fourth the length of her body.
    c. Kristen and Alex both learn to speak at exactly the same age.
    d. Roland first learns to use his upper arms, then his forearms, then his hands, and finally his fingers.

20. During his first months of life, Jamie is an alert baby who cries often and shows a variety of responses to his environment. Claudia, however, is a much less vigorous newborn; she is quiet and rarely active. Which of the following might we infer?
    a. By age 10, Claudia will become a more active child.
    b. By age 10, Jamie will become a more active child.
    c. Both infants will develop similarly.
    d. During infancy, Claudia's parents created an environment with a great deal of stimulation.

21. Which of the following statements regarding growth is most accurate?
    a. Physicians and parents should begin to worry when a young child's growth seems to have halted for several weeks.
    b. By the first birthday, children are generally still toothless.
    c. Growth is faster during the first 3 years of life than it will ever be again.
    d. Growth in young children is primarily smooth and continuous.

22. Jody and her obstetrician have just finished a discussion concerning the nutrition of Jody's newborn infant. The doctor has most likely indicated that the best food for newborns is
    a. milk-based formula
    b. goat's milk
    c. soy milk
    d. mother's milk

23. Which category of women is unlikely to breastfeed their newborn babies?
    a. minority women
    b. women who receive free samples of infant formulas from the hospital
    c. women who return to work full time after their babies' birth
    d. all of the above

24. Which sensory system is *least* well developed at birth?
    a. touch
    b. taste
    c. smell
    d. sight

25. Shelley is an obese 5-year-old American child. After reading recent research on obesity, Shelley's parents are most likely to believe
    a. there is a largely genetic basis for obesity
    b. they should put Shelley on a strict weight-loss diet immediately, eliminating all dietary fat
    c. Shelley may have an overactive metabolism
    d. Shelley should receive a diet containing approximately 60 percent of total calories from fat

26. Melinda, a 2-month-old baby, would most likely possess a visual preference for
    a. straight lines
    b. pictures of faces
    c. simple patterns
    d. familiar sights

27. In an experiment, a week-old baby boy is able to turn on a recording of his mother reading a story by sucking on a pacifier. At certain times, though, the baby's sucking instead turns on a recording of an unfamiliar woman reading a story. Research indicates that
    a. the baby cannot distinguish between the two different voices
    b. the baby will suck harder on the nipple when he hears his mother's voice
    c. the baby will suck harder on the nipple when he hears the unfamiliar woman's voice
    d. the baby's early sensitivity to sounds is not an indicator of later cognitive functioning

28. A physician in favor of routine circumcision theorizes that several medical conditions may be prevented by using the procedure on newborns. These include
    a. urinary tract infections
    b. genital ulcers
    c. bacterial growth
    d. all of the above

29. According to the Denver Developmental Screening Test, which of the following children is developmentally delayed?
    a. a child who is born with a low birthweight
    b. a child who cannot roll over by the time he is two months old
    c. a child who is unable to walk properly by the time he is 14 1/2 months old
    d. a child who cannot stand alone by the time he is 11 1/2 months old

30. About six months of age, most babies begin to get around by themselves. The methods of locomotion employed include:
    a. wriggling
    b. bear-walking
    c. walking on two feet only
    d. both a and b

31. Sarah's baby boy has begun to show striking changes: he is fearful of new situations, imitates complex behaviors, and appears most secure around Sarah and her husband. These changes seem to occur in the second half of the baby's first year of life and are initiated by
    a. precise hand control
    b. the new ability to crawl
    c. visual preferences
    d. the new ability to walk

32. Crawling babies often look at their mothers more than babies who have not yet begun to crawl, apparently trying to pick up emotional signals from their mothers' faces or gestures. These babies are displaying
    a. social referencing
    b. developmental delay
    c. the proximodistal principle
    d. social irritability

33. Quasia's baby boy has recently embarked upon the major motor achievement of infancy--walking. We can infer that the child is approximately
    a. 6 months old
    b. 12 months old
    c. 18 months old
    d. 24 months old

34. Motor skills such as sitting, standing, and walking
    a. proceed uniquely for each individual
    b. proceed in a preordained sequence
    c. depend only on environmental factors
    d. depend only on genetic factors

35. Delays in motor development can result from an environment deficient in
    a. nutrition
    b. physical freedom
    c. attention from adults
    d. all of the above

36. Byron is a 12-month-old child who has difficulty walking, standing alone, and even sitting up without support. It is likely that Byron
    a. is being raised by loving parents who are very attentive and provide their son with a great deal of stimulation
    b. is being raised in an orphanage, receiving proper nutrition, adequate attention, and a great deal of physical freedom
    c. is being raised in an understaffed orphanage, receiving little attention and stimulation
    d. can never achieve normal motor development skills

37. What is the general conclusion about using infant walkers?
    a. They are highly related to injuries in infants.
    b. They encourage early walking.
    c. They are usually safe.
    d. They always make for happy babies.

38. Which of the following is a conclusive statement about early toilet training?
    a. It is quite successful and easy to achieve.
    b. Elimination is originally voluntary.
    c. Maturation must occur before training can be effective.
    d. It is very difficult to achieve.

39. Katrina runs a day care center for newborns and toddlers. Experts in child development would instruct Katrina to do all of the following *except*:
    a. provide youngsters with freedom to explore and have some control over their world
    b. respond promptly to the babies' cries for help, providing them with lots of attention
    c. provide the youngsters with a variety of toys to play with
    d. leave the babies alone in their high chairs, to learn to feed themselves

40. Which of the following statements about physical differences is true?
    a. Boys are usually smaller than girls at birth.
    b. Boys are more physically vulnerable than girls throughout life.
    c. Infant boys and girls are very different.
    d. Boys and girls are very different in reaching such maturational milestones as sitting up and walking.

Completion

Supply the term or terms needed to complete each of the following statements.

1. For approximately the first four weeks of life, a newborn infant is called a/an ____________________.

2. A newborn's skin is quite pale and may have an oily covering referred to as ____________________ to protect the baby against infection.

3. Waste matter formed in the fetal intestinal tract and excreted during the first 2 days or so after birth is ____________________.

4. Until the middle of the 20th century, it was believed that brain development followed an unchangeable pattern. Now we know that the brain is more ____________________, especially while it is developing rapidly.

5. Automatic responses to external stimulation, such as blinking at a bright light, are called ____________________.

6. The Brazelton Scale assesses four dimensions of infant behavior, including ______________, ______________, ______________, and ______________.

7. Babies who, due to delayed fetal growth, weigh less than 90 percent of all babies of the same gestational age are termed ____________________.

8. Although the U.S. is more successful than any other country in saving ____________________ babies, the rate of such births in the U.S. is higher than those in 30 other European, Asian, and Middle Eastern nations.

9. ____________________ babies tend to be long and thin, because they have continued growing in the womb but have had an insufficient blood supply at the end of gestation.

10. The sudden death of an apparently healthy infant under one year of age, which remains unexplained after a complete post-mortem exam is called ____________________.

11. A comparison of immunization rates in 1985, 1986, and 1987 in the U.S., Denmark, France, West Germany, Netherlands, Norway, and England found that ______________ preschoolers are less likely to be immunized against the major childhood illnesses.

12. According to the ________________ principle, development proceeds from the head to the lower parts of the body.

13. According to the ________________ principle, development proceeds from the central parts of the body to the outer parts.

14. The periodic variations in an infant's daily cycle of wakefulness, sleep, and activity are called ______________________.

15. ______________________ is a complete source of nutrients for young infants, more digestible than ______________ and less likely to produce allergic reactions.

16. Although increases in breastfeeding rates have occurred across socioeconomic and educational levels, breastfeeding is still less popular among __________, ____________, and ________________ women.

17. The diet of children over age 2 should contain no more than 30 percent of total calories from _________ and less than 300 milligrams of ______________ daily.

18. Gibson and Walk learned through their ________________________ experiment that babies perceive depth from a very early age.

19. Because experiments have shown that babies have the ability to distinguish between sights and the ability to select what they view, we can identify some of their visual ____________________.

20. Because the nervous system of a newborn is more highly developed than we used to think, the American Academy of Pediatrics now recommends the use of ________________________ in most surgery on infants.

21. The __________________ Test may be used as a benchmark for normal development between the ages of one month and six years.

22. Between 7 and 9 months of age, babies show a new understanding of concepts like near and far; they imitate more complex behaviors; they show new fears, and they show a new sense of security around their caregivers. All these changes may result from a major reorganization of brain function, initiated by the new ability to ____________________.

23. In 1984, in a single hospital in Toronto, 139 children who had used infant ____________________ were treated for such injuries as skull fractures or fractures of exposed body parts.

24. Gesell's classic experiment, which studied a pair of identical twins, demonstrated the powerful influence of ____________________ on infants' behavior.

25. ________________ babies are slightly longer and heavier than ________ babies at birth and remain larger throughout adulthood, except for a brief time during puberty.

ANSWERS FOR SELF-TESTS — CHAPTER 3

Multiple-Choice

		Page	
1.	b	92	factual
2.	a	93	conceptual
3.	a	93	conceptual
4.	c	95	factual
5.	a	95	conceptual
6.	c	99	Box 3-1, factual
7.	c	99	Box 3-1, factual
8.	d	96	conceptual
9.	b	96, 98	factual
10.	b	100	conceptual
11.	d	102	conceptual
12.	d	102	factual
13.	a	103	factual
14.	c	104	factual
15.	b	105	conceptual
16.	b	105	factual
17.	d	107	conceptual
18.	a	107	factual
19.	a	108	conceptual
20.	b	110	conceptual

		Page	
21.	c	110	factual
22.	d	111	conceptual
23.	d	112	factual
24.	d	113	factual
25.	a	114	conceptual
26.	b	115	conceptual
27.	b	115	conceptual
28.	d	118	factual
29.	c	119	conceptual
30.	d	119	factual
31.	b	120	conceptual
32.	a	121	factual
33.	b	121	conceptual
34.	b	121	factual
35.	d	121	conceptual
36.	c	122	conceptual
37.	a	122	factual
38.	c	123	factual
39.	d	123	conceptual
40.	b	124	factual

Completion

		Page
1.	neonate	92
2.	vernix caseosa	93
3.	meconium	94
4.	plastic	95
5.	reflex behaviors	96
6.	interactive behaviors, motor behaviors, physiological control, response to stress	98
7.	small for date	100
8.	low birthweight	101
9.	postmature	103
10.	sudden infant death syndrome (SIDS)	104
11.	American	107
12.	cephalocaudal principle	107

		Page
13.	proximodistal	108
14.	states of arousal	108
15.	breast milk; cow's milk	112
16.	younger, poorer, minority	112
17.	fat, cholesterol	113
18.	visual cliff	114
19.	preferences	115
20.	pain relievers (anesthesia)	116
21.	Denver Developmental Screening	117
22.	crawl	120
23.	walkers	122
24.	maturation	123
25.	boy; girl	124

CHAPTER 4

Intellectual Development in Infancy and Toddlerhood

INTRODUCTION

Chapter 3 discussed the physical development of the baby from birth through toddlerhood. Chapter 4 continues the examination of that early stage of life but shifts the focus to intellectual development. Contrary to earlier beliefs, the infant is capable of significant learning and not only responds to the environment but works actively to alter it.

- This chapter explores the intellectual capabilities of the newborn and examines the processes by which the developing infant begins to interact with the environment in order to render it meaningful. Topics which are introduced include maturation, habituation, conditioning, and infant memory.

- Three different approaches to studying intellectual development will be evaluated: the psychometric, Piagetian, and information-processing approaches.

- The major intellectual accomplishment of infancy--the development of language--is outlined and will be examined from the view of learning theory and nativism. Also, a variety of factors influencing language development are discussed.

- The chapter concludes with a discussion of the child's emerging sense of competence and how it is acquired and develops relative to parents' child-rearing styles.

CHAPTER OUTLINE

I. **How Infants Learn**

- A. Learning and Maturation
- B. Types of Learning
  - 1. Habituation
  - 2. Conditioning
- C. Infant Memory

II. **Studying Intellectual Development: Three Approaches**

- A. Psychometric Approach: Intelligence Tests
  - 1. Why is it Difficult to Measure Infants' and Toddlers' Intelligence?
  - 2. What is Developmental Testing?
  - 3. Can Children's Scores on Intelligence Tests be Improved?
- B. Piagetian Approach: Cognitive Stages
  - 1. Piaget's Sensorimotor Stage (Birth to about 2 Years)
    - a. Substages of the Sensorimotor Stage
  - 2. Evaluation of Piaget's Sensorimotor Stage
    - a. Support for Piaget's Theory
    - b. Limitations of the Sensorimotor Stage Concept
- C. Information-Processing Approach: Perceptions and Symbols
  - 1. Information Processing during Infancy as a Predictor of Intelligence
  - 2. Influences on Information Processing and Cognitive Development

III. **Development of Language**

- A. Stages in Language Development
  - 1. Prespeech
    - a. Crying
    - b. Cooing
    - c. Babbling
    - d. Imitating Language Sounds
    - e. Recognizing Language Sounds
    - f. Gestures
  - 2. First Words
    - a. How Vocabulary Grows
  - 3. Creating Sentences
    - a. First Sentences
    - b. Learning Grammar
  - 4. Characteristics of Early Speech
- B. Theories of Language Acquisition
  - 1. Learning Theory
  - 2. Nativism
- C. Influences on Language Development
  - 1. Child-Directed Speech ("Motherese")
  - 2. The Impact of Different Aspects of Adult Speech
- D. Delayed Language Development

IV. Development of Competence

A. What Influences Competence?
B. Home: The Home Observation for Measurement of the Environment

KEY TERMS

Bayley Scales of Infant Development (page 134)

causality (138)

child-directed speech (151)

circular reactions (135)

classical conditioning (130)

cognitive development (135)

cross-modal transference (143)

deferred imitation (140)

habituation (129)

holophrase (148)

information-processing approach (142)

intelligent behavior (132)

invisible imitation (139)

language acquisition device (LAD) (151)

learning (128)

learning theory (150)

linguistic speech (148)

maturation (128)

nativism (150)

novelty preference (143)

object permanence (137)

operant (instrumental) conditioning (131)

Piagetian approach (135)

prelinguistic speech (146)

psychometric approach (133)

representational ability (138)

schemes (136)

sensorimotor stage (135)

visible imitation (139)

visual-recognition memory (142)

LEARNING OBJECTIVES

After finishing Chapter 4, you should be able to:

1. Distinguish between *learning* and *maturation*. (pp. 128-129)

2. Explain *habituation*. (p. 129)

3. Define and give an example of the following types of conditioning: (pp. 130-131)

   a. *classical conditioning*

   b. *operant (instrumental) conditioning*

4. Describe how *classical conditioning* and *operant conditioning* can combine to produce complex learning. (p. 131)

5. Describe the concept of infant memory. (pp. 131-132)

6. Briefly compare and contrast the three approaches to studying intellectual development: (p. 133)
   a. *psychometric approach*

   b. *Piagetian approach*

   c. *information-processing approach*

7. Define *intelligent behavior* and explain some problems in trying to measure intelligence in infants and toddlers. (pp. 132-134)

8. Explain the significance of developmental tests. (p. 134)

9. Explain *cognitive development* in Piaget's *sensorimotor stage* and define his terminology: (pp. 135-138)

   a. *circular reactions*

   b. *schemes*

   c. *object permanence*

   d. *causality*

   e. *representational ability*

10. List and briefly describe the 6 substages of Piaget's *sensorimotor stage*: (pp. 135-138)

    a. d.

    b. e.

    c. f.

11. Explain the pros and cons of the *sensorimotor stage* concept, and define the following terms: (pp. 138-142)

    a. *invisible imitation*

    b. *visible imitation*

    c. *deferred imitation*

12. Explain how information processing in infancy is related to intelligence, and give an example of each of the following: (pp. 142-143)

    a. *visual-recognition memory*

    b. *novelty preference*

    c. *cross-modal transference*

13. Briefly relate the cultural difference of the Chinese and American approaches to child development that Professor Gardner found in his 1989 study in China (Box 4-1). (p. 144)

14. Describe the development of *prelinguistic speech*. (pp. 148-149)

15. Explain the significance of the babbling of hearing-impaired children. (p. 147)

16. Describe the development of *linguistic speech* and explain how vocabulary grows in young children. (pp. 148-149)

17. Explain how children learn to create sentences and list 3 characteristics of early speech. (pp. 149-150)

18. Compare and contrast *learning theory* and *nativism* as approaches to language acquisition. (pp. 150-151)

19. Define *child-directed speech* ("motherese") and explain its influence on language development. (pp. 151-153)

20. Give three suggestions for talking with babies and toddlers at different stages of language development. (Box 4-3) (p. 154)

    a.

    b.

    c.

21. Briefly explain the topic of delayed language development. (p. 153)

22. Explain what influences competence, and give a few suggestions for enhancing a child's competence. (Box 4-4) (pp. 155-156)

23. Describe some findings of studies using the Home Inventory. (pp. 155-157)

SUPPLEMENTAL READING

The following article is reprinted with permission from Working Mother in ©March 1992. Betty Holcomb is Working Mother's articles' editor.

What Your Baby Really Knows

Betty Holcomb

Over the last decade, there has been an explosion of new research on infant intelligence. Here's how you can use the findings to enrich your child's mind.

Not so long ago, most scientists believed the mind of a newborn was a blank slate, governed mostly by reflexes. Infants could not learn much, researchers reasoned, until their brains developed enough to give them long-term memory and control over their bodies. But new studies now offer intriguing evidence that babies know a lot more than anyone gave them credit for--and that their ability to learn, right from the moment of birth, may be far more sophisticated than anyone guessed.

"We have an increasing respect for infants and their abilities," says Elizabeth Spelke, Ph.D., professor of psychology at Cornell University in Ithaca, New York. "The more we look, the more we're finding the seeds of later knowledge."

Even a squirmy newborn seems to be especially tuned in to language and can copy simple facial expressions the adults around him make. Under certain circumstances, babies as young as three months can recall events that occurred weeks earlier. Very young babies can anticipate future events and act on their expectations.

These abilities have led researchers to question standard theories of cognitive development and to pose revolutionary questions about what babies know: Is it possible that babies are born with some basic knowledge about the world--that certain objects are solid, others are not? Do they have expectations about the way things will behave? Do they know what is alive and what is not?

More likely, researchers say, babies are born with the "tools" or an "agenda" to learn rapidly throughout the first year of life. "Most of us can't say that babies are born with innate ideas about the world, but infants do seem to have a special endowment that allows them to make sense of things quickly," says Frank Keil, Ph.D., professor of psychology and co-director of the Cognitive Studies Program at Cornell University. "Even babies seem to think there are rules about how things behave and to make categories for sorting out things--just as adults do."

A New Window on Infants' Minds

To be sure, much of the new work is still controversial. "I don't think newborns know much about their world, says Marshall Haith, Ph.D., professor of psychology at the University of Denver and a leading researcher on infant perception. Still, he concedes, up until recently, scientists had asked only limited questions about what babies know--and therefore had gotten very limited answers.

Indeed, infant research has relied heavily on measuring babies' reactions to such things as a series of black-and-white pictures to see if they recognize ones they've seen before, or whether they can make out patterns and colors. "You get a lot of little facts that way--what colors babies can see, how good their focus is," says Haith. But you don't really get the big picture: How does a baby's perception of color help him learn about the real world? How do babies organize the information they see? How do they know that a Chihuahua and an Irish setter are both dogs and not separate species?

Some psychologists also believed such limited tests gave the wrong answers. "When I started out, everybody thought that babies couldn't remember anything for more than fifteen seconds. That didn't make sense to me. If that were true, then a baby wouldn't remember his mother when she went into another room," says Carolyn Rovee-Collier, Ph.D., professor of psychology at Rutgers University and editor of the journal *Infant Behavior and Development*.

Rovee-Collier suspected babies didn't remember many of the things scientists had shown them because the things were basically boring: black-and-white patterns, for example, aren't the stuff of which memories are made. "I thought we needed to give the babies a reason to remember something--to allow them to have some control over an event." So she began to give infants mobiles they could move themselves--and she soon found convincing evidence that babies could recall the mobiles for days or even weeks after they'd played with them.

Over the last decade, other psychologists have taken a similar tack--creating more interesting events to study an infant's learning patterns. W. Keith Berg, Ph.D., professor of psychology at the University of Florida, for example, switched from playing a simple musical note in his experiments to using musical toys. "We decided we needed to give babies a marvelous event, a sound-and-light show to remember," says Berg.

With more sophisticated methods and such fascinating questions about babies, the field of infant research has grown from a handful of scientists in the mid-1960s to nearly 2,000 today. And they are opening entirely new windows on the minds of infants.

Do Babies Know the Laws of Nature?

One of the most compelling new lines of inquiry probes an infant's basic knowledge of the world. Does a baby know, for example, that a rock is hard and a pillow soft? Can an infant predict which way a ball will roll? Is it possible that humans are born with some rudimentary understanding of the physical laws of nature?

Until a few years ago, most every psychologist or pediatrician would have answered with a resounding no. The widely accepted theories of French psychologist Jean Piaget hold that a baby has no sense that most objects are permanent until late in the first year. Indeed, most child-development books will tell you that the expression "out of sight, out of mind" is quite literal for kids; if you hid a ball from a four-month-old, he'll simply think it no longer exists.

But experiments by researcher Elizabeth Spelke suggest that babies as young as two and a half months not only know that a ball is solid and permanent but can predict how it should behave. Spelke showed babies a ball that rolled down a ramp and stopped at a barrier. Then she put a screen in front of the ramp and let the ball roll. When she lifted the screen, she arranged to have the ball appear on the correct side of the barrier--or at times on the wrong side. In nearly every case, the babies seemed puzzled and surprised when the ball was on the wrong side of the barrier.

Other experiments have elicited similar results. Scientists have set up optical tricks, for example, to make it appear as if a ball passed through the solid top of the table--and babies seemed surprised. (They also acted bored when the ball performs as one would expect it to and comes to rest on the tabletop instead of passing through--an indication that they know what the ball should do.)

But while babies understand certain laws of nature--that a solid object can't pass through another solid object--they do not seem to comprehend others. Spelke found, for example, that babies do not understand gravity before they are eight or 10 months old.

This research is especially intriguing to Spelke and others because she speculates that infants' knowledge parallels that of adults. "Adults understand that a ball will roll in a continuous path and that it can't pass through a solid wall," she says. "But adults also have a hard time with gravity. If you ask us how an object's speed should change as it falls, we often get it wrong. We don't understand gravity the way we understand the basic properties of the objects around us--that a rock is hard and solid, for example."

"The really central question here," she adds, "is do infants have some underlying understanding about the physical world that helps them learn? Babies may not know very much, but they do seem to know something."

Other researchers have also uncovered evidence that very young babies either learn quickly or already know things about the way the physical world should behave. Whether this proves that babies are born with some innate knowledge of the world is hotly debated--and a tantalizing new area of research.

Can Babies Think in an Organized Way?

Scientists are also exploring how infants organize the information they take in--a key skill in learning. If you did not know, for example, the difference between a dog and a lion, life would be confusing--and even dangerous.

"Infants' ability to group things together is essential to their survival. They have to relate each new object to prior experience. That prior experience might have been dangerous--so if babies couldn't relate present events to prior experiences, they wouldn't survive," says Leslie Cohen, Ph.D., professor of psychology at the University of Texas.

But until recently, most psychologists assumed that infants do not have the skills to organize their experience. To know that a seagull and a robin are birds, for example, you have to have the ability to notice details about each bird and the memory to compare them and conclude that they are similar enough to fit in the same category.

Now, however, experts see that an infant's ability to organize information into categories is there at birth; the skill simply grows more sophisticated over time. A newborn knows that baby bottles are similar, even if he sees the bottles from different angles. A four-month-old can group a series of triangles by color. And by seven months, a baby is already creating rather sophisticated categories.

Cohen and his colleagues showed pictures of a series of stuffed animals to seven-month-old babies. Then they added a picture of a stuffed rabbit and a picture of a flowerpot. "The babies look surprised when you add the flowerpot," says Cohen. In a more recent experiment, he gave 10-month-olds real toy trucks to play with. When the babies continue to get trucks, they grow bored. But when the researcher hands them a completely different type of toy, the babies act interested again. "They see it's a new category--something that doesn't belong," says Cohen.

What does a baby use as an organizing principle? Researchers don't know yet, but some differences are emerging. A baby will categorize things with similar forms--such as different-size cups--at 10 months. But it is not until about 14 months that a child uses both form and function to create a category.

Do They Anticipate the Future?

You probably don't think about it much, but most everything you do every day is governed by your sense of anticipation. "When you see the light turn yellow, you slow down because you know you need to stop. If you're a student and a test is coming up, you make a plan to study for it," says psychology professor Berg. "Anyone without the ability to anticipate is certainly at a serious disadvantage."

Yet most scientists didn't think infants were able to anticipate the future or form expectations about it. Researchers assumed that a baby could certainly not plan his behavior based on expectations. Since babies can't really act on the world anyway, it didn't even seem an important question to ask. But it turns out that babies as young as two months old can anticipate what will happen, based on their previous experience.

Some of the first glimmers of this ability emerged in research on infants' vision. Marshall Haith and colleagues at the University of Denver showed babies pictures that appear and reappear in predictable places. After just a few seconds of viewing, two-month-olds start to scan the screen and rest their eyes on the spot where they expect the next picture to appear. "We wondered why a baby would bother moving his eyes ahead of time," says Haith. "Then we realized, here are babies controlling their behavior based on what they think will happen next."

Many researchers are now studying how babies form expectations about the future. "It's one of the most exciting areas of research," Haith says. "We had assumed that babies just react to things as they happen. But now it seems they may have an idea of what will happen in the future--and even try to control their behavior based on what they expect will occur." This is a form of fairly sophisticated learning.

Can They Imitate Adults?

The accomplishment sounds relatively small: Newborns can mimic their parents by sticking their tongues out. But when Andy Meltzoff, researcher at the University of Washington, presented the evidence in the early 1980s, it sent shock waves through the room--and even through the profession of child development. How could this be when Piaget, the most respected developmental psychologist, had established long ago that babies do not have the capacity to imitate before the age of about seven months? "It was an amazing reaction. I remember hearing that the meeting degenerated into a yelling match," says developmental psychologist Merry Bullock, Ph.D., now a researcher at the Max Planck Institute in Munich, Germany.

But why should parents care about this finding? Because imitation is one of the most basic ways we learn. If you want to ski or play the piano, you find a teacher and try to copy her actions. And that's what babies do, right from the start: They watch and then try to imitate the actions they see you and other people taking.

Since Meltzoff's first experiments, other researchers have tried to explore just how sophisticated infants are at imitating the actions of those around them. Experts now know that babies are good at imitating facial expressions and sounds--indeed, the capacity to mimic is the earliest way babies learn to communicate.

Do Infants Have Much Memory?

Memory is basic to learning--if we couldn't recall what we saw or tasted yesterday, we couldn't do much. We'd be stuck reacting to each event as if it were brand new, and we'd have to figure everything out all over again.

Psychologists are just beginning to understand the way babies' memories work--how they retain and retrieve information--and they are finding that infants have some surprising abilities. Babies as young as two months have long-term memories under certain conditions, according to the latest research by Rovee-Collier. She found, for example, that if two-month-old babies played with a mobile for 15 minutes a day for three days in a row, they remembered the mobile on the fourth day--as long as they played with it exactly the same place in the same room the next day.

She now contends that an infant's memory works much like that of an adult--if a baby experiences an event that he cares about, he'll store it in long-term memory. And that memory can be dredged up with cues--putting the baby back in the same place, where the event happened the first time, for example.

That is not to say that an infant's capacity for memory is exactly the same as an adult's--Rovee-Collier believes that the ability to retrieve memories grows more efficient over time. Three-month-olds, for example, seem to need more prompting and take a few more hours to retrieve a memory than six-month-olds do. Still, many scientists are startled to learn that tiny infants are able to remember much of anything at all for more than a few seconds--Rovee-Collier's work indicates that babies may be retaining a lot more than any of us ever dreamed.

More to Learn

Researchers are studying many other aspects of what babies know and how they learn. In recent years, for example, scientists have discovered that infants tune in to human language differently than other sounds. Babies who are just a month old can recognize the difference between certain sounds, such as "pa" and "ba." Neural surgeons are trying to figure out if language is processed in a special part of the brain--and how brain development influences the way babies acquire an understanding of language.

Other scientists are focused on how a child's temperament influences his or her learning--does a baby who is shy and frightened take longer to learn new tasks? Does his fearful personality give him a totally different filter on the world--and make it harder for him to organize sights, sounds, and smells?

And there is the burgeoning new field of neural psychology: A group of research scientists are attempting to link the way the brain develops with a youngster's ability to learn. Some experiments in animals--kittens, for one--demonstrate that brain cells "turn on" as the kittens need to use them. If the kittens are deprived of stimulation, parts of their brains simply don't develop at all! Could the same be true of human infants?

With thousands of researchers studying the way babies learn, there is plenty of excitement about that complicated little being you hold in your arms each day. It seems the scientists are catching up with mothers who have suspected all along that their babies are pretty darn smart. "The rate of learning in the first year is nothing short of astonishing," observes Tiffany Field, Ph.D., professor in the departments of pediatrics, psychology and psychiatry at the University of Miami and author of *Infancy* (Harvard University Press). "We've just begun to ask the right questions and now we are getting the right answers."

Questions:

Which hypothesis do you believe is more accurate about infant intellectual abilities--that proposed by Dr. Spelke and Dr. Keil (infants are born with some basic knowledge about the world) or that by Dr. Haith (newborns don't know much about the world)? Support your response.

Based on this article, identify three suggestions for stimulating infant intellectual abilities during the first year of life.

SELF-TESTS

Multiple-Choice

Circle the letter of the response which best completes or answers each of the following statements and questions.

1. Which of the following statements about newborns' capacities is most accurate?
   a. Babies are blind at birth.
   b. Babies are born with the ability to learn.
   c. Newborn babies are unable to feel pain.
   d. Newborn babies' first cries represent learned behavior.

2. "A relatively permanent change in behavior that results from experience" is a good definition for
   a. maturation
   b. habituation
   c. learning
   d. development

3. Which of the following correctly states the relationship between maturation and learning?
   a. Learning cannot take place without maturation.
   b. Maturation cannot take place without learning.
   c. Learning and maturation are unrelated.
   d. Maturation and learning are indistinguishable from each other.

4. A 4-month-old baby boy is repeatedly exposed to a recording of a young woman's voice whenever he sucks on his pacifier. Eventually, the infant stops responding to this auditory stimulus. Habituation experiments indicate that when a new voice is introduced on the recording, the baby will
   a. still not respond to the recording
   b. be unable to distinguish between the two different voices
   c. become upset and begin to cry
   d. show revived interest and begin to suck hard on the pacifier

5. Anna was used to her father's taking pictures with a camera with a flashbulb. One day she actually blinked *before* the flash went off in the camera. Anna now associated her blinking with the camera. Anna's learned behavior is an example of
   a. classical conditioning
   b. spontaneous learning
   c. operant learning
   d. incidental learning

6. Jose, a 2-month-old baby boy, learns to smile at his parents in order to gain their attention. This type of conditioning, where the learner influences the environment, is called:
   a. habitual conditioning
   b. classical conditioning
   c. operant conditioning
   d. incidental conditioning

7. Which of the following statements about infant memory is *least* accurate?
   a. In order to learn, infants must possess at least a short-term ability to remember.
   b. One-day-old newborns possess the ability to remember specific sounds for up to 24 hours.
   c. Infants as young as 3 to 6 months of age can recognize differences in settings.
   d. The ability that memory provides to organize the world is unrelated to an infant's development of intelligence.

8. A string is attached to a 2-month-old baby's left leg and also attached to a bright mobile hung above his crib. The baby quickly learns that kicking his left leg will actuate the mobile. The mobile is removed from the crib for 4 weeks. When the mobile is rehung, however, the string is not attached to the baby's leg. Which of the following responses is most likely?
   a. The baby will not kick his legs.
   b. The baby will kick, especially his left leg, because he remembers that kicking starts the mobile.
   c. The baby will cry upon seeing the mobile, because its reappearance frightens him.
   d. none of the above

9. Intelligent behavior is generally considered to have two key aspects:
   a. It is goal-oriented and adaptive.
   b. It is goal-oriented and unadaptive.
   c. It is unconscious and adaptive.
   d. It is conscious and unadaptive.

10. Which approach to studying intellectual development emphasizes the quantity of intelligence as measured by intelligence tests?
   a. Piagetian
   b. quantitative
   c. information processing
   d. psychometric

11. Ratike, a 14-month-old boy, undergoes psychometric testing. Research leads us to believe:
   a. It is nearly impossible to predict Ratike's future manhood IQ from psychometric test scores.
   b. For infants Ratike's age, IQ predictions based on psychometric tests are highly unreliable.
   c. A more useful predictor of Ratike's future childhood IQ is his parents' IQ.
   d. all of the above

12. Bayley's Scales of Infant Development, used with children from 2 months to 2½ years old, is not used to
   a. measure abilities such as perception, memory, learning, and verbal communication
   b. predict later intelligence
   c. measure gross motor skills and fine motor skills
   d. examine test-taking behaviors

13. Katarina is a 6-month-old baby girl from a disadvantaged family. When given an intelligence test, her scores are quite low. After receiving extensive home and day care intervention, we can reasonably infer that
   a. Katarina's intelligence test scores will remain the same
   b. Katarina's intelligence test scores will improve
   c. the enhanced care Katarina receives at home and at day care is unlikely to affect her cognitive development
   d. none of the above

14. Kumi is a psychologist studying intelligent behavior. He is concerned with the quality of intellectual functioning and how children adapt to the environment. Kumi's way of studying intellectual development represents the
   a. psychometric approach
   b. information-processing approach
   c. developmental approach
   d. Piagetian approach

15. What is the first stage of cognitive development, according to Piaget?
    a. representational
    b. sensorimotor
    c. reflexive
    d. circular reactions

16. Tessa, a 2-month-old baby girl, happens to stick her thumb in her mouth and begin sucking on it. Because she enjoys sucking, Tessa continues to place her thumb in her mouth. This is an example of a
    a. primary circular reaction
    b. tertiary circular reaction
    c. object permanence
    d. causality

17. Which of the following youngsters, according to Piaget, exhibits fully developed object permanence?
    a. A 3-month-old baby boy, whose mother has left the room, begins crying loudly because he believes she no longer exists
    b. A 12-month-old baby girl sees her favorite doll being moved from her crib; however, when she later looks for the doll, the infant searches the crib only.
    c. A 20-month-old baby boy searches for his mother's keys. Although he cannot find them in any of his mother's normal hiding spots, he continues looking for them because he knows they exist
    d. all of the above

18. In a research study, babies saw films that showed physically impossible events, like a light going on before a person turned on its switch. Infants under 10 months of age showed no surprise, but older babies did. The older group is exhibiting awareness of:
    a. object permanence
    b. causality
    c. invisible imitation
    d. circular reactions

19. More recent research on Piagetian theories has found which of the following?
    a. Young infants may fail to search for hidden objects because they weren't capable physically to perform actions to find an object.
    b. Visible imitation using body parts the baby cannot see has occurred as early as within 3 days after birth.
    c. Babies aged 14 months could accurately imitate an action seen as much as one week earlier.
    d. all of the above

20. Which approach sees people as manipulators of perceptions and symbols and focuses on individual differences in intelligent behavior?
    a. Piagetian
    b. information-processing
    c. psychometric
    d. quantitative

21. Dr. Thompson has recently completed a research project studying how infants process information. His results will most likely show that which of the following infant abilities are related to future cognitive development?
    a. novelty preference
    b. habituation
    c. attention
    d. all of the above

22. Infants' ability to identify items by sight that they had felt with their hands earlier but did not see is called
    a. novelty preference
    b. habituation
    c. cross-modal transference
    d. causality

23. Leeza has recently given birth to a premature infant, Brianne. If Leeza remains sensitive, responsive, and positively involved with her child, Brianne will
    a. achieve higher scores on adolescent IQ tests than premature infants of less responsive mothers
    b. achieve low scores on adolescent IQ tests, regardless of her mother's intervention
    c. fail to overcome any negative effects of her premature birth, maintaining a low IQ throughout life
    d. none of the above

24. In Professor Gardner's investigation of early childhood education and creativity in China in 1989, which of the following did he find?
    a. American parents encourage more exploratory, independent behavior than Chinese parents do.
    b. Chinese parents encourage more exploratory, independent behavior than American parents do.
    c. Chinese parents do not believe in guiding their children's behavior in order to diminish the children's frustration.
    d. American parents believe in guiding their children's behavior in order to diminish the children's frustration.

25. Babies make a variety of sounds which progress in a fairly set sequence from crying to cooing and babbling, accidental imitation, and then deliberate imitation. These sounds are known as
    a. linguistic speech
    b. postlinguistic speech
    c. holophrastic speech
    d. prelinguistic speech

26. From their 1991 study of the babbling of hearing impaired babies, Petitto and Marentette concluded that
    a. Babies learn sign language in a very different manner than babies learn speech.
    b. Babbling is tied to maturation of the vocal cords rather than brain maturation.
    c. The brain lacks an inborn language capacity which underlies the acquisition of both spoken and signed language.
    d. Both nativists and learning-theory explanations for how children learn language are valid.

27. Midari is a 5-month-old Japanese baby girl. She can easily differentiate "ra" from "la." However, her father has trouble with this same discrimination. This is best explained by the fact that
    a. Japanese adults speak a language that does not have the "R" sound.
    b. Children lose the ability to differentiate sounds that are not relevant to their native language.
    c. Japanese adults speak a language that does not have the "L" sound.
    d. Both b and c

28. Stefan observes his 14-month-old son Johan holding up his arms to show that he wants to be held. Symbolic gestures such as these reveal that
    a. The child is acquiring the fundamentals of symbols.
    b. Stefan has played little or no role at all in his child's development of gestures.
    c. Even before children can talk, they understand that objects and concepts have names.
    d. Johan is a very gifted child. Most youngsters his age have not yet learned to use gestures.

29. A 12-month-old baby utters "Mama." The word "Mama" may mean the child wants a toy, wants to get out of his crib, or wants to see his mother. A word such as this, which expresses a complete thought in one word, is called
   a. sentence
   b. gesture
   c. babble
   d. holophrase

30. Karin tends to learn new words faster than Lakeeba. According to research, which of the following *does not* account for Karin's earlier vocabulary growth?
   a. Karin uses her first words primarily to refer to objects and events, whereas Lakeeba uses them to express social routines.
   b. Karin is from a better educated family than Lakeeba.
   c. Lakeeba's parents encourage labeling more so than Karin's parents by asking their child many questions.
   d. Lakeeba's parents speak to their child more often to tell her what to do.

31. Tyrone calls his favorite toy, a dump truck given to him by his older brother, "da-tuck." One day Tyrone's mother comes home with a new, bigger dump truck for him. However, Tyrone ran and got his truck from his brother and said "da-tuck." This is an example of
   a. underextending a concept
   b. overextending a concept
   c. developmental delay
   d. holophrase

32. Language learning based on experience is to ________________ as language learning based on an inborn capacity is to ________________.
   a. nativism; learning theory
   b. motherese; causality
   c. learning theory; nativism
   d. causality; motherese

33. According to nativists, which language acquisition statement is *most* accurate?
   a. Children learn language through conditioning and reinforcement.
   b. Human beings have an inborn capacity for acquiring language and learn to talk as naturally as they learn to walk.
   c. Children reared at home who presumably hear more adult speech than those who grow up in institutions, babble more.
   d. Human beings learn language through experience.

34. According to Noam Chomsky, an inborn language acquisition device programs children's brains to analyze the language they hear and to extract from it the rules of grammar. This belief is in accordance with which theory of language acquisition?
   a. nativist
   b. learning theory
   c. developmental
   d. environmental

35. Oprah communicates with her toddler using a high-pitched voice, short sentences, and speaking slowly. She is practicing
   a. motherese
   b. parent-directed speech
   c. holophrase
   d. infantese

36. Karen is the mother of a newborn baby girl. Candice is the mother of newborn twin boys. Research on child-directed speech leads us to believe that
   a. Candice's twins will speak earlier than Karen's baby girl.
   b. Candice's twins will speak later than Karen's baby girl.
   c. Candice will spend more time using directive speech with her twins, whereas Karen will ask her daughter more questions and have longer conversations.
   d. both b and c

37. A major factor in determining how quickly and how well babies and toddlers learn to speak is
   a. discouragement by parents of the babbling stage
   b. one-to-one conversations with adults in which youngsters are asked challenging open-ended questions
   c. watching and listening to television
   d. ensuring that conversation with the baby is based on commands, requests, and instructions

38. Which of the following environments is most conducive to raising competent children?
   a. A home in which the mother hovers over her children, being overprotective, and pushing them to learn
   b. A home in which the mother fosters learning, sets reasonable limits, and shows love and respect toward her children
   c. A home in which the mother limits her children's physical freedom so as to avoid accidents and allows them to frequently watch TV and listen to the radio
   d. none of the above

39. When researchers compared HOME scores with children's scores on the Stanford-Binet intelligence test, the single most important factor in predicting high IQ was found to be
   a. how early the child had begun to talk
   b. high socioeconomic status
   c. the mother's ability to create and structure an environment that fostered learning
   d. the quality and quantity of the father's involvement with his children

40. Ali, a developmentally delayed African-American baby is raised in a favorable home environment. Results from a 1989 study by Bradly, et al., indicate that
   a. It is likely that Ali's favorable home conditions will offset some of his developmental problems.
   b. Regardless of the nature of his environment, Ali's chances of improving developmentally are very slim.
   c. Ali is more likely than Mariana, a developmentally delayed Mexican-American baby raised in an unstimulating environment, to achieve higher IQ test scores.
   d. both a and c

Completion

Supply the term or terms needed to complete each of the following statements.

1. The visual cliff experiments demonstrated that learning must be preceded by ________________________, the biologically determined readiness to master new abilities.

2. ________________________ is the process by which repeated exposure to a particular stimulus results in a reduced response to the stimulus.

3. A baby learns to make a certain response in order to produce a particular effect. This is an example of ________________________.

4. ________________________ results in a person's being able to acquire, remember, and use knowledge; to understand concepts and relationships among objects, ideas, and events, and to apply knowledge and understanding to everyday problems.

5. One reason that early intelligence scores fail to predict later scores is the fact that the tests traditionally used for babies are primarily ____________ and ______________ whereas the tests used for older children are heavily _________________.

6. Comparing a baby's ability with the ability typical of infants of the same age is the basis for ____________________ testing.

7. The growth in children's thought processes that enables them to acquire and use knowledge about the world is called ____________________.

8. During Piaget's first cognitive stage, the _________________ stage, infants learn about themselves and their world through their own developing sensory and motor activity.

9. According to Piaget, a great deal of growth in the sensorimotor period occurs through ______________, in which the child learns how to reproduce pleasurable or interesting events originally discovered by chance.

10. The recognition that certain events caused other events was referred to as ____________ by Piaget.

11. _________________ is the basis for children's awareness that they exist apart from objects and other people.

12. ____________________, the ability to imitate an action a baby saw some time before, shows that a baby has a long-term memory for an event.

13. The goal of the ________________ approach is to discover what infants, children, and adults do with information from the time they perceive it until they use it.

14. The ability of infants to identify items by sight that they had felt with their hands earlier but did not see is referred to as _______________.

15. The use of spoken language to convey meaning is called _______________ speech.

16. According to the _______________ view, children learn language through reinforcement, but according to __________________, human beings have an inborn capacity for acquiring language.

17. When speaking to a baby, if you pitch your voice higher, use short words and sentences, speak slowly, ask questions, and repeat your words, you are speaking what is called ___________________.

18. In order for children to learn to speak and communicate, they need both ______________ and ______________; hearing speech on television is not enough.

19. The Harvard Preschool Project Study of 400 preschoolers in 1965 found that the most _______________ children exhibited such social skills as getting and holding the attention of adults in acceptable ways, and such cognitive skills as using language well and showing a range of intellectual abilities.

20. In a study of children from 3 different ethnic groups, researchers found that day-to-day aspects of a child's _________________ are more closely related to the child's development than such aspects of the child's wider environment as____________.

ANSWERS FOR SELF-TESTS — CHAPTER 4

Multiple-Choice

		Page	
1.	b	128	factual
2.	c	128	factual
3.	a	128	conceptual
4.	d	129	conceptual
5.	a	130	conceptual
6.	c	131	conceptual
7.	d	131	factual
8.	b	131	conceptual
9.	a	132	factual
10.	d	133	factual
11.	d	133	conceptual
12.	b	134	conceptual
13.	b	134	conceptual
14.	d	135	conceptual
15.	b	135	factual
16.	a	135	conceptual
17.	c	137	conceptual
18.	b	138	conceptual
19.	d	138	factual
20.	b	142	factual
21.	d	143	conceptual
22.	c	143	factual
23.	a	143	conceptual
24.	a	144	factual
25.	d	146	factual
26.	d	147	factual
27.	d	147	conceptual
28.	c	147	conceptual
29.	d	148	factual
30.	c	148	conceptual
31.	a	150	conceptual
32.	c	150	conceptual
33.	b	151	factual
34.	a	151	factual
35.	a	151	conceptual
36.	d	152	conceptual
37.	b	154	factual
38.	b	155	conceptual
39.	c	156	factual
40.	d	156	conceptual

Completion

		Page
1.	maturation	128
2.	habituation	129
3.	operant (instrumental) conditioning	131
4.	intelligence	133
5.	sensory, motor, verbal	133
6.	developmental	134
7.	cognitive development	135
8.	sensorimotor	135
9.	circular reactions	135
10.	causality	136
11.	object permanence	137
12.	deferred imitation	140
13.	information-processing	142
14.	cross-modal transference	143
15.	linguistic	148
16.	learning theory; nativism	150
17.	motherese (child-directed speech)	151
18.	practice, interaction	153
19.	competent	154
20.	home environment; socioeconomic status	156

CHAPTER 5

Personality and Social Development in Infancy and Toddlerhood

INTRODUCTION

Chapter 5 begins with a discussion of early personality development. According to Erik Erikson, infants and toddlers experience the first two crises in a series of eight that influence personality development throughout life. These include *basic trust versus mistrust* and *autonomy versus shame and doubt*. Suggestions on reducing negative behavior and encouraging self-regulation are provided.

- Emotions form a fundamental element of personality. Self-awareness appears to emerge in the following sequence: physical self-regulation, self-description, and emotional response to wrongdoing. The ability of infants to show their emotions through crying, smiling, and laughing is examined, and the mutual regulation model is presented to explain how emotions are communicated between infant and adult.

- Early differences in emotional response are indicative of future personality development. Some emotional reactions may stem from differences in temperament. Nine fairly stable components of temperament are given, as are a variety of temperamental influences.

- Also examined are personality differences between the sexes, which appear to be mostly socially influenced.

- The topic of socialization--how children learn the behaviors their culture deems appropriate--is looked at closely. Mothers play a central role in their child's development. The mother-infant bond and father-infant bond are critiqued, and research on mother-infant attachment is presented.

- Separation anxiety and stranger anxiety, which appear during the second half of the first year, are discussed. Research on disturbances in family relationships--including institutionalization, hospitalization, and child abuse/neglect are presented.

- Studies about the influence of sibling relationships are presented.

- The impact of early day care is discussed, with suggestions provided on selecting good child care. Research is summarized on how day care affects a child's cognitive, social, and emotional development.

CHAPTER OUTLINE

I. **Early Personality Development**

- A. Trust versus Mistrust
- B. Autonomy versus Shame and Doubt

II. **Emotions: The Foundation of Personality**

- A. How Infants' Emotions are Studied
- B. How Emotions Develop: The Emerging Sense of Self
- C. How Infants Show Their Emotions
  1. Crying
  2. Smiling
  3. Laughing
- D. How Emotions are Communicated between Infants and Adults
  1. Mutual-Regulation Model
     a. "Reading" the emotions of another person
  2. Social Referencing

III. **Differences in Personality Development**

- A. Temperamental Differences
  1. Components of Temperament
  2. Three Patterns of Temperament
  3. Influences on Temperament
  4. Effects of Temperament on Adjustments: "Goodness of Fit"
- B. Gender Differences

IV. **The Family and Personality Development**

- A. The Mother's Role
  1. The Mother-Infant Bond
     a. Is there a critical period for mother-infant bonding?
     b. What do babies need from their mothers?
  2. Attachment: A Reciprocal Connection
     a. Studying attachments
     b. Patterns of attachment
     c. How attachment is established
        (1) What the mother does
        (2) What the baby does
     d. Changes in attachment
     e. Long-term effects of attachment
     f. Critique of attachment research
- B. The Father's Role
  1. Bonds and Attachments between Fathers and Infants
  2. How do Fathers act with their Infants?
  3. What is the Significance of the Father-Infant Relationship?
- C. Stranger Anxiety and Separation Anxiety
- D. Disturbances in Family Relationships
  1. Institutionalization
  2. Hospitalization

3. Child Abuse and Neglect
    a. Causes of abuse and neglect
        (1) abusers and neglecters
        (2) victims
        (3) families
        (4) communities
        (5) cultures
    b. Effects of abuse and neglect
    c. Combatting abuse and neglect
    d. Preventing sexual abuse

V. Relationships with Other Children

A. Siblings
    1. How Children React to the Arrival of a New Baby
    2. How Siblings Interact
B. Sociability

VI. The Impact of Early Day Care

A. Cognitive Development
B. Social Development
C. Emotional Development

KEY TERMS

---

ambivalent (resistant) attachment (page 177)

attachment (176)

autonomy versus shame and doubt (163)

avoidant attachment (177)

basic trust versus basic mistrust (162)

battered child syndrome (185)

child abuse (185)

depression (170)

disorganized-disoriented attachment (177)

emotions (165)

ethological approach (174)

mother-infant bond (175)

mutual regulation model (168)

negativism (164)

neglect (185)

nonorganic failure to thrive (185)

personality (162)

secure attachment (177)

self-awareness (166)

self-regulation (164)

separation anxiety (183)

sexual abuse (185)

social referencing (169)

socialization (174)

strange situation (177)

stranger anxiety (183)

temperament (171)

LEARNING OBJECTIVES

After finishing Chapter 5, you should be able to:

1. Describe the significance of the following developmental stages, according to Erik Erikson: (pp. 162-164)
   a. *basic trust versus basic mistrust*

   b. autonomy versus shame and doubt

2. List and briefly explain the three stages in which *self-awareness* emerges. (pp. 166-167)

3. List and describe the three ways in which babies are able to show their *emotions*: (pp. 167-168)
   a.

   b.

   c.

4. Describe the significance of the *mutual-regulation model* and provide an example of what can happen when this model breaks down. (pp. 168-169)

5. Explain how babies "read" the emotions of others and display *social referencing*. (p. 169)

6. Define *temperament* and, in your own words, explain what is meant by each of the following terms pertaining to a baby's *temperament*: (pp. 171-173)
   a. easy child
   c. slow-to-warm up child

   b. difficult child
   d. goodness of fit

7. Describe how, in a research study on gender differences, strangers tended to react to a supposedly male baby and a supposedly female baby. (pp. 173-174)

8. Explain what babies need from their mothers by defining these two concepts: (pp. 174-175)

   a. *ethological approach*

   b. *mother-infant bond*

9. Define *attachment* and briefly describe the four patterns of attachment observed in the *strange situation*. (pp. 176-177)

10. Compare and contrast the mother's role, as well as the baby's role, in establishing attachment. (pp. 178-179)

11. Describe recent findings about fathers' interactions with young children. (pp. 180-182)

12. Distinguish between *stranger anxiety* and *separation anxiety*. (p. 183)

13. Briefly describe how babies may react to the following changes in their lives: (pp. 183-185)

    a. institutionalization

    b. hospitalization

14. List some of the causes of *child abuse* and *neglect*, as well as some of the ways in which they can be prevented. (pp. 185-187)

15. What is the reaction of most children to a new sibling? (pp. 187-188)

16. Describe sociability and its significance in a child's development. (p. 189)

17. Explain how day care may affect the following aspects of a youngster's development: (pp. 190-194)

    a. cognitive development

    b. social development

    c. emotional development

SUPPLEMENTAL READING

J. Ronald Lally, Ed.D., is director of the Center for Child and Family Studies at Far West laboratory for Educational Research and Development in Sausalito, California. This article is reprinted with permission, Gruner + Jahr Publishing, Parents, ©March 1994.

What "NO" Really Means

J. Ronald Lally

I can't count the number of times I've had a conversation with a concerned parent that goes roughly like this:

Parent: I can't understand it. My child and I have had a wonderful time together until just lately. Now he resists doing *anything* that I want him to do. Let's get dressed. "No!" We have to go now. "No!" I even ask him if he wants some ice cream. "No!" We're constantly in a power struggle. Sometimes I think he's trying to drive me crazy!

Me: Is your child around 18 months old?

Parent: Why, yes. How did you know?

Me: I know because there are two times in a child's life when saying no and fighting parents' wishes are most prevalent. One, as we all know, is during adolescence. The other is between 15 and 30 months. What is interesting to me is that at both of these ages, the child resists his parents for more or less the same reason. Like the adolescent, the older toddler is trying to define himself by showing that he can be different from his parents, that he doesn't have to go along.

Parents often misinterpret their toddler's "No." Practically every parent has been bewildered by the experience of offering a doll, receiving a resounding "No!" and seeing her child playing with the same doll ten minutes later.

Maybe the best way to understand it is to realize what "No" does not mean to a child this age. It very rarely means that he doesn't want to do what is being asked, or that he doesn't like the food, toy, or activity, or whatever it is that has just been offered to him. If you take "No" too seriously and imagine that your child is showing a strong preference or voicing a deeply held opinion, you will just be creating frustration for yourself.

The other thing is that "No" doesn't signify is that your toddler is out to "push your buttons." To take his resistance personally is to miss the point of it; his seeming rejection of everything has little to do with you. Your child's motivation is to figure out--and in a way, to create--where his sense of identity starts and your influence leaves off.

Saying no is proof of a toddler's individuality

At this age your child is beginning to see with increasing sophistication that she is an individual being, separate from you. Even though she is capable of expressing that sense of separateness by initiating an action (such as wandering into the neighbor's yard unaccompanied) or creating something of her own (such as crayoning on the wall), the easiest way for her to express it is to say no. Simply by resisting you, she has gotten her message across: "I am my own person."

Saying no is an important first step in your child's awareness that she can make her own choices. That awareness is essential to--and always developmentally precedes--her understanding of the concept of responsibility. If she doesn't have the chance to stand on her own two feet at times, she will never see that she is accountable for her actions.

When you see a toddler's propensity for saying no in this light, you can eliminate one of the most frequent--and misguided--responses to "no" dealing with it quickly and strongly in order to show your child who's the boss. Very often, parents mistakenly see a challenge to their word as a challenge to their authority and worry that unless firm action is taken, they will lose control of their child, who will eventually become willful and spoiled.

Your child isn't declaring a war of wills; only you can turn it into one

A child's "No" is not an indication of a power struggle between him and his parents. Rather, it is a power quest on his part; as his sense of himself grows, so does his urge to exercise his distinctive personality. Your toddler still sees you as all-powerful and is simply searching for some authority of his own. Your relationship will become a power struggle only if *you* make it into one.

One way that you can avoid opposition is by giving your toddler several choices instead of insisting that he follow your bidding. He'll be so busy asserting his independence by making his choice that resistance is unlikely. And remember, you can control the situation by controlling the choices.

When your toddler flat out resists you, instead of meeting that resistance head on, stay confident that you will remain in charge, and don't push a contest of wills. You'll only make your child more determined not to do what you want. You would be surprised how effective refusing to force the issue can be. Sometimes it isn't even necessary to reintroduce the toy, morsel of food, or article of clothing that your child refused; he will seek it out for himself. (It doesn't hurt, however, to leave it in plain view.)

Shaming a toddler makes her question herself

When your child decides to eat the apple slice or wear the hat she violently rejected before, don't point out to her that she has changed her mind. Sometimes, especially in moments of frustration, it's difficult to not show your toddler how inconsistent her actions seem to be. Doing so, however, can shame a child and lead her to believe that she is incapable of making good decisions. It can also trigger a bout of renewed stubbornness. Bear in mind that by her standards, your toddler is being perfectly consistent; after all, the object of her refusal is far less important to her than her ability to refuse it.

When you must override your child's "No"--for example, when she *must* put on her coat, or when she cannot take another child's toy--be firm and state simply why it is necessary that she do as you say. Tell her that you understand her dislike of bending to your rules, but also help her understand that sometimes others' needs have to be considered. This isn't a concept that goes over well with an 18-month-old, but in time she will come to see that she is not alone in having to accommodate other people.

During toddlerhood, your child will come to learn that she shares the world with others who have choices, too, and that sometimes they will resist her attempts to assert her independence. If she has been treated with understanding during her early phase of saying no--if your relationship has been one of give-and-take rather than "win or lose," if she has not been continually over-powered--she will have a pretty good sense of her own power and worth. She'll also have the confidence she needs to enter into the peer relationships of her preschool years.

Overcoming resistance with play

The key to handling battles with your toddler is to keep things light. Using humor to counter his resistance is often a good way to prevent a battle of wills, as long as you don't overplay the humor card and give your child the idea that you don't take his concerns seriously. Here are some ways that you can meet resistance playfully. The idea with all of these gambits is not to make fun of your child but to turn his opposition into a game that the two of you can share.

Exaggerate your own reaction. Say something to your child such as, "Oh, my goodness! You're not going to lie down for your nap? What am I going to do?" Pretend to start crying (but don't do it so realistically that you frighten him), or fall back in your chair in mock despair.

Imitate the resistance. If your toddler won't eat, then say with a wink, "If you won't eat, then I won't, either. Nosirree! You can't make me do it! Don't even try!"

Beg dramatically. Say to your child, "Oh, pleeeeease! Pleeeeease, oh powerful one, put on your coat for me!"

Play the yes-no game. When your child says no, question it in a singsong voice: "Nooooo? Do you mean yessssss?" When he hears no again, say, "Yesssss..." After several rounds, quickly say, "Okay, no!" Often children respond by laughing and saying, "Yes!"

Questions:

Do the concepts presented in this article support Erik Erikson's theories about autonomy versus shame and doubt?

What kind of response would you give if a child refuses to get into his or her carseat when riding in the car?

SELF-TESTS

Multiple-Choice

Circle the letter of the response which best completes or answers each of the following statements and questions.

1. A person's unique and relatively consistent way of feeling, thinking, and behaving is called
   a. self-awareness
   b. personality
   c. emotion
   d. self-regulation

2. Clarisse and Johan are both 10 months old. Clarisse's mother is sensitive, responsive, and consistent in attending to her daughter's needs. Johan's mother is insensitive and unpredictable in attending to her son's needs. According to Erikson, which child is most likely to develop the virtue of hope?
   a. Johan
   b. Clarisse
   c. both Johan and Clarisse
   d. a mother's behavior does not affect her child's inclination to develop hope

3. Trust versus mistrust is to the virtue of __________ as autonomy versus shame and doubt is to the virtue of ______________.
   a. hope; will
   b. will; hope
   c. joy; fear
   d. fear; joy

4. Rhonda, a 2-year-old, runs into a busy street after her ball. Jesse, a 3-year-old, however, waits for his father to retrieve the ball. Erikson refers to Jesse's control of his own behavior as
   a. trust
   b. self-awareness
   c. autonomy
   d. self-regulation

5. Which of the following, according to Erikson, represents an important step toward autonomy?
   a. toilet training
   b. language
   c. walking
   d. all of the above

6. According to research on infants' emotions, which of the following statements is most accurate?
   a. In the first few months of life, babies express a fairly wide range of emotions.
   b. Five-month-old babies cannot yet recognize such emotions as joy, sadness, and fear.
   c. It is relatively easy to learn how babies feelings first develop.
   d. none of the above

7. Charlie, who is 2½ years old, wants a cookie. However, he understands that his mother will be very upset with him if he opens the forbidden cookie jar. Thus, he refrains. Charlie has
   a. developed self-awareness
   b. not yet developed self-awareness
   c. developed an early sense of conscience
   d. both a and c

8. Which of the following statements about a baby's developing emotional language is false?
   a. The most powerful way that babies can express their needs is by crying in a variety of patterns.
   b. Babies gain confidence when they realize that they get a response to their crying or smiling.
   c. By the end of the first year, babies whose mothers have regularly answered their crying with compassion and sensitivity cry more.
   d. Babies who cry a lot need less attention from a caregiver.

9. Anna's crying is consistently responded to with tender, soothing care; research indicates that, consequently, Anna will
   a. continue to cry as much
   b. cry even more
   c. stop crying completely
   d. actually cry less

10. Lucinda does not smile frequently at her parents. Viktor, however, smiles and gurgles often in response to his parents' caretaking. We can thus infer that
    a. Viktor is likely to form a more positive relationship with his parents than is Lucinda.
    b. Viktor and Lucinda's smiling frequency will affect their respective relationships with their parents.
    c. Viktor is less likely to form a more positive relationship with his parents than is Lucinda.
    d. Viktor is likely to become a more spoiled child than Lucinda.

11. According to the mutual-regulation model,
    a. infants take an active part in regulating their emotional states
    b. all babies require the same amount of stimulation
    c. overstimulation will not negatively affect a child's development, but understimulation will
    d. all of the above

12. Which of the following statements regarding how infants' read the emotions of others is least accurate?
    a. The ability to decipher other people's feelings seems to be an inborn ability.
    b. Most babies passively receive other people's actions; for example, a 9-month-old will not look sad when his mother seems sad.
    c. Infants lacking the ability to read the feelings of others will often become socially and emotionally handicapped.
    d. A failure to notice the emotional signals of people around them is common in autistic children.

13. Ahmad, an 18-month-old, is surprised when his father brings home a new puppy. Hesitant to approach the dog, he looks to his parents for guidance. As they smile and show enthusiasm, Ahmad begins to pet the puppy. Ahmad is exhibiting
    a. social referencing
    b. self-recognition
    c. temperament
    d. autonomy

14. How does a mother's depression affect her baby?
    a. The baby will most likely learn to be unresponsive and sad.
    b. The baby will probably grow slowly and perform poorly on cognitive measures.
    c. The baby is more likely to have accidents and present behavioral problems into adolescence.
    d. all of the above

15. A child's characteristic style of approaching and reacting to people and situations is called
    a. self-recognition
    b. temperament
    c. social referencing
    d. personality

16. Svetlana, who is 3 years old, likes to dress herself. She puts on her pants, then her shirt, and then her shoes. Her twin sister, Marlena, however, likes to put her shirt on before her pants. In approaching the task of dressing in unique ways, the twins are displaying differences in
    a. referencing
    b. attachment
    c. self-recognition
    d. temperament

17. Based on results of the New York longitudinal study, which of the following components of temperament show up soon after birth?
    a. activity level
    b. distractibility
    c. attention span
    d. all of the above

18. Melinda is a calm baby who eats and sleeps at regular times and smiles often. Her twin brother, Andrew, sleeps and eats very little, throws frequent tantrums, and is quite shy. According to the New York Longitudinal Study, Melinda is a ___________ child, whereas Andrew is a __________ child.
    a. easy; difficult
    b. easy; slow-to-warm up
    c. slow-to-warm up; difficult
    d. easy; mean

19. A 10-year-old boy was classified as an infant as a "difficult" child. Recently, to his parents' delight, Roberto has become very active in sports, showing rare athletic talent. From studies on changes in temperament, we can reasonably infer that
    a. Roberto will remain a difficult child, because temperament is determined solely by heredity.
    b. Roberto will become a more well-adjusted individual as a result of a more positive interaction with his parents.
    c. Roberto's "difficult" behavior will not improve since environmental factors do not influence temperament.
    d. none of the above

20. The key to adjustment of temperament between parents and children appears to be
    a. parenthood classes
    b. goodness of fit
    c. to be authoritarian
    d. to be punitive

21. Roxanne talks with a psychologist regarding her youngster's behavior problems at nursery school. The psychologist is likely to point out to Roxanne that the best thing parents can do when dealing with their child's temperament is to
    a. be permissive
    b. try to mold the child's personality
    c. be authoritarian
    d. give the child time to adjust to new situations and ride with his basic temperament

22. A main finding in a study where adults played with boy and girl babies without knowing the babies actual gender was that
    a. "boys" were encouraged to play actively
    b. "girls" were encouraged to play actively
    c. adults talked more to "boys"
    d. there was no difference in the ways adults behaved

23. Tonya is a graduate student researching personality differences. She has learned that parents' behavior toward babies is affected by
    a. the babies' gender
    b. the babies' age
    c. the parent's gender
    d. all of the above

24. To study the mother-infant bond, some researchers use an approach which considers behavior to be biologically determined and is concerned with the evolutionary basis of behaviors. We call this the
    a. ethological approach
    b. sociability approach
    c. maternal approach
    d. environmental approach

25. When a newborn puppy first opens his eyes, he sees his mother. He thus begins to follow her everywhere, becoming increasingly attached. This is an example of what type of behavior?
    a. referencing
    b. autonomizing
    c. imprinting
    d. ambivalence

26. From their early research on the mother-infant bond, Klaus and Kenborn hypothesized that if mother and baby are separated during the first few hours after birth, the bond may not develop normally. Today several researchers such as Stella Chess
    a. agree with Klaus and Kenborn's critical period for mother-infant bonding
    b. cite Klaus and Kenborn's findings as the reason many adoptive parents have difficulty getting close to their child
    c. generally discredit Klaus and Kenborn's "critical period concept," stating that long term effects are unlikely as a result of early extended contact between mother and baby
    d. believe that bonding is an irrelevant issue; attachment to a mother figure has little effect on a child's development

27. Findings from Harlow's experiment with infant monkeys, a "wire" mother and a "cloth" mother, seem to imply that
    a. animals seek their mothers only to be fed
    b. animals seek their mothers to be touched and held as well as fed
    c. animals can learn nurturant behavior instinctively without observing and imitating
    d. animals can thrive without bodily contact

28. The laboratory technique devised by Mary Ainsworth to elicit behaviors of closeness between an adult and an infant is called the
    a. strange situation
    b. attachment situation
    c. separation situation
    d. none of the above

29. Chelsea, an 18-month-old, cries when her mother leaves and is happy when she returns. In addition, Chelsea is angry only rarely and freely explores her environment. According to the strange situation concept, Chelsea is a/an
    a. avoidant baby
    b. securely attached baby
    c. resistant baby
    d. disorganized baby

30. Which of the following characteristics is *not* common to mothers of avoidant babies?
    a. irritability
    b. positive feelings toward their children
    c. lack of self-confidence in their mothering skills
    d. anger

31. China, who is a 4-month-old, exhibits signs of anxious attachment. We can reasonably infer that
    a. regardless of how China's mother acts, her daughter will remain anxiously attached
    b. China was a low-birthweight baby
    c. for China to become securely attached, it is critical that her mother interact positively with China
    d. China is a hearing-impaired baby

32. Stetson is a 12-month-old boy, securely attached to his mother. Research on the long-term effects of attachment leads us to believe that
    a. Stetson will grow into a very dependent adult
    b. around age 4 Stetson will have difficulty getting along with other children
    c. around age 5 Stetson is unlikely to exhibit hostile behavior toward other children
    d. as an adult, Stetson will have an easier time leaving his parents due to his secure childhood attachment

33. In our culture, fathers tend to do which of the following with their babies?
    a. play with them
    b. care for them
    c. ignore them
    d. be gentle with them

34. Which of the following factors affects the way in which a father interacts with his child?
    a. the mother's attitude
    b. the mother's employment
    c. cross-cultural differences
    d. all of the above

35. Which of the following statements regarding the father-infant relationship is *most* accurate?
    a. Fathers play the part of family disciplinarian in a stereotypical family.
    b. Fathers act less differently toward boys and girls than mothers do.
    c. Fathers, more than mothers, seem to affect the development of gender identity and gender typing.
    d. Fathers have little influence on their sons' cognitive development.

36. Suzette used to be a friendly baby, who approached strangers readily. As long as someone was around, Suzette remained happy. However, she recently began screaming loudly whenever a new person comes near her. Suzette is experiencing
    a. stranger anxiety
    b. emotional disturbances
    c. attachment anxiety
    d. none of the above

37. If a child must be hospitalized, the stress can be reduced if
    a. the parents can stay overnight with the child
    b. prior to hospitalization, the child spends time staying with his grandparents
    c. family members visit daily
    d. all of the above

38. Which of the following applies to abused, battered, and neglected children?
    a. They are resilient, especially if they have a supportive family member to whom they can form an attachment.
    b. They tend to be sexually maladjusted, have low-self-esteem, and have difficulty trusting others.
    c. They are more likely to repeat a grade, to do worse on cognitive tests, and to be discipline problems in school.
    d. all of the above

39. When Sean is three years old, his mother gives birth to a baby boy. As a result,
    a. Sean's mother is likely to play less with him.
    b. Sean is likely to exhibit behavioral problems, such as wetting his pants and refusing to talk; these problems are likely to disappear by the time his brother is one year old.
    c. Sean will adjust better to his new sibling's arrival if his father provides Sean with extra time and attention.
    d. all of the above

40. Isabelle is considering enrolling her daughter in the local day care center since she has obtained a full-time job. It is important that the day care facility Isabelle selects
    a. employs adult caregivers with a master's degree
    b. employs adult caregivers with formal training in childhood education and/or psychology
    c. employs mostly female staff members
    d. all of the above

41. Which of the following statements regarding day care is *most* accurate?
    a. Children from low-income families benefit the most from a good day care program.
    b. Children aged 2 to 4 in adequate group day care tend to do much worse than children raised at home by parents on a number of intellectual measures.
    c. Day care is usually severely detrimental to a child's cognitive development.
    d. Boys from high-income families in full-time infant care may be at risk for lower intellectual development.

42. Researchers studying children's attachments to their mothers have found that
    a. the greatest risk to the mother-child bond lies in poor-quality care and poor family environments.
    b. the first year of the child's life seems the most critical for establishing the mother-child bond.
    c. when infants get poor-quality day care, they are more likely to avoid their mother and develop future emotional problems.
    d. all of the above

43. Which of the following statements is *least* accurate regarding child care in Sweden.
    a. Every Swedish family receives an allowance from the state for each child, from birth through age 16.
    b. Both mothers and fathers can take parental leave from work to raise their newborns.
    c. Parents pay an average of 90 percent of the real cost of child care.
    d. The most important factor in a child's future development seems to be how well the child is cared for in his/her own home.

44. Ben is 5 month's old. His mother, Louisa, has recently returned to her full-time job. From her studies of parent-infant attachment, Lois Hoffman concludes that
    a. Ben will become very insecurely attached to his mother due to her full-time employment.
    b. The relationship between Louisa's employment during her son's first year of life and Ben's attachment security is very weak.
    c. Despite Louisa's full-time employment, Ben is likely to become securely attached to his mother if he is raised in a nurturing environment.
    d. both b and c

Completion

Supply the term or terms needed to complete each of the following statements.

1. The first of Erikson's eight crises, or critical developmental stages, ____________ ____________________, begins in infancy and continues until about 18 months of age.

2. The tendency to say "No" just for the sake of resisting authority is called ____________________________.

3. Around age three, babies develop _________________, which is the ability to control their own behavior to conform with social expectations.

4. ____________________ are expressed in characteristic ways, are accompanied by certain neurochemical processes in the body, and arise in response to various situations and experiences.

5. Around the second year of life, babies typically develop the understanding that they are separate from other people and things. This is called ___________________.

6. Self-awareness usually emerges according to the following sequence: ___________, ____________________; and _____________________.

7. ________________________ is the most powerful way, sometimes the only way, by which infants can communicate their vital needs.

8. The _________________________ model shows how infants as young as three months of age take an active part in regulating their emotional states.

9. Through __________________, one person forms an understanding of an ambiguous situation by seeking out another person's perception of it.

10. A child's ______________________ is his/her characteristic style of approaching and reacting to people and situations.

11. According to the New York Longitudinal Study, a _________________ child is irritable, irregular in biological rhythms, and intense in expressing emotion.

12. The key to healthy adjustment is _________________ between children and the demands made upon them.

13. When strangers think that a crying baby is a male, they are likely to assume that "he" is crying from ______________; when they believe that the baby is female, they think that "she" is ________________.

14. How children learn the behaviors their culture deems appropriate is referred to as __________________________.

15. _______________________ is an active, affectionate, reciprocal, enduring relationship, between two people; in unscientific circles we call it love.

16. The ____________, a famous technique devised to elicit behaviors of closeness between an adult and an infant, is now the most common way to study attachment.

17. Babies with _________________ attachment often show inconsistent, contradictory behavior; they greet their mother brightly when she returns but then turn away, or approach without looking at her.

18. A number of critics question the validity of the strange situation to study attachment. A more complex method may be needed to measure it more sensitively, especially to see how mother and infant interact during natural, non-____________ situations.

19. Swedish infants show more attachment behaviors to mothers than to fathers, whereas ____________ babies show attachment fairly equally to both parents.

20. The wariness of a person a child does not know is called ____________; the distress a child shows when a familiar caregiver leaves her is called ________.

ANSWERS FOR SELF-TESTS — CHAPTER 5

Multiple-Choice

		Page	
1.	b	162	factual
2.	b	163	conceptual
3.	a	163	conceptual
4.	d	164	conceptual
5.	d	164	factual
6.	a	165	factual
7.	d	166	conceptual
8.	c	167	factual
9.	d	167	conceptual
10.	a	168	conceptual
11.	a	168	factual
12.	b	169	factual
13.	a	169	conceptual
14.	d	170	factual
15.	b	171	factual
16.	d	171	conceptual
17.	d	171	factual
18.	a	171	conceptual
19.	b	172	conceptual
20.	b	173	factual
21.	d	173	factual
22.	a	173	factual

		Page	
23.	d	173	conceptual
24.	a	174	factual
25.	c	175	conceptual
26.	c	175	factual
27.	b	175	factual
28.	a	177	factual
29.	b	177	conceptual
30.	b	178	factual
31.	c	179	conceptual
32.	d	179	conceptual
33.	a	181	factual
34.	d	182	factual
35.	c	182	factual
36.	a	183	conceptual
37.	d	184	conceptual
38.	d	186	factual
39.	d	188	conceptual
40.	b	190	conceptual
41.	d	191	factual
42.	d	192	factual
43.	c	193	factual
44.	d	194	conceptual

Completion

		Page
1.	basic trust v. mistrust	163
2.	negativism	164
3.	self-regulation	164
4.	emotions	165
5.	self-awareness	166
6.	physical self-recognition; self-description; emotional response to wrongdoing	166
7.	crying	167
8.	mutual regulation	168

		Page
9.	social-referencing	169
10.	temperament	171
11.	difficult	171
12.	goodness of fit	173
13.	anger; afraid	173
14.	socialization	174
15.	attachment	176
16.	strange situation	177
17.	disorganized-disoriented	177
18.	stressful	180
19.	American	181
20.	stranger anxiety separation anxiety	183

CHAPTER 6

Physical and Intellectual Development in Early Childhood

INTRODUCTION

The discussion of physical and intellectual development in early childhood in Chapter 6 begins a pattern that will continue through most of the remainder of the textbook. Each period of development (early childhood, adolescence, etc.) will be discussed in two chapters: the first will deal with physical and intellectual development during that period, and the second, with personality and social development during that period.

- Chapter 6 begins by describing the physical growth and change of children aged 3 to 6 and examines the effect of nutrition on growth and health.

- The early childhood years are basically healthy; yet, some health problems do exist. Various minor and major illnesses, as well as common accidental injuries are described, with particular attention given to the topic of children with AIDS. Several factors affecting children's health are discussed.

- Children's sleep patterns and sleep disturbances and how they change during early childhood are discussed, as well as the topic of bedwetting.

- Large-muscle, small-muscle, and hand-eye coordination are briefly described.

- In the area of intellectual development, Chapter 6 examines how memory, speech, and intelligence develop and function during early childhood. It focuses on Piaget's preoperational stage of cognitive development and modifies his theories with recent research findings.

- Recent research is presented and evaluated on the effects of the quality of day care, preschool, and kindergarten programs.

CHAPTER OUTLINE

PHYSICAL DEVELOPMENT

I. Physical Growth and Change

A. Height, Weight, and Appearance
B. Structural and Systemic Changes
C. Nutrition

II. Health

A. Health Problems in Early Childhood
  1. Minor Illnesses
  2. Major Illnesses
    a. AIDS in children
  3. Accidental Injuries
B. Influences on Health
  1. Exposure to Illness
  2. Stress
  3. Poverty

III. Sleep Patterns and Problems

A. Normal Sleep Patterns
B. Sleep Disturbances
C. Bed Wetting

IV. Motor Skills

A. Large-Muscle Coordination
B. Small-Muscle and Eye-Hand Coordination

INTELLECTUAL DEVELOPMENT

V. Aspects of Intellectual Development

A. Development of Memory: Information Processing
  1. Influences on Children's Memory
    a. General knowledge
    b. "Mastery motivation" and study activities
  2. Unusual Activities and New Experiences
  3. Social Interactions
B. Cognitive Development: Piaget's Preoperational Stage
  1. The Symbolic Function
    a. Indications of the symbolic function
  2. Achievements of Preoperational Thought
    a. Understanding of identities and function
  3. Limitations of Preoperational Thought
    a. Centration
    b. Irreversibility
    c. Focus on States Rather than on Transformations
    d. Transductive Reasoning
    e. Egocentrism

4. Assessing Piaget's Theory
   a. Do Young Children Understand Cause and Effect?
   b. How Animistic are Young Children?
   c. How Egocentric are Young Children?
   d. How Well Can Young Children Classify?
   e. Can Cognitive Abilities be Accelerated?

C. Development of Language
   1. Using Words, Sentences, and Grammar
   2. Speaking to Others: Social Speech
   3. Speaking to Oneself: Private Speech

D. Development of Intelligence
   1. Assessing Intelligence by Traditional, Psychometric Measures
   2. What do Scores on Intelligence Tests Mean?
      a. Stanford-Binet Intelligence Scale
      b. Wechsler Preschool and Primary Scale of Intelligence, Revised (WPPSI-R)
   3. The "Zone of Proximal Development"
   4. Parents' Influence on Children's Intelligence
      a. Providing an Environment for Learning
      b. "Scaffolding"
      c. The Father's Role
      d. The Mother's Role: When Mothers are Employed

VI. The Widening Environment

A. Preschool and Day Care
   1. How Good Preschools Foster Development
   2. Montessori Preschools
   3. Compensatory Preschool Programs
      a. Project Head Start
      b. Long-Term Benefits of Compensatory Education

B. Kindergarten

KEY TERMS

animism (page 218)

centration (215)

conservation (215)

decenter (215)

deferred imitation (214)

egocentrism (217)

enuresis (208)

fine motor skills (209)

gross motor skills (209)

intelligence quotient (IQ) tests (224)

irreversibility (215)

preoperational stage (214)

private speech (223)

Project Head Start (233)

recall (212)

recognition (212)

reliable (224)

scaffolding (214)

social speech (223)

standardized norms (224)

Stanford-Binet Intelligence Scale (225)

symbol (214)

symbolic function (214)

symbolic play (214)

transduction (214)

transitional objects (208)

valid (224)

Wechsler Preschool and Primary Scale of Intelligence (WPPSI-R) (225)

zone of proximal development (ZPD) (225)

LEARNING OBJECTIVES

After finishing Chapter 6, you should be able to:

1. Describe changes during early childhood in the following areas: (pp. 200-201)

   a. height

   b. weight

   c. muscular

   d. structural

2. Explain the vital role of nutrition on children's health. (p. 201)

3. List some of the common childhood illnesses, accidental injuries, and other factors that influence health. (pp. 201-204)

4. Discuss some of the physical and psychological effects of AIDS on children. (p. 202)

5. How does poverty affect young children, and what recommendations are made to improve the situation for children most at risk? (pp. 204-206)

6. Describe patterns of sleep and some common sleep disturbances in early childhood. (pp. 207-208)

7. List some biological and environmental facts about bedwetting and explain some of the approaches used to deal with this. (pp. 208-209)

8. Describe eye-hand coordination and some of the characteristic motor skills, both large- and small-muscle, that are present or develop in early childhood. (pp. 209-210)

   a. eye-hand coordination

   b. motor skills

9. Explain how memory is developed and operates in early childhood and define the following terms: (pp. 212-213)

   a. *recognition*
   b. *recall*
   c. general knowledge
   d. mastery motivation

10. Describe children's thinking process during the *preoperational stage* of cognitive development. (p. 214)

11. Explain the following concepts associated with *preoperative* thinking: (p. 214)

    a. *symbol*
    b. *symbolic function*
    c. *deferred imitation*
    d. *symbolic play*

12. Compare and contrast the achievements and limitations of *preoperational* thought and explain the following terms: (pp. 215-218)

    a. *centration*
    b. *irreversibility*
    c. *transduction*
    d. *animism*
    e. *egocentrism*

13. Briefly critique Piaget's theory and comment on the following questions: (pp. 218-221)
    a. How *animistic* are young children?
    b. How *egocentric* are young children?
    c. How well can young children classify?
    d. Can cognitive abilities be accelerated?

14. Describe the development and use of language in early childhood. (pp. 221-222)

15. What are the cognitive benefits a child derives from speaking to others and from speaking to himself or herself. (pp. 223-224)

16. Describe the purpose of measuring young children's intelligence, then name and describe the three major psychometric intelligence inventories mentioned in the text. (pp. 224-225)

17. How do parents influence children's intellectual development? (pp. 225-227)

18. Explain how preschools foster development and describe the views of both Montessori and compensatory preschool programs. (pp. 228-234)

19. What is kindergarten like in American schools today? (pp. 234-235)

SUPPLEMENTAL READING

Michael Lipson, Ph.D., is senior psychologist at Harlem Hospital in New York City, New York. This article is reprinted with permission from The Hastings Center Report, ©March-April 1993, The Hastings Center.

What Do You Say to a Child with AIDS?

Michael Lipson, Ph.D

As more children with Human Immunodeficiency Virus (HIV) live to older ages, the question of when and how to talk with them about their illness becomes more pressing and more widespread. The Centers for Disease Control currently estimates that there are over 4,100 children with AIDS in America, with three times that number of HIV-positive children. Perhaps even without the innovations of improved antiretroviral treatments and early diagnosis, many of these children will live at least to school age.

At the younger end--say, before four years of age--few guardians or caregivers desire to tell children the name or other details of their illness. It is said that they are "not old enough." At the older end--say, after fourteen years--few guardians or caregivers seriously doubt that children must be told. It is said that now they are "old enough," and sexual maturity presents an issue of public health. Between these ages lies a decade of ethical and clinical obscurity.

Observations forming the experiential basis of this article were made in the Harlem Hospital pediatric AIDS facility (Family Care Center) and draw on the (scant) literature about pediatric AIDS disclosure. As psychologist to the pediatric AIDS team, I have been struck by how few parents have told their cognitively normal school-age children about their diagnosis. This has been the case even for the majority of symptomatic children, with silence surrounding the issue through the child's death. Of the approximately thirty school-age children treated at Harlem since 1985, only three had been told their diagnosis as of summer 1991. Informal reports from other New York City and Boston hospitals suggest varying (but low) rates of disclosure and a similar range of ethical questions.

These ethical questions include the following. Substantively, when is it right to tell children they have a life-threatening illness, in particular the AIDS virus with its high mortality and terrible stigma? What are the ethical grounds for telling or not telling? Is the possible increased anxiety that diagnosis may bring offset by possible gains in intimacy or longer-term psychological adjustment? Are other ethical grounds, such as respect for autonomy, decisive at any point? Procedurally, who should decide whether a child is "ready" to discuss diagnosis? If parents want silence and others want discussion, under what circumstances should each prevail? Is there a difference, for example, between the (generally infected) natural parent's and a (generally uninfected) foster or adoptive parent's reservations about disclosure? Does the health professional's therapeutic responsibility to the child conflict with a responsibility to the parent?

Some factors tend to move the adults who form a child's environment toward disclosure and discussion, while others move them toward silence. In this article I will not examine each of these ethical questions in detail, but sketch common motivations and circumstances that form the context within which the ethical issues arise. A part of this context beyond the scope of the present discussion is the disclosure of children's serostatus to their school and disclosures between parents or within families more generally.

My emphasis is clinical rather than legal. As a question of the quality of life for a minor, and given the brief time span in which the question is relevant, disclosure will probably seldom come to adjudication, though it is possible to imagine ways in which that might occur. In New York State, a minor's legal guardian has the prerogative to disclose or conceal the HIV diagnosis.

Although it is both somewhat artificial and somewhat problematic to do so, I will begin my sketch of the issues by casting them in terms of a conflict between parents (natural, foster, or adoptive) and health professionals (pediatricians, nurses, social workers, psychologists). Parents, who want to delay disclosure, confront health professionals, who want to hasten it. To speak in terms of this opposition is somewhat artificial because motives on both sides are mixed and are sometimes the reverse of those just mentioned. It is somewhat problematic because this opposition exists in large measure precisely to the degree that actors in a child's environment perceive the issues in polarized terms. To discuss them as a polarity is therefore to risk reinforcement of adversarial stereotypes. Nevertheless, I will make use of this schema both for clarity of exposition and to acknowledge its frequency in treatment settings. Later we shall see that overcoming the perception that there is an adversarial element in the relationships among children, parents, and health care staff holds out the best hope for answering the ethical questions involved.

Parents

Parents have many reasons to be reluctant about disclosure of diagnosis to their HIV-positive children. Yet I have never encountered a parent of a perinatally infected child over six years of age who had not at least considered disclosure. The question has a long history by the time it becomes pressing. Part of its history is the mother's experience of hearing her own and her child's diagnosis; another part is her experience of telling or not telling others about the infection. To the extent that these experiences were painful or disappointing (and they almost always are, to some degree), the mother will tend to be averse to further disclosures.

We must go further back still, however. The overwhelming majority of pediatric HIV cases occurs in urban minority families that have experienced poverty, early or violent family deaths, racial discrimination, lack of basic services, drug addiction, and unstable family configurations. Strategies for coping with the pervasive losses these families have encountered on all fronts generally do not include full and open discussion. In a significant number of such families, denial, unresolved mourning, and a resultant depression may become the norm. Discussing HIV might be both a difficult-to-achieve exception to the accustomed pattern and a threat to the whole system of avoidance a family has developed adaptively in onerous circumstances.

In families affected by HIV, as in others, children are loved. They often represent all hope for the future. They are incalculably precious as individuals. To discuss their infection with a fatal virus is to bring its presence and their likely premature death into consciousness, while to avoid mentioning it is to keep the illness mentally at bay. I have frequently seen parents who are impassive when discussing their own or their child's death directly, but who break down in tears, both for themselves and their child, when contemplating disclosure of serostatus to the child.

At the extreme, this reluctance includes the idea that disclosure will do immediate body harm. One woman told me that if she spoke to her daughter about HIV, the child would get sick and die sooner. Since the prognosis is poor, the mother will probably find her prediction confirmed should she bring herself after all to speak with her daughter about HIV. Such concerns are only rarely associated with an explicit causal link in mind--that the knowledge will sap the child's will to live, for example, or that a resulting depression will lower immune response. Yet these links may be implicit, even if they are irrelevant to the validity of the parent's fear as a basis for caution, or they simply may be an alternate form in which fear of disclosure's psychological consequences is clothed.

Parents, then, resist disclosure of HIV in part to shield their children and themselves from the full impact of the child's illness. For infected parents, the further apparent mental equation must be noted: discussing my child's infection *equals* discussing my own infection *equals* my guilt, illness, and likely death.

Unlike cancer or even other inheritable diseases such as hemophilia, HIV is associated with taboo sexual and drug-related behaviors. Parents often fear their children's questions about the source of the infection because they are ashamed of their own past high-risk conduct, and they feel guilty for transmitting the disease through this conduct. A former intravenous drug user, mother of an infected child, with past sexual partners of unknown serostatus, is unable to say for sure how she became infected, which may contribute to her hesitancy in discussing infection with her child.

AIDS has a unique social stigma. Parents fear that if they tell their children, the children will tell others, and they will be ostracized. This fear is realistic up to a point. Children's capacity for secrecy on such topics is impressive but unreliable. At six years or earlier, children can sometimes be aware they have HIV yet not mention it to their closest family members, having tacitly absorbed and followed the family code of silence. Nevertheless, they may also blurt out the word "AIDS" or "HIV" or "AZT" at an inappropriate moment, irrevocably changing a school teacher's or relative's attitude toward the family. Although public health education and the increasing incidence of the disease will continue to ameliorate social reactivity to HIV-positive individuals, these factors have not made AIDS safe public territory to date. And there is no age at which health professionals can guarantee a child's respect for the disclosure limits set by parents.

Parents often say children are not "old enough" to know about HIV. They mean this in any combination of at least three senses. First, they mean the child cannot yet keep the diagnosis a secret. Second, they mean the child will not understand the disease itself--its aetiology, course, treatment, stigma, and so on. Third, they mean the child is not capable of understanding death.

The first of these has been discussed. The second and third are paradoxical, since it is on the basis precisely that children *will* understand aetiology and prognosis that the same parents at other moments justify nondisclosure on the grounds of beneficence. The apparent paradox is resolved when we realize that behind the fear of telling children something they "will not understand" is the view that children will in fact grasp the diagnosis emotionally (as devastating) but not be able cognitively to engage it and so master or at least endure it. Health professionals will vary in their estimation of whether these "not old enough" arguments are valid, misinformed, or substitutes for less easily articulable reservations.

Among the latter may be the kind of reluctance discussed by Myra Bluebond-Langner in her pivotal study, *The Private Worlds of Dying Children*. In that account of children with cancer, Bluebond-Langner describes the loss of secure social roles that threatens both parents and children when they talk about a terminal illness in the child. Normally, countless interactions with children center on their preparation for adulthood. It is on this footing that they are urged to eat well, learn school conduct, and perform at school. When this element of training is missing from the relationship, parents and children can feel profoundly dislocated, making the kind of frank discussion Bluebond-Langner calls "open awareness" difficult to maintain.

Health Professionals

Health professionals working in the HIV field live in an unusual atmosphere of relative verbal openness about the illness. Their resistance to talking about it with infected children and adults tends to be low, because of special preparation and the attrition of repeated discussion. They are initially self-selected for relative willingness to work with disease and death; they mention the course of the disease and its treatments constantly; they have seen children live and die with it.

Health professionals also work in a setting that has gradually undergone a profound change in attitude toward disclosure of all life-threatening illnesses in adults and children. In the 1960s it was still common to withhold the diagnosis of pediatric cancer right through the patient's death. By the mid-1980s the custom of early disclosure of such a diagnosis had become near-automatic. In the intervening years, many studies had demonstrated that, for example, children with cancer are more anxious and more death-focused that other chronically ill children even when they have not been "told." By contrast, positive results of disclosure were shown to include reduction of anxiety, improved family functioning, and (for survivors to adulthood) long-term gains in psychosocial adjustment.

An extensive developmental literature on children's concepts of illness (including AIDS) and death indicates that children older than four years of age do in fact understand these phenomena--in accordance with their stage of emotional and cognitive development. They do not understand AIDS or death as an adult would. But then, which of us could claim complete understanding of these things? Like our own, children's knowledge is in process. To those familiar with the developmental literature or its applications, the clinical question becomes not *whether*, or even *when*, but *how* to speak with children about any disease.

In addition to this shared professional history, health care workers may have accumulated individual experiences of disclosure and nondisclosure. Often, a child will talk about HIV to a favorite nurse and to no one else. Such nurses have sometimes said to me in exasperation, "She knows. She *knows*. We talk about it all the time." From the perspective of intimacy they enjoy with a patient who can talk openly about the disease, they cannot comprehend a parent's refusal to have the topic officially broached. After much debate, one family decided to tell their eleven-year-old daughter and were met with her fury; she had known about this for years, she said. Why did everyone treat her as if it had to be a secret?

Hospital staff experiences with disclosure include the many cases in which children were not told of their HIV infection and then died of AIDS. If children at the terminal stage ask about their condition, they typically focus on their solitude, pain, or death. In the last weeks or days of life, the name of a fatal disease can therefore seem quite irrelevant to all concerned. Health professionals who have witnessed extreme dependence, confusion, and anxiety in such children may want to prevent a sudden, harsh, and lonely confrontation with death that could have occurred more gently. The gentleness in question would require discussion of a child's illness long before its final stages.

Although parents may think children are ignorant of their condition, health professionals may be privy to children's explicit references to HIV or AIDS. There are many intermediate kinds of knowledge, however, that health professionals may also encounter. Children show a curiosity or knowledge about treatments, at times, that they do not put into words. They may try to listen in on a conversation between doctors, hint to or ask other patients about their condition, refer in conversations to AZT with a challenging glance, and otherwise indicate curiosity and partial knowledge.

In these and other ways, health professionals see children acting as autonomous individuals attempting to achieve cognitive mastery over their bodies and lives. They may feel that respect for this autonomy requires disclosure--and that most school-age children have the capacity to deny or avoid the disclosed diagnosis if its contemplation is injurious to them. Regard for the child's autonomy, on this view, does not conflict with the principle of beneficence (which motivates the parental position), but coincides with it. Benefits of disclosure are thought to include, beyond this recognition of autonomy, increased intimacy with those close to the child and the possibility of improved psychological adjustment.

If a central element of the relationship between parents and children is that of training for adulthood, as Bluebond-Langner asserts, this amounts at times to treating a child as a means to the end of their future, adult selves. Parents' delay of disclosure reflects their view that the child is *not yet* that being with whom full openness is appropriate. Health professionals' bias toward disclosure reflects their view that the child is *already* endowed with a measure of autonomy, self-awareness, and rationality.

Particularity

To some degree, the benefits or risks of disclosure are an empirical matter. The growing body of evidence from pediatric oncology should be met by research specifically in HIV and AIDS to determine infected children's responses to the spectrum of disclosure and nondisclosure styles. We need such research to help us weigh the likely merit of disclosure in each case.

Yet research results are generalizations; as

clinicians we have to do always and only with individual patients and specific moments. So as neither to inflict needlessly painful and psychologically harmful knowledge on patients, nor to deprive them of helpful knowledge they need and desire, we must give heed to the special methods, timing, and circumstances required by children's developmental level.

We have to do, in normal children, with a *developing* autonomy, and so the risks and benefits of a specific intervention also change over the course of a child's development. Paternalistic interventions in the name of a child's well-being ought to decrease as the child's autonomy is seen to increase.

As a physical disease, HIV/AIDS tends to fall under the sway of medical protocol. The nature of research and procedural innovation in the hospital context makes it likely that disclosure of their diagnosis to infected children will eventually occur on a programmed schedule. Yet there is an *ethical* principle militating against such regimentation, and that is respect for human uniqueness. Not only does each child differ from every other in style and rate of development, but cognitive and emotional capacity varies from moment to moment. At times, children with life-threatening disease will regress below the threshold of readiness for disclosure; at other times, disclosure will quite properly constitute a challenge occurring at the crest of their cognitive capacity. The distinction among such moments is a matter for clinical responsiveness, not for forced performance according to a medical or ethical protocol.

In principle, parents' reasons for nondisclosure, to the extent that they are based on self-interest alone (however understandably, as, for example, to avoid anticipatory grief), are not oriented toward the child's best interest and do not qualify as grounds for silence. In practice, this distinction is impossible to maintain; what harms or benefits the parent has an effect upon the well-being of the child in numerous ways. As an extreme example of this, I saw a parent become so anxious about a planned disclosure that she did not bring her child to the hospital for needed services. To confront parents' attitudes as if they are in conflict with the interests of the child, as occurred in this example, is to run the real risk of making them so.

Most children with AIDS live in families with nonnuclear configurations. Many are in foster care or adoptive placement, either with a relative or person outside the natural family. This gives rise to special ethical tensions regarding disclosure of diagnosis.

Foster parents may not feel entirely secure in their relationship to a child and are uncomfortable with the intimacy and ultimacy of disclosure for that reason. Their desire to provide a "better home" can also stimulate foster and adoptive parents to avoid discussion of the disease because it links the child to the past. Alternatively, a child's foster parent, now caring for a child whose natural mother infected but did not rear it, may feel inclined toward disclosure in part due to her resentment of the natural mother. Thus, whether foster parents seek disclosure or seek to avoid it, their impulse often stems from an effort to make reparation for conditions brought about through the natural parent. They may feel an obligation not to love or care for the child in just the manner of the natural parents, but precisely to offer a healthier alternative. In this offering, motives of resentment or even revenge can mingle with motives of compassion.

For example, I counseled a mother-grandmother pair on the issue of disclosure to the mother's nine-year-old son. The grandmother, now having custody of her grandson, urged disclosure. It later became apparent that her motive was partly to stimulate guilt in her daughter over drug abuse and over the child's infection. At the disclosure meeting, when the boy was told he had HIV since birth, he asked, "How did I get it?" Although his mother had been coached in constructive answers to this question, under the pressure of the moment she responded, "I didn't know I was positive when I got pregnant with you." Her son met this protestation with a puzzled look, and no one explained it to him. The disclosure process, in which the grandmother has since become uninterested, came to seem most of all like a move in the mother-daughter conflict. As it turned out, disclosure has brought social and psychological benefits to this boy, despite the mixed circumstances of its initiation.

Siblings in the foster family, even more than in the family of origin, may find the acknowledgement of an infected child's medically sensitive and therefore privileged condition to be a burden. In the short run, HIV gives the newcomer sibling a hatefully high status as deserving of maternal care, while in the long run it frighteningly overindulges siblings' worst fantasies of revenge against the young family intruder. Of course, the same foster siblings can also be wonderfully accepting and protective.

The special family circumstances of HIV-positive children in each case are an aspect of the child's individuality or uniqueness, and respect for this uniqueness is one principle that should guide disclosure decisions. Another such governing principle, as I will explore more thoroughly in the next section, involves a reconceptualization of disclosure as something quite different from the provision of *information*. It is not so much the vocabulary that matters from an ethical standpoint, nor the conceptual content of the message, nor even its style and tone, but rather the whole relationship within which disclosure occurs. As we have seen, consideration of a child's developing autonomy will tend to require a gradual and increasing openness about HIV *as information*, but this is, after all, less than sufficient as an ethical minimum. Beyond this informational level we must give heed to the dialogue within which disclosure comes about.

From Disclosure to Dialogue

The ethical and clinical difficulties surrounding disclosure find their solution when we begin to think and treat less in terms of *points* and more in terms of *processes*. Rather than a pointlike moment of development at which children "understand" HIV, for example, there is a continual process of potential cognitive involvement with their illness and its consequences. Rather than an instant at which autonomy is attained, there is an evolution of the cognitive and emotional components of autonomy. And rather than a traumatic moment of disclosure, there can be a gradual and increasingly open dialogue about the events, terms, and relationships that children's HIV-positive status entails.

In my characterization of both parents' and health professionals' attitudes, there is a conflictual or adversarial tendency whose root lies in the conception of disclosure as a point in time. In fantasy, this moment is conceived as either a beneficial or deleterious shock that would change a child's adaptation to illness all at once and once and for all.

In my experience, both parents and staff benefit from changing their concept of a disclosure moment into the idea of participation in a dialogue, a process of discussion, that will be lifelong. Parents, professionals, and children can consult one another frequently; share fears and pleasures as well as information, invite one another's speech, and respond to one another's invitations. All parties change through such a process--if it goes well. It is generally incumbent on health professionals to initiate the change in conceptualization from disclosure-point to disclosure-process; this change being itself a negotiated, dialogical, and gradual evolution. It can begin with the exploration of disclosure fantasies on all sides.

When we say of a parent, "She doesn't want her child to know," we should be aware that such statements are partial and momentary truths at most. Through dialogue a parent's views will often change so that, for example, she *does* want to disclose; meanwhile the health professional may realize that, for example, the mother was right and it *is* too early for this child even to begin the disclosure process. We are in danger of locking ourselves and our patients into established (therefore adversarial) positions especially when, as in these cases, emotions are strong. Every assertion of a "position" is capable of being stated with such vehemence or certainty that it creates and perpetuates both its own solidity and its own opposition. To stand on an ethical principle in defense of, say, the child's autonomy is often to sacrifice the engagement with the parent that the child needs, most often, much more than any nugget of information.

At times, the stated position of a parent can run counter to the parent's apparent true feelings. While we must take parents seriously and give respect to their wishes, it requires sensitivity and discussion to discover what those wishes really are, and to track them as they evolve. For example, it is not uncommon to see parents rush into disclosure, having previously resisted it, in the apparent hope that they will thereby more thoroughly dismiss the topic. Openness becomes a refinement of denial. Conversely, some parents will loudly "protest" that their child is not ready--but it is the parent, and no one else, who brought up the issue of disclosure. The announcement of a need for secrecy becomes a backhanded approach toward openness.

Although the specific delineation of treatment methods lies outside the scope of this paper, a few indications can suggest the lines along which a dialogical solution may run. It is crucial to our work at Harlem Hospital that families have already come to trust the pediatric AIDS team because the hospital has provided years of medical, social work, and psychological services. Such helping relationships are the best institutional basis for the establishment of disclosure dialogues.

When disclosure issues arise, we need not start by blurting out the words "HIV" or "AIDS" to the child, but by discussing with the parents their attitudes toward the disease and its consequences in their lives. When parents (most often, and most importantly, the mother or foster mother) are ready, when some of their fears and grief have been addressed, they can be encouraged to talk with their children about the children's feelings toward their doctor, hospital, or medication. General information about viruses or about a specific opportunistic infection the child has encountered can be introduced. When comfortable exchanges between parent and child have been established, it may seem right to all concerned to identify the virus by name. Depending on the child's educational level, "HIV" may be mentioned and explained before any reference to "AIDS." If dialogue with a parent proves impossible, and the needs of the child require it, this process can be undertaken by professional staff with relatively little parental involvement, though this is not the best course. The order of these stages and their specific content is much less important than the idea that they occur in stages, with sensitivity to the changing meanings of the terms being used. Children at different cognitive and emotional levels will respond best to different kinds of information and different styles of presentation (in accordance, for example, with Piagetian principles of cognitive development, as suggested by Walsh and Bibace).

An important element in adult fantasies of disclosure, imagined as a point in time, is that children will receive in a single instant the full meaning of HIV/AIDS as it exists for the adults. But this too is and can only be a process. During disclosure discussions we continually observe that children do not see in a word or circumstance the same significance that adults do. To communicate the full spectrum of meanings and implications of HIV/AIDS to a child is a long and only partially (though increasingly) necessary task. Before talking with their children, parents can be encouraged to think through which issues they will discuss with children and approximately in what order. Among the disclosure topics that unfold gradually may be the following: Who knows and does not know about family infections; with whom the infected child should discuss HIV/AIDS; what past family events have been linked to HIV/AIDS that can now be more fully explained; who else in the family has HIV/AIDS; who has died of it; how family members acquired HIV; the child's and other family members' prognosis; the parent's feelings about HIV/AIDS and its effect on the family.

Children

Two clinical vignettes will illustrate some of the variety of disclosure issues relevant to pediatric HIV (names and other identifying details have been changed).

Johnnie. Johnnie was a seven-year-old, perinatally infected African American boy, referred for psychotherapy because of persistent nightmares, depression, and rumination about his mother who had died four years previously. He was now in the care of his maternal grandmother, along with his twelve-year-old half-sister (same mother) and six-year-old sister.

Johnnie's mother had died of AIDS, contracted from her husband. Johnnie's father was an intravenous drug abuser. The father was now in prison, having been convicted of sexually abusing Johnnie's older half-sister, who now tested HIV-positive from the repeated abuse. Of the children, only the half-sister knew about the role of HIV in the family.

When I met Johnnie, I said I was a worry-doctor (a formulation borrowed from Steven Tuber, of City University of New York) and asked if he had any worries. He thought long and hard, then answered: "I saw my father beat my mother to death with a baseball bat." As we talked about his concerns, I marveled at the explanatory efficiency of Johnnie's version of events. While accounting for both his mother's death and his father's imprisonment, it eliminated HIV and sexual abuse from the story. Johnnie's one concern about himself was his height--like many perinatally infected HIV-positive children, he was below the norm in height and weight.

It was clear that to confront Johnnie with the adult version of events would be to tamper with a good defensive adaptation to his highly traumatic family history. Only after much discussion with Johnnie and other family members might I have begun to reexamine with him some of this history's contours. As it turned out, events overtook us. He was admitted to the pediatric intensive care unit with pneumocystic pneumonia.

In the ICU, I asked him what it meant that he was so sick, expecting an answer like, "I have pneumonia." Instead, Johnnie said, "It means I am going to die." As we talked, Johnnie went on to say he was scared of dying and wanted to know what it would be like. I said I did not know but offered him some prevalent theories, in age-appropriate language. I also wondered aloud whether he would like to talk about all this with his grandmother. He said he would, and when next his grandmother was present, I facilitated her teaching him her own view of the afterlife. She told him there was no need for fear, that it would be painless there, and that he would rejoin his mother and her mother. He died the next day.

In Johnnie's case, the relevant disclosure issue became death, not HIV, and it needed immediate treatment. It is an example of the acceleration of issues that can take place in such an unpredictable disease and also of the precocious grasp of life-and-death questions we sometimes see in terminally ill children. It presented me with the ethical problem of whether to confirm for Johnnie that he was in fact dying, as I had been told by his doctors he might be. I had no parental permission to say such a thing to him, yet I thought he might well be dying and needed to engage in a frank discussion of this question. At the relevant moment, I said only that I hoped he would not die, but that I knew he was very sick; that we all die sometime; and that I too would be frightened in his place. This allowed for empathic connection and seemed to help him. For the rest, I facilitated an interaction with his guardian.

Amy. Amy was infected shortly after her premature birth by blood transfusion. When I met her, she was a very cheerful nine-year-old African American girl, the fourth grade teacher's pet, now in a period of remission from the enuresis that had brought her to psychotherapy with a previous therapist. Her mother did not want to "tell" her about her AIDS, though Amy had many times been at the point of death from various infections and had openly discussed both death and her AIDS diagnosis with nurses and other patients. It was the view of all hospital staff that the mother and daughter would benefit from open discussion and that the mother's resistance to this stemmed from her attachment to Amy and her belief that discussion would lead to Amy's death. Direct instructions, for example from the pediatrician, had no effect on Amy's mother and made her angry and resentful. This situation had persisted for several years. Once, when the mother had been about to disclose, Amy came close to dying from an opportunistic infection. After that, her mother fiercely resisted any reference to disclosure.

At a meeting of the mother, the pediatrician, and one of Amy's nurses, the pediatrician suggested the mother herself needed support for her anticipatory grief. This offer of assistance made the mother burst into tears and brought about a gradual change in attitude. It was some months after this meeting that she agreed her daughter could enter a children's group in which all the children had HIV and knew about it. Still, she said, she would not herself discuss the illness with Amy. We had long since stopped mentioning disclosure and agreed wholeheartedly that she need not address the issue until she felt ready. The next week, after Amy's first day in the children's group, the mother came up to me and said, "I told her!" I asked how the discussion had gone. She said, "It wasn't no big deal"--and we both laughed.

Over the months that followed, Amy participated actively in the children's therapy group. When we tried the group exercise of writing down the name of something we feared on a slip of paper and then attaching the papers to helium balloons and releasing them out the window to show we were ready to give up the fear, Amy asked one of the group leaders to write "HIV" on her slip of paper. Though all the children knew of and discussed their illness, she alone had the courage at that moment explicitly to unleash the topic--which the others noted with shy looks and perhaps some envy. Her gesture was multilayered: she was demonstrating courage in the face of fear; she was showing a willingness both to contain and to release her concern with HIV; she was showing how much she wanted adult support in the endeavor.

Through this and other moments in her treatment, Amy approached HIV and her death in ways that were often complex and indirect. When she lay on the hospital bed in the ICU during her final admission in early December, she seemed perfectly lucid, yet one day began wishing everyone Merry Christmas. It was as if she knew she would not be around to extend the greeting on Christmas day. She died that night.

In Amy's case, mother, child, and hospital staff went through a long process of conflict and accommodation. The potential ethical standoff between what we saw as the child's best interests on the one hand and the mother's understandable intransigence on the other became a cooperation through dialogue. This dialogue seemed to us afterwards to have helped Amy release some of her fear of dying, and finally to encounter death in a spirit of love for those around her. The quality of Amy's openness and generosity on her deathbed was deeply felt by her family whose burden of grief and loss, while not lightened, was made a little easier to bear.

Questions:

Since Piaget would say that children in the early years are in the preoperational stage of development, what kinds of questions do you think children affected with HIV/AIDS are going to ask of a parent or "worry doctor?"

Do you think a child should be informed of this illness? If so, why? If not, why?

SELF-TESTS

Multiple Choice

Circle the letter of the response which best completes or answers each of the following statements and questions.

1. Which of the following statements is most correct regarding children's body composition during early childhood?
   a. Per pound of body weight, boys tend to have more fatty tissue; girls tend to have more muscle.
   b. Per pound of body weight, boys tend to have more muscle; girls tend to have more fatty tissue.
   c. Both boys and girls tend to be chubby, with more fatty tissue than muscle per pound of weight.
   d. Both boys and girls tend to develop noticeable "definition" with more muscle than fatty tissue per pound of weight.

2. All of the following descriptions are true of physical growth and development during early childhood except one. Which one?
   a. By the age of 3, few of the primary teeth are in place, and children have difficulty chewing several foods.
   b. Bones become harder, giving children a firmer shape.
   c. Both large-muscle and small-muscle motor skills increase.
   d. The increased capacities of the respiratory and circulatory systems improve physical stamina.

3. Kindah is a licensed dietician who runs clinics which teach parents how to provide children with adequate nutrition. She is most likely to inform parents that
   a. the nutritional demands of early childhood are very difficult to satisfy
   b. children over age 2 should receive about 30 percent of their total calories from fat
   c. a small child's daily protein requirements can be met with 2 glasses of milk and one serving of meat
   d. both b and c

4. Which of the following statements about childhood illness is not accurate?
   a. Suffering minor illness helps children to be more sympathetic toward ill siblings and peers.
   b. Many children believe that sickness is a result of bad behavior.
   c. After recuperation from a minor illness, most children's self-esteem is lowered, and they feel less competent.
   d. Exposure to common childhood illnesses can strengthen a child's immunity.

5. Bobby is a 6-year-old who was born with AIDS. Which of the following can we infer?
   a. With minor precautions, Bobby will not transmit the disease to family members.
   b. Bobby's classmates are at a high risk of contracting AIDS.
   c. Bobby's family will receive a great deal of emotional support from their community.
   d. Bobby will behave normally and suffer developmental delays only during the final stages of the disease.

6. Anson, a five-year-old, refuses to eat almost anything but cold cereal and milk. In addition, his appetite has shown a significant decrease over the past year. Which statement most accurately explains Anson's behavior?
   a. Anson's parents should be concerned; a diminished appetite in early childhood is abnormal.
   b. Anson's parents need not be overly concerned; a diminished appetite in early childhood is quite common.
   c. Anson's parents should be concerned if their son is often weak and lethargic, has dry hair, and poor muscle tone. Anson may be suffering from inadequate nutrition.
   d. both b and c

7. In the United States, the leading cause of death in children is/are:
   a. cancer
   b. inadequate nutrition
   c. accidents
   d. AIDS

8. Which of the following is the most accurate statement about health during childhood?
   a. Children in small families are sick more often than children in large families.
   b. Events which produce stress in a family tend to adversely affect the health of children in those families.
   c. Because of welfare and health care programs for the poor, the relationship between poverty and childhood illness is insignificant.
   d. The highly developed immune system in early childhood reduces the risk of illness due to exposure to other children.

9. Johanna is 6 years old and resides in the Netherlands. Tomeka also is 6 years old and lives in Chicago. Both are the daughters of poor, single mothers. Research on childhood death rates leads us to believe that
   a. Johanna will receive preventive health services and medical care regardless of her family's financial resources.
   b. Children from Johanna's country are far less likely to suffer from low birthweight and death due to violence than children growing up in Tomeka's country.
   c. Tomeka is less likely to receive proper immunization than is Johanna.
   d. all of the above

10. Karen's 4-year-old daughter has frequent temper tantrums at bedtime. To help alleviate this, Karen and her husband should
    a. punish their daughter by taking away her favorite toy
    b. send their daughter to bed an hour earlier than the time when she usually falls asleep
    c. establish a routine of bedtime stories and activities
    d. all of the above

11. Enuresis, repeated urination in clothing or in bed,
    a. tends to run in families
    b. is most common among children who were toilet-trained before the age of 18 months
    c. is a serious childhood problem
    d. is more common among girls than boys

12. Which of the following statements is most accurate regarding children's motor skills?
    a. Children under the age of 6 are rarely ready to take part in any program preparing them for organized sports.
    b. The best way to help children develop physically is to encourage them to be active at an appropriate level for their state of maturity, in unstructured situations.
    c. As children gain control of their small muscles, they feel an increased sense of competence and independence.
    d. all of the above

13. A young boy is introduced to a number of relatives he has not previously met. Later, when he correctly identifies his Aunt Jane, he is demonstrating
    a. deferred imitation
    b. reencounter
    c. recall
    d. symbolic play

14. A group of 3-year-olds are shown two different sets of pictures. The first set contained random pictures of such objects as people, dogs, and flowers. The second set contained pictures of a variety of differently sized red balls. Research on children's memory indicates that
    a. the children are no more likely to recall one set of pictures over the other
    b. the children are more likely to recall the pictures of the balls because they are related objects
    c. the children are more likely to recall the pictures of the people, dogs, and flowers because they are of unrelated objects
    d. none of the above

15. The best predictor of how well a child remembers specific objects and events is the child's tendency to be independent, self-directed, and generally resourceful. This is known as
    a. knowledge
    b. mastery motivation
    c. transduction
    d. animism

16. Four women take their 4-year-old sons to a dinosaur exhibit at a local museum. According to research on childhood memory, which of the following children is most likely to remember objects seen at the museum?
    a. Lyle, whose mother does not open discussions with her son but instead responds to his comments.
    b. Mark, whose mother talks naturally with her son, using a narrative style of speech.
    c. Rupert, whose mother talks to her son very infrequently.
    d. none of the above

17. Sensorimotor stage is to ______as preoperational stage is to ________.
    a. learning by sensing and doing; learning by thinking symbolically
    b. learning by reflections on actions; learning by acting alone
    c. learning by thinking symbolically; learning by recall
    d. learning by recall; learning by recognition

18. Johnny sees a movie about the "teenage mutant Ninja turtles." Within a week, he is imitating their martial arts. This imitation of an observed action after time has passed is known as
    a. latent modeling
    b. post hoc reenactment
    c. deferred imitation
    d. representational modeling

19. In symbolic play, children will
    a. discuss their mental symbols with each other
    b. make jokes in which there is a play on words
    c. mentally rehearse a game that they have played earlier
    d. make an object stand for something else

20. Jose, a 5-year-old in the preoperational stage, fills two identical pails with sand. His mother then pours sand from one pail into a taller, thinner pail. According to Piaget, which of the following is true?
    a. After conceptualizing pouring the sand into the original pail from the taller one, Jose will understand that the two differently shaped pails contain the same amount of sand.
    b. Jose will perceive either the taller or the wider pail as containing more sand because one of them is "bigger."
    c. Jose will focus simultaneously on the height and width of the pails and realize that the amount of sand in the two differently shaped pails is the same.
    d. none of the above

21. In his most famous experiment, Piaget tested children's ability to sense that two things that are equal remain so if their shape is altered so long as nothing is added or taken away. This is called:
    a. conservation
    b. irreversibility
    c. egocentrism
    d. transduction

22. According to Piaget, which of the following statements is *least* accurate?
    a. Egocentrism explains why young children often talk to themselves.
    b. Most young children lack the ability to see things from another's point of view.
    c. Preoperational children understand that an operation can go two ways.
    d. Preoperational children cannot think simultaneously about many aspects of a situation.

23. Which of the following scenarios best exemplifies Piaget's principle of transduction?
    a. Claudia knows many people who ate too much food and got sick. Claudia eats too much food, and so she thinks she may get sick.
    b. Lamont ate too much candy, and her mother became angry with her. Lamont's brothers ate too much candy, and they also were punished. Therefore, Lamont understands that eating too much candy is bad.
    c. Stephen got into an argument with his little sister and broke one of her toys. The next day Stephen has a stomachache. Stephen believes that if he misbehaves again, he will feel sick again.
    d. Erica's parents buy her nice presents on her birthday. Her friends also get nice presents on their birthdays. Erica understands that people should get presents on their birthday.

24. Which of the following statements most accurately reflects recent findings concerning the egocentricity of young children?
    a. Between the ages of 3 and 5, children begin to think about how other people are thinking and feeling.
    b. Between the ages of 3 and 5, children's understanding of other people's actions grows significantly.
    c. Children who come from families in which feelings are often discussed tend to be better able to recognize emotions in other people.
    d. all of the above

25. Which of the following is a characteristic of the speech of children over the age of 3?
    a. telegraphic speech
    b. single-word utterances
    c. simple, active, declarative sentences
    d. plurals and the use of the past tense

26. Which of the following statements is most accurate regarding the ability of young children to communicate?
    a. Children's speech is quite social from an early age.
    b. Children's ability to communicate is related to their popularity with their peers.
    c. Children's general knowledge affects their ability to communicate.
    d. all of the above

27. Whitney, a 6-year-old, talks to herself in school. From Vygotsky's research on private speech, which of the following can we infer?
    a. Whitney is antisocial and unable to communicate with her peers.
    b. Whitney uses private speech in order to think better, not because of social inadequacy.
    c. Whitney's development of language is delayed.
    d. Whitney will continue to talk aloud to herself throughout grade school.

28. Test developers must try to devise tests that measure what they claim to measure; we call this criterion
    a. validity
    b. reliability
    c. standardization
    d. a norm

29. In recent years, people in general have been performing at higher levels on the Stanford-Binet IQ test, probably as a result of
    a. better educated parents
    b. exposure to educational TV
    c. genetic changes in the population
    d. both a and b

30. Charlotte, a teacher, uses the "zone of proximal development" (ZPD) approach to direct her students' learning. This approach aids in assessing children's intelligence because
    a. it enables researchers to measure the extent to which children can learn solely on their own
    b. it enables researchers to measure and test children's abilities only in completed areas of development
    c. it enables researchers to measure what children can learn with minimal tutoring, focusing on both completed areas of development, and areas still in the process of development
    d. it enables researchers to measure what children can learn after rigorous tutoring, focusing solely on areas still in the process of development

31. Reed and Allison work with their 5-year-old son James on a difficult task: having James retell his favorite bedtime story. According to the concept of "scaffolding,"
    a. Reed and Allison should not provide James with direction regardless of his abilities
    b. Reed and Allison should help James less and less as he is able to accomplish more of the task on his own
    c. Reed and Allison should help James with the task every step of the way, providing their son with complete direction
    d. none of the above

32. Which of the following statements is the most accurate regarding a father's influence on his children's intelligence?
    a. A father will tend to influence his sons more than his daughters.
    b. A strict, authoritarian father is most likely to have an intellectually developed child.
    c. A father's absence has no effect on his children's cognitive development.
    d. A father who is nurturing and approving will probably not be imitated by his son.

33. Charisse is a full-time nurse who has two young children, Janelle and Devon. Research on a mother's employment leads us to believe that
    a. Janelle and Devon's overall cognitive development will be far less than that of children whose mother is at home
    b. Charisse's employment is unlikely to have any gender-related influence on Janelle and Devon's cognitive, social, and emotional development
    c. Janelle and Devon's overall cognitive development will be as good as that of children whose mother is at home
    d. none of the above

34. Which of the following statements best describe the difference between preschool and daycare?
    a. Preschool provides children with educational experience; day care does not.
    b. Day care provides a safe place where children can be cared for, usually all day, while parents are at work or school; preschool does not.
    c. The distinction between preschool and day care has blurred; today both programs attempt to meet children's intellectual and emotional needs, while offering longer days
    d. none of the above

35. According to many educators and psychologists, which of the following children would benefit most from a good day care program?
    a. Sally: 3 years old, white, upperclass family, mother does not work
    b. Ricardo: 2½ years old, hispanic, middle-class family, father works full time, mother does not work
    c. Oksana: 3 years old, white, lower-class family, parents divorced, mother collects welfare
    d. Christopher: 2 years old, black, upperclass family, mother works full time, father works at home

36. A good preschool for young children
    a. helps children learn and grow in many ways and is fun as well
    b. emphasizes academic skills more strongly than social and emotional skills
    c. focuses solely on strengthening social and emotional skills
    d. emphasizes basically the same values in all cultures

37. Which of the following is a finding of the recent study of preschools in three different cultures?
    a. Chinese preschools stress academics more than American preschools do.
    b. The U.S. stresses learning basic skills, concentration, and getting along with the group.
    c. The Japanese emphasize play experiences and creativity.
    d. none of the above

38. The Montessori curriculum
    a. is child-centered, based on respect for the child's natural abilities
    b. allows preschoolers to learn from their own experiences, with the guidance and support of skilled teachers
    c. aims to foster moral development
    d. all of the above

39. Xavier, a 4-year-old, is from a deprived socioeconomic background. Recently, he has been enrolled in Project Head Start, a compensatory preschool program. As a result:
    a. Xavier will be less likely than other needy children to be held back in school
    b. Xavier will be less likely than other needy children to require special education classes
    c. Xavier will be more likely than other needy children to finish high school and enroll in college
    d. all of the above

40. Jerome will soon be entering kindergarten. In which program should his parents enroll him?
    a. a kindergarten program with an emphasis on cognitive and academic skills
    b. a kindergarten program which expands social interactions and stresses learning when children are self-motivated
    c. a kindergarten program that exposes children to many community activities
    d. an all-day kindergarten

Completion

Supply the term or terms needed to complete each of the following statements.

1. One cause of children's dietary deficiencies is the impact of television commercials for foods heavy in ____________________ and ____________________.

2. In the U.S., death rates for ____________ children and teenagers are considerably higher than for whites for every cause except suicide, car injuries, and accidental poisoning and falls.

3. A toy or an animal that a child holds at bedtime is referred to as a ________________________.

4. Repeated urination, during the day or night in clothing or in bed is called ____________________.

5. ______________________ is the ability to identify something that has been encountered before.

6. In the ___________________________ stage, children can think about objects, people, or events in their absence, by using mental representations of them.

7. Failure to understand that an operation can go both ways is known as ________________________.

8. Reasoning that goes from the general to the particular is called _______________.

9. Reasoning that goes from the particular to the general is called __________________.

10. ________________________ reasoning, typical of preoperational children, goes from one particular to another particular, not taking the general into account.

11. The inability to see something from another's point of view is known as ________________________.

12. Programs to teach specific cognitive abilities seem to work when a child is already ______________________ the concept being taught.

13. A young child who is overregularizing the rule for forming the past tense of verbs is likely to say __________________ as the past tense of the verb *run*.

14. Standardized ______________ are standards obtained from the IQ test scores of a large, representative sample of children of the same age who took the test while it was in the process of preparation.

15. Because they are made up largely of _________________ items, intelligence tests for use with young children (ages 3 to 5) provide more stable scores than tests for toddlers.

16. According to Vygotsky, children in the ____________________ for a particular task can almost, but not completely, perform the task on their own.

17. Daughters of working mothers tend to be more _______________ than daughters of mothers who are at home.

18. The ______________________ curriculum is child-centered and based on respect for the child's natural abilities.

19. _________________________, begun in 1985 as part of the "war on poverty," is the best-known compensatory preschool program in the U.S.

20. During the 1970s and 1980s, the kindergarten curriculum became more like that of ___________________________.

ANSWERS FOR SELF-TESTS — CHAPTER 6

Multiple-Choice

		Page	
1.	b	200	factual
2.	a	200	factual
3.	d	201	conceptual
4.	c	201	factual
5.	a	202	conceptual
6.	d	203	conceptual
7.	c	203	factual
8.	b	204	factual
9.	d	205	conceptual
10.	a	208	factual
11.	c	209	conceptual
12.	d	210	factual
13.	c	212	conceptual
14.	b	212	conceptual
15.	b	212	factual
16.	b	213	conceptual
17.	a	214	conceptual
18.	c	214	conceptual
19.	d	214	factual
20.	b	215	conceptual
21.	a	215	factual
22.	c	215	factual
23.	c	217	conceptual
24.	d	219	factual
25.	d	222	factual
26.	d	223	factual
27.	b	223	conceptual
28.	a	224	factual
29.	d	224	factual
30.	c	225	conceptual
31.	b	226	conceptual
32.	a	226	factual
33.	c	227	conceptual
34.	c	227	factual
35.	c	228	conceptual
36.	a	228	factual
37.	a	232	factual
38.	d	233	factual
39.	d	233	conceptual
40.	b	234	factual

Completion

		Page
1.	sugar, fat	201
2.	African American	205
3.	transitional object	208
4.	enuresis	208
5.	recognition	212
6.	preoperational	214
7.	irreversibility	215
8.	deductive	217
9.	inductive	217
10.	transductive	217
11.	egocentrism	217
12.	on the verge of acquiring	221
13.	"runned"	222
14.	norms	224
15.	verbal	224
16.	zone of proximal development (ZPD)	225
17.	independent	227
18.	Montessori	233
19.	Project Head Start	233
20.	first grade	234

CHAPTER 7

Personality and Social Development in Early Childhood

INTRODUCTION

Chapter 7 presents several theories about personality development in early childhood to help us understand how young children begin to perceive their place in the world around them. Many factors can influence a child's development in this stage--fears, friends, parenting styles, siblings, etc.

- According to Erikson, the chief developmental crisis of early childhood is the development of a balance between initiative and guilt. The ways in which parents deal with their children strongly influences this stage.

- Several types of theories attempt to explain how young children acquire gender identity: the psychoanalytic approach, the social-learning approach, the cognitive developmental theory, and the gender-schema theory.

- Gender differences, gender roles, and gender stereotyping are discussed in detail from both the biological and environmental perspectives.

- Childhood fears are examined briefly. The development of aggressive (or passive) tendencies is explained along with a section devoted to the detrimental effects of televised violence and a practical section on guiding children in watching television.

- Parents' influence on the development of prosocial (or altruistic) behavior--or the lack of it--is covered in detail, as is the effect of rewards and punishment on children's behavior.

- In addition, parenting styles--authoritarian, permissive, and authoritative--are presented, with some practical suggestions on effective parenting.

- Research on siblings' influence--or the lack of it--is also covered. The discussion includes findings of a study on China's policies toward the one-child family.

- Finally, play is examined as both a social aid and a cognitive activity. Play is influenced by parents, type of day care, and gender.

CHAPTER OUTLINE

I. Important Personality Developments in Early Childhood

A. Initiative versus Guilt
B. Identification
C. Gender Identity
D. Psychoanalytic Theory
E. Social-Learning Theory: Observing and Imitating Models
  1. How Identification Occurs
  2. Effects of Identification
  3. Evaluating Social-Learning Theory
F. Cognitive-Developmental Theory: Mental Processes
  1. Gender Identity and Gender Constancy
G. Gender-Schema Theory: A "Cognitive-Social" Approach
  1. Evaluating the Cognitive Theories

II. Aspects and Issues of Personality Development

A. Gender
  1. How Different are Girls and Boys?
  2. Attitudes Toward Gender Differences
    a. Gender roles and gender typing
    b. Gender stereotypes
    c. Androgyny: A different view of gender
  3. How do Gender Differences Come About?
    a. Biological influences
    b. Family influences
    c. Media influences
    d. Cultural influences
B. Fears
  1. What Do Children Fear and Why?
  2. Preventing and Dealing with Fears
C. Aggression
  1. Triggers of Aggression
  2. Reinforcement
  3. Frustration and Imitation
  4. Televised Violence
  5. Reducing Aggression
D. Altruism: Prosocial Behavior
  1. Origins of Prosocial Behavior
  2. Encouraging Prosocial Behavior: What Parents Do
E. Child-Rearing Practices
  1. Parents' Use of Reinforcement and Punishment
    a. Reinforcement
    b. Ineffective Punishment: "Rewarding with Punishment"
    c. Effective Punishment: When Does Punishment Work?
  2. Parents' Styles and Children's Competence: Baumrind's Research
    a. Three Parenting Styles
    b. Evaluation of Baumrind's Conclusions
  3. Determinants of Child-Rearing Styles
  4. Parents' Love and Maturity

F. Relating to Other Children
   1. The Only Child
   2. Brothers and Sisters
   3. First Friends
      a. Behavior Patterns and Choice of Playmates and Friends
      b. Family Ties and Popularity

G. Play
   1. The Importance of Play
   2. Perspectives on Play
      a. Social and Nonsocial Play
      b. Cognitive Play
      c. Imaginative Play
   3. Influences on Play: Parents, Day Care Centers, and Gender

---

KEY TERMS

---

aggressive behavior (page 250)

androgynous (247)

authoritarian parents (257)

authoritative parents (257)

behavior modification (255)

cognitive play (263)

gender (241)

gender constancy (gender conservation) (241)

gender differences (246)

gender identity (241)

gender roles (241)

gender schema (241)

gender-schema theory (241)

gender stereotypes (246)

gender-typing (246)

identification (241)

imaginative play (265)

initiative versus guilt (241)

permissive parents (257)

prosocial behavior (254)

sex differences (245)

social play (263)

LEARNING OBJECTIVES

After finishing Chapter 7, you should be able to:

1. Explain Erikson's third psychosocial crisis, *initiative versus guilt*, and its resolution. (pp. 240-241)

2. Define the following terms as they relate to a child's personality development: (p. 241)
   a. *identification*

   b. *gender identity*

   c. *gender roles*

3. Briefly explain Freud's psychoanalytic theory as it pertains to child development at this age. (p. 242)

4. Describe and evaluate the social-learning theory of personality development. (pp. 242-243)

5. Briefly explain and evaluate Kohlberg's cognitive-developmental theory of *gender differences* and behavior. (pp. 244-245)

6. Describe and evaluate the *gender-schema* theory of gender development. (pp. 244-245)

7. List some *gender differences* and some similarities between boys and girls. (pp. 245-246)

8. Explain some factors that might contribute to *gender stereotyping*. (pp. 246-247)

9. Define *androgyny* as it relates to gender. (p. 247)

10. Explain what research tells us about the following influences on *gender differences*: (pp. 247-249)
    a. biological influences
    b. family influences
    c. media influences
    d. cultural influences

11. List some common childhood fears, and explain why young children seem to develop fears. (pp. 249-250)

12. Explain why *aggressive behavior* seems to appear in early childhood. (pp. 250-251)

13. Explain what research tells us about violence on television and the relationship between children's behavior and the programs they watch. (pp. 252-253)

14. List some suggestions for reducing children's violence and aggression. (pp. 253-254)

15. Define altruism (or *prosocial behavior*) and explain some influences that encourage it. (pp. 254-255)

16. Briefly explain the following terms and explain how they influence a child's personality development: (pp. 255-256)
    a. *behavior modification*

    b. ineffective punishment

    c. effective punishment

17. Identify the three styles of parenting researched by Baumrind and briefly describe typical behavior patterns of children raised primarily according to each style: (pp. 257-258)
    a.

    b.

    c.

18. Referring to Box 7-2, "Window on the World," describe the findings from the studies of raising only children in China. (p. 260)

19. Explain the research pertaining to relationships between siblings. (pp. 259, 261)

20. List some suggestions for helping children make friends. (pp. 261-263)

21. How does play benefit children at this stage of development, and differentiate between *cognitive play* and *imaginative play*? (pp. 263-266)

22. Compare and contrast how a child's play is influenced by parents, day care centers, and gender. (pp. 266-267)

SUPPLEMENTAL READING

This article is reprinted with permission from Psychiatry, ©February, 1993. Dr. Emde's work is supported in part by a National Institute of Mental Health project grant, Research Scientist Award and the John D. and Catherine T. MacArthur Foundation Network in Early Childhood Transitions.

The Horror! The Horror! Reflections on Our Culture of Violence and Its Implications for Early Development and Morality

Dr. Richard Emde

This commentary draws on two dimensions of chronic community violence with thoughts that have been mobilized by the foregoing contributions. One concerns the importance of culture and the other concerns the importance of thinking about early development. Culture permeates all of our actions, and we are in a culture of violence. In other papers in this issue, Richters and Martinez point out that the United States is the most violent country in the industrialized world, and Ciccheti and Lynch state that violence "is becoming a defining characteristic of American society." We are fascinated by violence and in an implicit way we love violence--a fact that we need to acknowledge. Our fascination with violence in American culture is permeating and deep, and, as horrible as it is, I believe we need to face it in order to counter it.

I was reminded of this permeating dimension of our culture as I arrived at the hotel for the conference from which these papers emerged. On the table in my room was a magazine. It was a guide to cable TV and on its cover was a man who was pictured with a rather strained, smiling expression who looked at you with a clinched fist. The caption said, "Murder! A Battery of Killer Films! Assault TV!," trying to excite the reader. A number of films were then listed and at the bottom it added: "Plus...the small screen's 20 biggest murders ever!" More than a decade ago, while studying abroad in London, I had similar thoughts about our American cultural fascination and our implicit acceptance of violence. One could walk rather freely in London at that time without the same kind of fear of guns and other violence that are typical of many U.S. cities. During that time, the news came that our president had been the victim of an assassination attempt. His remarks at the time were reported and positively connoted as reflecting his equanimity and good grace. The remarks did reflect these qualities, but I found them nonetheless shuddering, as I did the reaction of many in the United States. The wounded president's statement to the press, "I forgot to duck," also reflected a gamesmenlike quality along with what some interpreted as expectations of violence and murder.

One more illustration. On the day of my putting together this commentary, the *Sunday Denver Post* began the series "Kids and Guns" (see Roberts and Lipsher 1992). The text reports interviews from many who are carrying guns. Among the quotes, a 16-year-old girl says, "Everybody knows somebody who has a gun and carries it...it's just the way it is now." Many talk about the meaning of the power of having a gun. A 17-year-old, speaking of the .38 semiautomatic he carried two years earlier stated, "It was like my Mom...it protected me." Another quote: "Whenever I go out with some of my friends, someone has a gun with them, a .22 or a .25...there's always occasions to use them. We do drive-bys mostly or shoot them at the air or at a dog or any car that passes by." A girl aged 15 stated, "There's really nothing to learn about a gun...all you need to do is make sure it's with you and it's loaded. The only time you have it on 'safety' is when you're in your own house or a relative's house." Guns are readily available in Denver as in most other American cities--inexpensively bought or, as with young children, often obtained from parents. (Note a similar theme about gun availability shown on national television recently when CBS's "60 Minutes" portrayed the use of guns by young children.)

Unless we become aware of our fascination and acceptance of guns and violence, we will not have the opportunity to investigate alternatives, let alone mobilize the will for change. I will return to this theme in my conclusion.

A second dimension of my commentary concerns early development and morality. Our research group has constructed a theoretical model of early development that incorporates recent infancy research. We envision a set of inborn basic motives that are activated within the context of consistent caregiving that in turn lead to exploration, learning, and internalized shared meaning. These basic motives portray the infant as fundamentally active, self-regulating, and social, and as monitoring experience according to what is pleasurable and unpleasurable. Moreover, from the start, the infant explores the environment, seeking what is new in order to make it familiar (Emde 1988; Emde, Biringen, Clyman, and Oppenheim 1991). Our theory also describes how, in the course of everyday routines of consistent caregiving, basic motives become organized into more complex motives. Among these are: (1) the consolidation of an "affective core of the self" that gives the infant a patterned sense of consistency through developmental change (Emde 1983), (2) derived relationship motives that give the infant a sense of wanting to repeat what is familiar in particular relationship experiences (Sander 1985) and (3) early moral motives.

Early moral motives are a consequence of internalizations that take place within the context of caregiving. Such internalizations have to do with the "dos" of experience as well as "don't's." A brief consideration of what we have come to appreciate about infants raised in relatively low-stress environments forms a background for thinking about early development in the midst of chronic community violence.

The infant typically learns a great variety of "rules" as a shared aspect of the caregiving experience, before there is conflict and quite naturally as a positive aspect of such experience. These learned or internalized rules have a dual origin, including both (1) an inborn propensity for initiating, maintaining, and terminating social interactions; and (2) expectable caregiver relationship experiences. Intricate sets of rules that govern "reciprocity" in face-to-face turn-taking interactions and other forms of communication operate well before language develops (for example, note documentations in Brazelton and Als 1979; Bruner 1982; Kaye 1982; Stern 1977; Trevarthen 1979; Tronick 1980). These developments are rudiments for a basic form of morality. All systems of morality are centered around reciprocity with some version of The Golden Rule: "Do unto others as you would have them do unto you." Moreover, a tendency for turn-taking in communication and for social cooperation may also be connected developmentally to another positive feature of early morality, namely, empathy. Toward the end of the child's second year, the infant typically comes to feel distress at another's expressed discomfort and may show a propensity to want to help or comfort the other (Radke-Yarrow, Zahn-Waxler, and Chapman 1983; Zahn-Waxler and Radke-Yarrow 1982).

Toward the end of the second year, another feature of what we consider to be "basic morality" becomes differentiated. The tendency for "getting it right" about the world expresses itself in a new affective way. When faced with a familiar object that is flawed or dirty, the child sometimes shows anxiety when internal standards or expectations are violated. The child may evidence distress along with an urge to correct what is perceived as a discrepancy (Dunn 1988; Kagan 1981). Kagan has highlighted this developmental milestone to the onset of reflective self-awareness and has emphasized that all systems of morality require internalized standards--along with a sense of uneasiness when prototypic standards are violated.

Thus our theory proposes that by the end of the second year a child has elements of a basic positive morality, by virtue of internalizing the dos of everyday interactions with caregivers. An internalized sense of reciprocity, a sense of everyday rules (for example, about what to do, when to do it, and what belongs where), empathy, and some internalized standards are part of this development. Typically, affect plays a major role as pleasure in "getting it right," which is confirmed by the caregiver's expression of pride and as lingering experiences of shame and disappointment in the course of interactions also begin to have a role.

The child's internalizing of don'ts also occurs through repeated interactions with caregivers. Observations of caregiver-infant interactions during the child's second year highlight processes of social referencing and negotiation in mediating self-regulation. Social referencing occurs when the child encounters situations of uncertainty and the child seeks out emotional information from a significant other in order to resolve the uncertainty and to regulate behavior. Thus, when a stranger approaches or a strange toy is presented, the child will look to the caregiver and if the latter smiles or expresses interest, the result will be encouragement to explore and touch; if the caregiver expresses fear or anger, the child will tend to avoid the new situation. We find a similar searching for emotional signals during situations when prohibitions are given by caregivers. Repeated looking occurs following vocalized prohibitions, and the child seeks a resolution of uncertainty or a confirmation for a decision about acting. Indeed, we have found that negotiation in the context of repeated prohibitions makes use of social referencing in this way and leads to internalized procedures for moral (and self) regulation. Typically, negotiation occurs when parents offer initially unclear emotional messages (depending on the context of what is prohibited), along with mild prohibitions; these messages are then "tested" by the infant. Sequences of such experiences are then internalized and made use of in subsequent encounters. We tend to say that shared meaning is negotiated in the course of back-and-forth exchanges with significant others; the young child thereby comes to internalize strategies of action with particular others in varying contexts. Thus, more than we had imagined, early development is revealed to be creative; it not only involves processes of construction on the part of the child and coconstruction on the part of the child-with-caregiver, but it also involves the child's internalizing remarkably dynamic experiences and procedures of negotiation.

Longitudinal observations indicate that by the end of the second year, children typically show evidence of having internalized rules for don'ts; they evidence restraint in the midst of prohibitions so long as the caregiver is physically present and available for social referencing. Internalization of don'ts without the parent being present in the midst of temptation, however, requires further development. Such development may also depend upon the acquisition of moral scripts that have narrative and emotional coherence, an acquisition that occurs during the child's third year and beyond (Buchsbaum and Emde 1990).

Although direct research has not been done with respect to such processes in the context of chronic community violence, the foregoing contributions in this issue suggest some stark realities and their consequences. In this issue, the picture drawn by the work of Richters and Martinzez, as well as that of Osofsky, Wewers, Hann, and Fick, and that of Bell and Jenkins, give indication of the devastating effects of the violent scene on caregiving--whether in Washington, DC, New Orleans, or Detroit. Such effects necessarily lead to caregiver restriction of activity in young children in order to ensure safety and survival. Garmezy commented that mothers who keep their children safe in our besieged urban ghettos are the unacknowledged moral heroes of our time (Garmezy 1991). Still, one wonders about the restricted breadth of values, goals, attitudes, and aspirations that must necessarily occur from the decreased developmental opportunities under such circumstances. As Friedlander has pointed out in his contribution to this issue, chronic violence undermines the child's potential basic trust and sense of reliable support for learning, as well as the child's potential sense of security because of unresolvable fear. In addition to fear, one can add the stresses of loss and grief that are likely to disrupt everyday interactions of caregivers; all of these stresses are likely to disrupt everyday interactions of caregivers; all of these stresses are likely to lead to a relative deficit of opportunities for internalizing experiences of reciprocity, to a restriction of opportunities of internalizing a variety of "rules and expectations," and to a restriction of opportunities for experiencing empathy, repairs, and other kinds of positive shared meaning.

But one also wonders about other kinds of risks for development along these lines. In addition to deficit, one wonders about deviant developmental pathways. What are the different kinds of expectations and goals along with later kinds of internalized scenarios that will develop in young children in such an atmosphere of chronic fear, loss, and restriction? In this issue, the contribution of Lorion and Saltzman comments on the general desensitization to threat and even addictive risk-taking behavior that can develop later under these circumstances.

Research has not yet been done that can give us direct knowledge about such influences from chronic violence. But research has been done on influences from family violence and child maltreatment. In this issue, the contributions of Cicchetti and Lynch and of Putnam and Trickett document findings with respect to distortions of emotional regulation that can occur in the child in such circumstances. Children and adults can suffer a variety of disturbances in affiliation and reciprocity in different social relationships, including those involving peers, spouses, and parenting. Putnam and Trickett comment on potential psychophysiological consequences related to elevated cortisol responses to chronic stress and its possible influences on neuronal loss. This also puts this commentator in mind of recent advances in our knowledge of early brain development, wherein we have learned there is normally an overproduction of cells and synapses with functional connections that undergo a "pruning" during early development. Although it is a matter of some scientific debate, early experiences and functional use may have a role in determining which synaptic connections and pathways "survive" in the brain (Edelman 1987).

In concluding, I would like to mention what we have recently come to refer to as a "Jeffersonian Principle" of early moral development (Emde and Clyman in preparation). The rudiments of early moral development, according to our view, take place procedurally, before the acquisition of language and before internalized knowledge can be represented in declarative fashion. Early internalized rules are not represented consciously, even though they come to govern behavior in coherent ways. Thus, rules about the way the world is and should be, as well as rules about reciprocity and tendencies to repair internalized standards that are discrepant from one's expectations, are based on procedural knowledge and are nonconscious. In the course of later development, these rudiments become part of a more complex process of "getting it right about the world." But they persist. And here we come to our Jeffersonian principle. There is a sense, as Thomas Jefferson put it, of internalized "truths" that we hold to be "self-evident." The evocation of this phrase, from the founding days of our Republic, also brings with it Jefferson's predications: "among these are life, liberty, and the pursuit of happiness." What opportunities do young children suffering from chronic community violence in the U.S. today have for such predication? What truths do they hold as self-evident?

Jefferson's framework for our thinking brings us back to the opening theme of my commentary. This concerns our coming to grips with our culture of violence today and its consequences for moral development. My title is taken from Coppola's movie, "Apocalypse Now," and from Joseph Conrad: "The Horror! The Horror!" But acknowledging the horror in ourselves and in our circumstances means that we have both incentive and opportunity to tap another feature of our American culture and democracy--mainly that of optimism and a willful activity to overcome adversity. Friedlander, in his contribution, points out that we have made significant progress with respect to national social problems such as in stigmatizing smoking and advancing women's rights. The problem we are addressing in this issue of Psychiatry is every bit as urgent.

Questions:

The authors of your text state that some children mask fears in aggressive activity, which surfaces in a new way in childhood. In what ways are children--not only children in inner-city environments but in the suburbs as well--acting more aggressively out of their fears?

Even though the ability to show some aggression may be a necessary step in the social development of human beings, not all children learn to control their aggression. List some factors mentioned in this chapter which can trigger aggression.

List several consequences of chronic violence on either the child's behavior and/or the caregiver's behavior.

SELF-TESTS

Multiple Choice

Circle the letter of the response which best completes or answers each of the following statements and questions.

1. Charlotte, who is 5 years old, loves to go through her mother's purse. However, Charlotte understands that her mother becomes very upset when Charlotte does so. According to Erikson, Charlotte's conflict between her desire to do and her desire for approval is called
   a. identification
   b. initiative vs. guilt
   c. gender identity
   d. altruism

2. Awareness of one's maleness or femaleness is called
   a. values clarification
   b. gender identity
   c. "goodness of fit"
   d. altruism

3. Morgan, age 5, insists on wearing oversized jeans and baggy T-shirts because his older brother Raphael dresses this way. This process, in which Morgan has adopted the behavior of another person, is called
   a. identification
   b. gender constancy
   c. altruism
   d. socialization

4. Freud's psychoanalytic theory proposes that identification results from
   a. social success
   b. imitating the parent of the opposite sex
   c. repression or abandonment of the wish to possess the parent of the opposite sex
   d. becoming aggressive toward the parent of the opposite sex

5. Proponents of social learning theory believe that children's identity is formed by
   a. observing a model
   b. acting like a model
   c. wanting to be like a model
   d. all of the above

6. Jerome sees that he is physically more like his father than his mother. He imitates his father by trying to act powerful and by protecting his younger sister. Thus, Jerome is rewarded for acting "like a boy." This scenario is exemplary of which theory of personality development?
   a. psychoanalytic
   b. cognitive-developmental
   c. gender schema
   d. social-learning

7. Who is more likely to differentiate between boys and girls?
   a. fathers
   b. mothers
   c. neither a nor b
   d. none of the above; no studies done

8. Which psychologist believes in the cognitive developmental theory, i.e., that children actively think about how they fit into the male or female role?
   a. Freud
   b. Kohlberg
   c. Erikson
   d. Bem

9. Huong is a preschooler who believes that wearing a dress and makeup will transform him into a girl. Huong has not yet developed
   a. gender constancy
   b. gender discrimination
   c. identification
   d. gender schema

10. Victoria and Brian, both American children, learn that it is important for girls to be nurturant and for boys to be strong and aggressive. These children are observing their culture's
    a. gender constancy
    b. gender discrimination
    c. gender schema
    d. none of the above

11. According to Bem's "cognitive-social" approach, since the gender schema is learned, it can be modified. Thus, to free children from the constraints of gender stereotypes, parents should
    a. give girls trucks for gifts
    b. emphasize clothing and behavior as the main distinctions between males and females
    c. emphasize anatomy and reproduction as the main distinctions between males and females
    d. both a and c

12. The clearest gender difference in personality, which shows up in early childhood, is that males tend to be more
    a. aggressive
    b. cooperative
    c. friendly
    d. compassionate

13. Pauline and Michael, both 4 years old, enjoy playing house. Pauline always is the homemaker, and Michael always pretends to leave for work. When Michael returns from "his job," Pauline has his dinner ready and waits on him. These children have absorbed their culture's
    a. gender discrimination
    b. gender roles
    c. "goodness of fit"
    d. none of the above

14. ____________ is/are a child's learning of his or her gender role; ____________ is/are exaggerated generalizations about male or female behaviors.
    a. gender stereotypes; gender typing
    b. gender constancy; gender schema
    c. gender typing; gender stereotypes
    d. gender schema; gender constancy

15. Roberto, the father of three young children, exhibits assertiveness and dominance--both so-called masculine traits. In addition, he showers his youngsters with love, compassion, and understanding--so-called feminine traits. Bem would describe Robert's personality as
    a. altruistic
    b. androgynous
    c. stereotypical
    d. gender specific

16. What influences gender differences?
    a. biological and genetic factors
    b. cultural factors
    c. the media
    d. all of the above

17. Felipe is a 6-year-old whose father abandoned his mother before Felipe's birth. It is likely that Felipe will
    a. become very aggressive and independent as a result of his mother's strong emphasis on gender-typing
    b. develop more exaggerated gender stereotypes than a child raised in a two-parent family
    c. be less gender-stereotyped, as a result of his father's absence
    d. develop the same attitudes toward gender-typing as if he were being raised in a two-parent family

18. Girls tend to be more fearful than boys, possibly because
    a. fear is an inherited tendency
    b. girls really have more fears
    c. girls are encouraged to be more dependent and boys are discouraged from admitting fears
    d. parents are more likely to accept boys' fears

19. Samantha, a 4-year-old, often grabs toys away from her playmates. Instrumental aggression such as this indicates which of the following?
    a. Samantha is a competent youngster, and her behavior is a natural part of social development.
    b. Samantha's parents are overly strict and domineering.
    c. Samantha has been raised in the absence of her father.
    d. Samantha will become increasingly aggressive with time and have great difficulty establishing friendships.

20. Which of the following factors contribute to the development of aggression in young children?
    a. testosterone
    b. imitation of aggressive models
    c. frustration
    d. all of the above

21. One preschooler prefers to watch Sesame Street while a second prefers to watch more violent television shows like Beavis and Butthead. We can reasonably predict that
    a. the first child will be less social than the second
    b. the first child will show concern more rapidly if a sibling or friend is injured
    c. the second child will be less aggressive toward a sibling
    d. the first child is more likely than the second to be spanked by parents

22. Nina is a generous, warm child and very sensitive to the needs of others. What can we reasonably infer from this?
    a. Nina's family is financially well off.
    b. Nina lacks self-confidence and thus lacks any aggressive tendencies.
    c. Nina has been raised solely by her mother and thus has not been influenced by the male characteristics of a father.
    d. Nina's parents encourage her to empathize with others and emphasize values such as sharing and cooperation.

23. Which of the following statements is most accurate regarding altruistic behavior?
    a. The most altruistic children have parents who discipline them by inductive techniques.
    b. The most altruistic children have parents who discipline them through strict punishment.
    c. Children who receive empathic, nurturant care as infants later develop these qualities themselves.
    d. both a and c

24. Reinforcement studies have found that children learn more by being
    a. rewarded for good behavior than by being punished for bad behavior
    b. punished as a consequence of undesirable behavior
    c. ignored after desirable behavior
    d. none of the above; children's behavior is unpredictable

25. Adam's parents ignore him most of the time when he behaves well. However, when Adam misbehaves and fights with his younger sister, they scold or spank him. In effect,
    a. Adam's parents are reinforcing his misbehavior by paying attention to it.
    b. Adam's parents are teaching their son not to misbehave by scolding him regularly
    c. By scolding Adam when he misbehaves, his parents are employing a very effective form of punishment.
    d. none of the above

26. Maria has just completed a course in effective parenting. Research tells her that if punishment must be used on young children,
    a. the shorter the time between misbehavior and punishment, the more effective the punishment
    b. punishment is more effective when accompanied by a short explanation at a level children can understand
    c. the better the relationship between the punishing adult and the child, the more effective the punishment
    d. all of the above

27. In her study of parenting styles and children's personalities, Baumrind concluded that children with permissive parents
    a. are the most mature
    b. tend to be highly exploratory and content
    c. lack self-control and are the least exploratory
    d. are the most withdrawn

28. Miranda and Donyell have two small children, 3 and 5 years of age. As parents, they respect their children's individuality, while simultaneously stressing social values. Miranda and Donyell are loving, consistent, demanding, and firm in maintaining standards. Baumrind would classify them as
    a. authoritarian parents
    b. permissive parents
    c. authoritative parents
    d. ineffective parents

29. Of the three kinds of parenting styles described by Baumrind, which one seems to rear children that are discontented, withdrawn, and distrustful?
    a. authoritative
    b. authoritarian
    c. permissive
    d. imaginative

30. Savannah is raised with authoritarian parents whereas Mia's parents are authoritative in child rearing. From Baumrind's research, we can reasonably infer that
    a. Savannah will become a more self-reliant, self-assertive, and exploratory child than Mia
    b. Mia will have difficulty making conscious choices regarding her behavior due to her parents' strict control
    c. Savannah will often become anxious about whether she is doing the right thing, due to her parents' lack of guidance
    d. Mia will be able to decide when it is worth risking her parents' displeasure to pursue a certain goal

31. Which of the following statements regarding parenting styles is most accurate?
    a. Cultural background, more than any other factor, seems to indicate whether a woman will spank her child or not.
    b. More religious women tend to be more sensitive to their children's needs.
    c. Younger, less educated single mothers, who were less involved in organized religion, tend to emphasize obedience and respect for elders to their children.
    d. all of the above

32. In the long run, specific parenting practices during a child's first five years may be less important than
    a. parents' socioeconomic status
    b. parents' level of education
    c. the number of friends a child has
    d. how the parents feel about their children and how they show those feelings

33. Reggie is an only child. According to research comparing only children to children with siblings
    a. Reggie will become a selfish, spoiled, maladjusted child
    b. Reggie will develop a lower intellect than children his age with siblings
    c. Reggie will surpass children with several siblings in terms of educational achievement and character
    d. none of the above

34. Which of the following statements most accurately reflects the existence of only children in China?
    a. More only children live in China than in any other country.
    b. In tests for academic achievement and physical growth, only children in China did about the same as or better than children with siblings.
    c. Census findings for 1990 suggest that 5 percent of all infant girls born in China are not accounted for.
    d. all of the above

35. Barbara is four years old, and her older brother, Damien, is five years old. From research on siblings, we can most reasonably infer that
    a. Barbara and Damien will play together more peaceably than same-sex siblings
    b. Barbara and Damien will get along better when their mother is not with them; fighting is often a bid for parental attention
    c. Barbara will tend to imitate her older brother Damien
    d. both b and c

36. Which of the following statements is most accurate regarding childhood personality?
    a. Popular children are less likely to be involved in angry conflict than unpopular children.
    b. Popular children are more likely to hit back or tattle than unpopular children.
    c. Popular children have difficulty controlling their anger.
    d. all of the above

37. Felicia, who is four years old, is a very popular preschooler. She has many friends and is quite agreeable most of the time. We can reasonably infer that
    a. Felicia has a warm, positive relationship with her parents
    b. Felicia's parents use an authoritative approach to childrearing
    c. Felicia's parents have a healthy, happy relationship
    d. all of the above

38. Which of the following statements about childhood play is most accurate?
    a. Lowerclass children interact more with other children in play.
    b. Solitary play generally indicates poor social adjustment.
    c. Solitary play can be a sign of maturity and independence.
    d. Solitary play is common only among very young children.

39. Tiya, who is two years old, pretends to feed and talk to her favorite doll. This type of behavior is called
    a. imaginative play
    b. cognitive play
    c. solitary play
    d. social play

40. According to recent research, __________ do not pay attention to requests and suggestions from ____________.
    a. boys; fathers
    b. boys; girls
    c. girls; mothers
    d. girls; boys

Completion

Supply the term or terms needed to complete each of the following statements.

1. Erikson's third crisis occurs during early childhood and is called ____________________ versus ____________________.

2. At approximately age two, a child becomes aware of being male or female, and this is called ________________ awareness. Usually about age 5 to 7, a child realizes his or her sex will remain the same, and this is called gender ______________.

3. According to Bem, the ______________ theory is a "cognitive-social" approach that contains elements of both cognitive-developmental and social learning theory.

4. Despite the variety of behavioral sex differences, both males and females believe that they are more ___________________ than they actually are.

5. The clearest gender difference between boys and girls is that males tend to be more ____________________ than females.

6. Gender ________________ are the behaviors, interests, attitudes, and skills that a culture considers appropriate for males and females and expects them to fulfill.

7. Bem coined the term ________________ to describe the healthiest people, those who have a balance of characteristics from those thought appropriate for males and females.

8. Because variations among people of the same sex are larger than the average differences between the sexes, ______________ fails to explain large behavioral differences between the sexes.

9. The reasons many young children are so fearful may stem from their intense fantasy life--their inability to distinguish ______________ from ______________.

10. A tendency for a child to show hostile actions intended to hurt somebody or to establish dominance is called __________________.

11. Research suggests that children are influenced more by seeing ___________ violence than by seeing real people acting aggressively.

12. Acting out of concern for another person, with no expectation of reward, is called ________________________.

13. A new name for the old practice of providing positive consequences when children do what parents want them to do and negative consequences when they do something the parents disapprove of is ______________________________.

14. The less time elapses between the behavior and punishment, the _____________ ____________________ the punishment will be.

15. According to Baumrind, ___________________ parents tend to have children who are withdrawn and distrustful; whereas self-reliant, self-assertive, exploratory, content children tend to have ___________________ parents.

16. If children's relationships with their _______________ are marked by an easy trust and companionship, they may carry this pattern over to their dealings with playmates, classmates, and eventually friends and lovers in adulthood.

17. It seems that children who can regulate their ___________________ can handle social situations better than children who cannot; this translates into popularity.

18. When parents actively arrange their children's social lives, the children have more ________________________.

19. Play in which children interact with others is called ________________ play, whereas the forms of play which enhance children's cognitive development are called ___________________ play.

20. Parents of children who play _______________________ tend to get along well with each other, expose their children to interesting experiences, talk with them, and not spank them.

ANSWERS FOR SELF-TESTS — CHAPTER 7

Multiple-Choice

		Page	
1.	b	241	conceptual
2.	b	241	factual
3.	a	242	conceptual
4.	c	242	factual
5.	d	242	factual
6.	d	243	conceptual
7.	a	243	factual
8.	b	244	factual
9.	a	244	conceptual
10.	c	244	conceptual
11.	d	244	factual
12.	a	246	factual
13.	b	246	conceptual
14.	c	246	factual
15.	b	247	conceptual
16.	d	247	factual
17.	c	248	conceptual
18.	c	249	factual
19.	a	250	conceptual
20.	d	251	factual
21.	b	252	conceptual
22.	d	254	conceptual
23.	d	254	factual
24.	a	255	factual
25.	a	256	conceptual
26.	d	256	conceptual
27.	c	257	factual
28.	c	257	conceptual
29.	b	257	factual
30.	d	258	conceptual
31.	d	258	conceptual
32.	d	258	factual
33.	c	259	conceptual
34.	d	260	factual
35.	d	261	conceptual
36.	a	261	factual
37.	d	262	conceptual
38.	c	264	factual
39.	a	265	conceptual
40.	b	267	factual

Completion

		Page
1.	initiative; guilt	241
2.	identity; conservation (or constancy)	241, 244
3.	gender schema	244
4.	different	246
5.	aggressive	246
6.	roles	246
7.	androgynous	247
8.	biology	248
9.	pretending (fantasy); reality	249
10.	aggression	250
11.	filmed	252
12.	altruism (prosocial behavior)	254
13.	behavior modification	255
14.	more effective	256
15.	authoritarian; authoritative	257
16.	siblings (or brothers and sisters	261
17.	anger	261
18.	playmates	262
19.	social; cognitive	263
20.	imaginatively	266

CHAPTER 8

Physical and Intellectual Development in Middle Childhood

INTRODUCTION

In Chapters 6 and 7, the development of children through kindergarten was discussed. Now, in Chapter 8, the discussion is shifted to the child of elementary school age. Whereas Chapter 6 focused on the physical and intellectual development of the preschooler, Chapter 8 examines the physical and intellectual development of the 6- to 12-year-old.

- Elementary school years are marked by further growth, strength, and agility and the mastery of skills that first appeared or were just learned during early childhood.

- Health, fitness, and safety represent important aspects of a child's development. Such topics as vision, dental health, general fitness, and childhood accidents are covered.

- Studies conducted several decades ago suggest that boys excel in motor skills, but more recent research indicates that boys and girls have similar motor abilities.

- Probably the most significant aspect of development at this age is the fact that children spend a large proportion of their time in school. Intellectual development takes place in the context of formal schooling, entry into which coincides with significant changes in the way children think and organize knowledge. Piaget's stage of concrete operations is discussed in detail in Chapter 8.

- Moreover, in middle childhood, moral and ethical thinking begins to develop in significant ways that are related to the changes in the way children understand their world. Piaget's and Kohlberg's theories of moral reasoning are compared and contrasted in this chapter.

- The development of memory, intelligence, and language during middle childhood are examined closely. The topics covered include mnemonic devices, rehearsal, elaboration, and external memory aids as well as the effects of race and culture on IQ tests and metacommunication.

- Childcare professionals and educators often disagree on how school can best enhance children's development. Teachers as well as parents influence how well children do in school. In addition, children with disabilities require special educational assistance. Learning disabilities and hyperactivity are examined closely, as is the topic of mainstreaming.

- Chapter 8 concludes with a discussion of giftedness, with suggestions for educating and nurturing gifted children. Bilingual speech is also covered.

CHAPTER OUTLINE

I. **Physical Development**

A. Growth During Middle Childhood
   1. Growth Rates
   2. Nutrition and Growth
      a. Malnutrition
      b. Obesity
B. Health, Fitness, and Safety
   1. Children's Health
      a. Minor medical conditions
      b. Vision
      c. Dental health
      d. General fitness
      e. Improving health and fitness
   2. Children's Safety
C. Motor Development in Middle Childhood

II. **Intellectual Development**

A. Aspects of Intellectual Development in Middle Childhood
   1. Cognitive Development: Piaget's Stage of Concrete Operations
      a. Operational thinking
      b. Conservation
         (1) How is conservation developed?
   2. Moral Reasoning: Two Theories
      a. Piaget and Two Moral Stages
      b. Kohlberg and Moral Reasoning
         (1) Kohlberg's moral dilemmas
         (2) Kohlberg's 3 levels of moral reasoning
         (3) Evaluating Kohlberg's theory
   3. Development of Memory: Information Processing
      a. How Memory Works: Encoding, Storing, and Retrieving
      b. Mnemonic Devices: Strategies for Remembering
         (1) Rehearsal
         (2) Organization
         (3) Elaboration
         (4) External memory aids
   4. Development of Intelligence: Psychometrics
      a. IQ tests
      b. Norms, Reliability, and Validity
      c. Race, Culture, and IQ tests
         (1) Intelligence testing of African American children
      d. Cultural Bias
         (1) "Culture-Free" and "Culture-Fair" tests
         (2) The test situation
   5. Development of Language: Communication
      a. Grammar: The Structure of Language
      b. Metacommunication: Understanding the Processes of Communication

B. Children in School
   1. Educational Trends
   2. Teachers' Characteristics and Expectations
   3. Parents' Influence
   4. Education for Special Needs
      a. Children with Disabilities
         (1) Mental retardation
         (2) Learning disabilities
         (3) Hyperactivity
         (4) Educating children with disabilities
      b. Gifted, Talented, and Creative Children
         (1) Defining and identifying giftedness
         (2) Educating and nurturing gifted children
   5. Bilingualism and Bilingual Education

KEY TERMS

---

attention deficit hyperactivity disorder (ADHD) (page 298)

bilingual education (301)

bilingualism (301)

code-switching (302)

concrete operations (279)

conservation (279)

conventional morality (280)

convergent thinking (300)

culture-fair (289)

culture-free (289)

decenter ((279)

divergent thinking (300)

dyslexia (296)

elaboration (286)

external aids (286)

giftedness (299)

horizontal decalage (280)

learning disabilities (LDs) (296)

mainstreaming (298)

mental retardation (296)

metacommunication (292)

metamemory (286)

mnemonic devices (285)

morality of constraint (280)

morality of cooperation (280)

operational thinking (279)

organization (286)

Otis-Lennon School Ability Test (287)

preconventional morality (280)

rehearsal (285)

self-fulfilling prophecy (294)

Wechsler Intelligence Scale for Children (WISC) (286)

LEARNING OBJECTIVES

After finishing Chapter 8, you should be able to:

1. Briefly describe the growth rates of middle childhood and explain the importance of nutrition and fitness for continued healthy growth. (pp. 272-274)

2. List some medical conditions common in middle childhood that might jeopardize growth and development. (pp. 274-276)

3. Identify the most common causes of childhood accidents. (pp. 277-278)

4. Explain the typical progression of motor development in middle childhood. (p. 278)

5. Explain Piaget's stage of concrete operations and define the following terms: (pp. 279-280)
   a. *operational thinking*
   b. *decenter*
   c. *conservation*
   d. *horizontal decalage*

6. Compare and contrast Piaget's and Kohlberg's theories of the development of moral reasoning. (pp. 280-282, p. 284)

7. Explain how the memory process works and describe the following *mnemonic* strategies: (pp. 285-286)
   a. rehearsal
   b. organization
   c. elaboration
   d. external memory aids

8. Compare and contrast the purpose and use of the WISC-R and the Otis-Lennon School Ability Test, both of which are used to assess "intelligence." (p. 287)

9. Explain why Black American children tend to score about 15 points lower on IQ tests than white American children. (p. 288)

10. Describe the ongoing controversy over IQ scores and *culture bias* and define the following terms: (pp. 288-289)

    a. *culture-free tests*

    b. *culture-fair tests*

11. Explain why Asian children are able to make such a strong showing on academic tasks. (pp. 290-291, Box 8-3)

12. Describe the development of language in children of elementary school age, and explain the concept of *metacommunication*. (pp. 289, 292-293)

13. List some strategies for developing thinking and reasoning skills (Box 8-4). (p. 294)

14. Explain how teachers' expectations can influence children's achievement. (pp. 293-295)

15. List some of the ways parents can influence their children to succeed in school. (pp. 295-296)

16. Briefly explain the ways in which children with mental retardation can benefit from mainstreamed schooling. (p. 296)

17. Describe how various disabilities, such as dyslexia and ADHD, affect children's ability to learn and provide some recommendations for educating these children. (pp. 296-299)

18. Define giftedness, and describe what educational opportunities schools provide for children who are gifted, talented, or creative. (pp. 299-301)

19. Briefly describe the two approaches schools use to encourage bilingualism. (pp. 301-302)

SUPPLEMENTAL READING

The following article is reprinted with permission from Maclean's Magazine, Maclean Hunter Ltd., ©March 1, 1993.

Good Touch, Bad Touch
How to Guard Against Sex Abuse

Diane Brad

Over the past decade, parents, teachers, and youth workers have intensified their efforts to protect children from sexual assault and to identify incidents of abuse as soon as possible. Countless books, teaching materials, and community programs now offer sound advice on reducing the risk of sexual assault. Here is a checklist of some of the key ways that parents can help protect their children--and uncover incidents of abuse:

Foster a Child's Self-Esteem

More than 90 percent of assaults are committed by relatives, close family friends, and other adults known to the child. Such abusers frequently use flattery, bribery and threats to coerce vulnerable children, whose emotional needs may not be met by their families. Psychologists and social workers emphasize that children require a solid sense of self-worth to help them make difficult judgments about confusing adult behavior. A consistent pattern of positive reinforcement by parents is an important element in strengthening a child's emotional security. "Research suggests that abuse prevention programs work much better for kids with self-esteem," says Leslie Tutty, assistant professor of social work at the University of Calgary. "Such children are able to trust their own feelings and to tell an adult if they have run into a problem--or to be assertive and tell someone else if they are not believed."

Just Say No

Many experts recommend that children be taught the differences between appropriate and inappropriate touching. Several programs across the country use plays, puppet shows or illustrated materials to teach children about the parts of the body, their right to refuse physical contact--and what to do if an adult attempts to touch them in unwelcome ways. Explains Suzanne Mulligan, executive director of a Hamilton, Ontario, area community child abuse council: "We do a disservice to our kids if we do not arm them with the information they need.

Understand a Child's World

Busy parents sometimes fail to see the physical world from their child's perspective. Experts recommend that parents tour their neighborhoods, identifying places such as parks, vacant lots, empty buildings, and wooded areas where children may be away from adult supervision--and more prone to assault. According to Personal Safety for Children: Parent Information, published by the Child Abuse Research & Education Productions Association of Surrey, B.C., parents frequently assume that other people are trustworthy--with sometimes tragic results. Parents should get to know their neighbors as well as members of their children's peer groups. Babysitters should be carefully screened, while parents should also make the effort to review the time that a sitter spends with their child. Adults who participate in children's extracurricular activities and supervise outings such as school trips should also be closely scrutinized.

Stranger Awareness

In general, children should be taught to avoid contact with strangers, whether young or old, well-dressed or poorly dressed, male or female--except in the company of a parent or another trusted adult. But because some strangers, such as those in uniform, can be helpful in threatening situations, simply instructing a child not to talk to strangers is seldom enough. Susan Laverty, an acting staff sergeant with the Ontario Provincial Police in Orillia, notes that children should be made aware of so-called safe strangers, including security guards in shopping malls and police officers. Says Laverty: "Children need to know the difference between the policeman and the man in the car with a puppy. They should be instructed to say no to such people and to go to a safe place and tell someone."

Playing "What If"

Because children often do not understand--or they forget--adult explanations and instructions, many experts recommend that parents participate in role-playing games with their children, using questions that begin with "What if?" Topics could include a wide range of situations, such as unwelcome touching by adults, the offer of candies or other gifts in exchange for such touching, or commands to keep incidents between an adult and a child a secret. Children also need to be assured that sometimes it might be impossible to prevent becoming a victim of abuse and that if it occurs it is not their fault. Says Tutty: "Kids are egocentric and tend to self-blame, so it is important to stress the opposite."

Be Aware of the Signs of Abuse

Many children are ashamed to talk about being abused, frequently because of their tendency to blame themselves. They may also fear retribution from the abuser if they speak out. In the event of abuse, however, it is likely that a child's everyday behavior will undergo marked changes. Although sleep and eating patterns may be disrupted, the clearest indicator that abuse has occurred is a child's acting out of sexual conduct that is inappropriate for his or her age. Children should be questioned in a calm, clear and straightforward way. Parents should not show excessive worry--if they do, a child may not reveal what has happened for fear of worrying parents even more. It is often necessary to persist in the face of initial denials or lack of response and, in the case of small children, to use acting-out games to get at the truth.

What to do if Abuse Occurs

Children should be told that they have done the right thing by reporting the actions--and that they have nothing to fear from threats. They should also be reassured that they will be protected from further assault and that the blame lies entirely with the abuser. Parents should report incidents to the police or child protection agencies. Because many abusers are repeat offenders, prompt action may help to protect others. Medical attention may also be necessary, as well as counseling.

Repeat the Lessons

Experts point out that close, continuing involvement by parents often makes a critical difference in helping a child avoid sexual assault. Says John Pearce, a psychologist with the child-abuse program at the Alberta Children's Hospital in Calgary: "Parents are missing the boat if they think that a one-hour street-proofing program at age five is going to protect their child." Frequent review is essential. Pearce also cautions that parents should always shoulder the responsibility for protecting their children, never transferring it to the child. Said Pearce, "Kids may know what to do, but they may not be able to do it under physical and emotional pressure from a much larger person." According to Pearce and many other experts, even the most thorough prevention program is no substitute for the never-ending vigilance that only parents, or their surrogates, provide.

Questions:

If over 90 percent of child abuse is committed by someone the child knows (relative, caregiver, neighbor, etc.), how do you explain to a child the difference between appropriate touches and inappropriate touches?

What are the legal responsibilities of many professionals (teachers, nurses, doctors, dentists, dental hygienists, etc., who work with children) for reporting child abuse in your own state?

SELF-TESTS

Multiple-Choice

Circle the letter of the response which best completes or answers each of the following statements and questions.

1. Which of the following statements about growth is most accurate?
   a. Boys grow faster than girls from birth through adulthood.
   b. Girls grow faster than boys from birth through adulthood.
   c. Girls' growth rate outdistances boys' rate starting about age 10; but boys overtake girls in growth about age 12 - 13.
   d. Growth rates around the world are similar for all races, national origins, and socioeconomic levels.

2. Colleen's 8-year-old daughter Allison eats a relatively well-balanced diet. However, Allison has a tendency to choose foods which have a high sugar content. From recent research, we can infer that
   a. Allison is a hyperactive child due to her abundant sugar consumption
   b. Allison suffers from severe mood swings due to her abundant sugar consumption
   c. Allison's abundant intake of sugar will not have adverse effects on her behavior or temperament
   d. none of the above

3. Ali is a well-nourished 6-year-old. His friend, Raphael, however, suffers from malnutrition. Nutritionists are most likely to theorize that
   a. Ali will be a happier, feistier, and more sociable child because he is better nourished than Raphael
   b. Raphael will have improved achievement test scores if he is better nourished
   c. As a result of malnourishment, Raphael will be a more passive, anxious child who is likely to depend more on adults
   d. all of the above

4. Which of the following statements about obesity is most accurate?
   a. Some people seem to be genetically predisposed toward obesity.
   b. Obesity is less common among lower socioeconomic groups.
   c. Fat children usually outgrow being fat; they tend to become thin adults.
   d. Obesity in children does not represent a major health issue in the U.S.

5. Recent research findings on children's health indicate that
   a. the death rate in middle childhood is the highest in the life span
   b. respiratory infections are common during middle childhood because youngsters pass germs freely at school
   c. approximately 1 in 4 children aged 4 to 8 show some kind of psychosocial or developmental problem
   d. both b and c

6. Josephine and Robert have two young children: Madeline, who is in preschool, and Donald, who is in fifth grade. They have had several conversations with their children regarding the topic of AIDS. When interviewed at school about the disease, it is likely that:
   a. Madeline nor Donald will know practically anything about the causes and prevention of AIDS
   b. Donald will remember a fair amount of accurate information about the causes and prevention of AIDS because he is older than Madeline
   c. both Madeline and Donald may believe inaccuracies, such as AIDS can be prevented by good nutrition
   d. both b and c

7. Lack of physical fitness among today's schoolchildren is mainly due to
   a. poor nutrition
   b. insufficient activity
   c. inherited weaknesses
   d. overeating

8. Which of the following can reduce high blood pressure in children?
   a. weight loss
   b. aerobic exercise
   c. reduced salt intake
   d. all of the above

9. Which of the following statements is most accurate regarding children's safety?
   a. The most common cause of death in young children is being hit by a motor vehicle.
   b. Children with siblings have fewer injuries than only children.
   c. Most kindergartners and first-graders possess the skills to safely walk alone to and from school.
   d. all of the above

10. Differences in physical skills and motor abilities between boys and girls aged 6 to 12 are largely due to
    a. inherent differences in anatomy
    b. hormone differences that affect the development of muscle
    c. differences in eating patterns and nutrition
    d. differences in participation and expectations

11. Tessa, who is 6 years old, has begun to think more logically. For example, she no longer believes that the cartoon characters on television are real people. According to Piaget, Tessa has entered the
    a. sensorimotor stage
    b. preoperational stage
    c. concrete operations stage
    d. formal operations stage

12. Alex is shown two equal balls of playdough. He agrees that they are equal. When one ball is rolled into a different shape, Alex recognizes that the two balls still have an equal amount of matter. Alex has developed which ability?
    a. conservation
    b. decentration
    c. cooperation
    d. formation

13. Concrete operational children possess which of the following characteristics?
    a. Their thinking is reversible.
    b. They show a qualitative cognitive advance over preoperational children.
    c. They can decenter.
    d. all of the above

14. Piaget and Kohlberg say that sound moral judgments are not likely until children have
    a. become capable of symbolic mental representations
    b. fully developed the ability to conserve
    c. matured beyond egocentric thinking
    d. mastered the fundamentals of symbolic logic

15. Suzette, a kindergartner, believes that behavior is either totally right or totally wrong. In addition, she has difficulty putting herself in the place of others. According to Piaget, Suzette is in which stage of moral development?
    a. morality of cooperation
    b. morality of constraint
    c. conventional morality
    d. postconventional morality

16. Julian and Thomas are 5-year-old twins. Julian notices that the table needs to be set and decides to help his mother by putting out the dishes. In the process, Julian breaks his mother's china plate. Thomas, upon seeing the dishes, picks one up to play with. Thomas drops a dish which leaves a small chip in the dish. A child in which stage of moral development is likely to consider Thomas a greater offender than Julian?
    a. preoperational thinking
    b. operational thinking
    c. morality of cooperation
    d. morality of constraint

17. The technique of using moral dilemmas to study moral development is most associated with
    a. Piaget
    b. Freud
    c. Chomsky
    d. Kohlberg

18. From a research perspective, one shouldn't generalize about the results of Kohlberg's study of moral development because the subjects
    a. were males only
    b. were from Western cultures
    c. might say they would only act a certain way when considering a hypothetical moral dilemma but in actuality might act differently
    d. all of the above

19. Shanicka, who is 6 years old, is trying to remember her grandparents' phone number. She repeats the number ten times a day for a week to accomplish this. She has used what type of strategy for remembering?
    a. a mnemonic device
    b. a memory encoder
    c. a metamemory
    d. none of the above

20. Which of the following is *not* a mnemonic strategy?
    a. formalization
    b. rehearsal, repetition
    c. organization
    d. elaboration

21. Greg, who is in second grade, has been scoring low on his spelling tests. He tells his mother that he is going to start studying his spelling words more often to raise his grades. Greg's understanding of his memory processes is called
    a. operational thinking
    b. preoperational thinking
    c. metamemory
    d. operational memory

22. Achievement tests assess children's ____________, whereas group intelligent tests aim to measure children's _________________.
    a. progress; aptitude
    b. aptitude; progress
    c. general intelligence; progress
    d. general intelligence; aptitude

23. Marcia, an elementary school principal, is in favor of IQ testing. Which of the following statements is Marcia likely to make at a school board meeting regarding the use of intelligence tests?
    a. IQ scores are good predictors of achievement in school, especially for highly verbal children.
    b. IQ tests help identify youngsters who are especially bright or who need special help in school.
    c. IQ tests measure abilities which are highly valued in our verbal society.
    d. all of the above

24. Kindah, a 5-year-old Black girl, scores 15 points lower on an IQ test than Rose, a white 5-year-old. Research on the influence of culture on intelligence tests leads us to most accurately infer which of the following?
    a. Because she is black, Kindah is innately less intelligent than Rose.
    b. Because she is white, Rose is innately less intelligent than Kindah.
    c. The difference in scores between Kindah and Rose probably reflects typical differences in environments--especially in education and living conditions between the two girls.
    d. none of the above

25. Which of the following factors can introduce cultural bias to tests designed to measure innate intelligence?
    a. language
    b. test questions which favor children from advantaged homes
    c. arbitrary decisions by test developers about which answers to accept
    d. all of the above

26. Which of the following statements is most accurate regarding the development of culture-fair tests--tests that deal with experiences common to various cultures?
    a. Separating inborn potential from the impact of life experience is a goal that, for the most part, has eluded test designers.
    b. So-called "culture-fair" tests almost invariably call for skills which are more familiar to some groups than others.
    c. Different cultures usually define intelligent behavior similarly.
    d. both a and b

27. Bihn is an Asian second grader who lives in China, and Jesse is an American second grader who lives in Florida. From research studies of the achievement levels of Asian children, we can most reasonably infer that
    a. Bihn is a more obedient student than Jesse
    b. Jesse spends more time doing his homework and enjoys doing it more than Bihn
    c. Jesse spends more time in school each year and more time being taught mathematics than Bihn
    d. Bihn will experience more feelings of stress, academic anxiety, and aggression than Jesse

28. Ludmilya, who is seven years old, is given two sentences to read: "Dad promised Mom to do the laundry," and "Dad told Mom to do the laundry." Ludmilya cannot see the structural differences between these two sentences and believes that both mean Mom is to do the laundry. Ludmilya has not yet mastered
    a. metamemory
    b. syntax
    c. mnemonic devices
    d. bilingualism

29. Which of the following statements regarding children's ability to understand the processes of communication is most accurate?
    a. Young children usually understand all of what they see, hear, or read.
    b. Young children do not understand all of what they see, hear, or read, but often they do not know they do not understand.
    c. By age 6, most children understand fully the processes of communication.
    d. none of the above

30. Howard is a second-grade teacher who opposes the "back-to-basics" approach to educating young children. He chooses to teach in a way that builds on children's natural talents. Howard is most likely to
    a. teach reading and writing in the context of a history project
    b. expose his students to hands-on experience
    c. teach his students to think for themselves--to reason
    d. all of the above

31. The principle that students live up to (or down to) the expectations that other people have for them is called the
    a. self-fulfilling prophecy
    b. convergence of expectations and achievement
    c. expectancy effect
    d. Hawthorne effect

32. Vanessa, a middle-class, 30-year-old woman, teaches a class of 22 first-grade students. Half of Vanessa's students are from minority groups and very poor families; the other half are from middle-class families. Which of the following statements best agrees with the principle of the self-fulfilling prophecy?
    a. Vanessa's minority and poor students will reach the same level of achievement as her middle-class students.
    b. Vanessa's middle-class students will achieve a higher level of achievement than Vanessa's minority and poor students.
    c. Because Vanessa is convinced that her minority and poor students have intellectual limitations, she will get very little achievement from them.
    d. both b and c

33. A 1990 study of nearly 1000 black, white, and Hispanic mothers and their elementary school children found that
    a. the white mothers showed more concern about their children's education than the black and Hispanic mothers
    b. the black and Hispanic children showed little enthusiasm about school and had low expectations for their future success
    c. although a high proportion of the black and Hispanic children expected to go to college, the rates of dropping out of school are very high among minority students in senior high schools
    d. all of the above

34. Below-average intellectual functioning, a deficiency in adaptive behavior appropriate to current age and the appearance of such characteristics before age 18 is defined as
    a. dyslexia
    b. mental retardation
    c. hyperactivity
    d. learning disability

35. Lester, who is 10 years old, confuses up and down and left and right. In addition, he has difficulty with reading and arithmetic. When looking at the word *bat*, Lester read *tab*. Lester could probably be identified as having
    a. convergent thinking
    b. attention deficit hyperactivity disorder
    c. dyslexia
    d. mental retardation

36. Sakinah, in third grade, has a learning disability. We can most accurately state she
    a. has a below average intelligence and trouble with her vision
    b. will outgrow her learning disability by the time she is a teenager
    c. can learn skills to help her use her strengths to compensate for her weaknesses and lead a satisfying, productive life
    d. all of the above

37. Which of the following is accurate about attention deficit hyperactivity disorder?
    a. Hyperactive children often have learning disabilities.
    b. Children with ADHD are inattentive, impulsive, and have frequent temper tantrums.
    c. ADHD is probably caused by a combination of genetic, neurological, biochemical, and environmental factors.
    d. all of the above

38. Public Law 94.142, landmark legislation passed by Congress in 1974, guarantees
    a. full mainstreaming of all retarded children
    b. a high school diploma for every disabled child
    c. appropriate public education for all children with disabilities, paving the way for mainstreaming and integration
    d. federal money for programs to provide year-round vocational training for any disabled learner

39. A teacher asks one of his young students to answer the question, "Where does snow come from?" Instead of using the traditional response "the sky" used by the student's classmates, the boy gives an unusual answer: "A magician tells the clouds it is wintertime and makes them open their pores and create snow." This child is demonstrating which kind of thought?
    a. convergent thinking
    b. divergent thinking
    c. operational thinking
    d. preoperational thinking

40. Children identified as "gifted" usually
    a. have well-educated, emotionally supportive parents
    b. possess a drive to excel
    c. receive freedom and responsibility from their parents
    d. all of the above

Completion

Supply the term or terms needed to complete each of the following statements.

1. The widespread use of fluoride in tablets, toothpaste, and mouthwash accounts for the fact that American children today have about 1/3 fewer ________________ than children at the beginning of the 1980s.

2. ________________ average more injuries than ____________, probably because they take more physical risks.

3. When third-, fourth-, and fifth-grade boys and girls who had been in excellent co-ed physical education classes for at least a year were compared on their scores for sit-ups, running, and jumping, ________________ improved with age.

4. Sometime between 5 and 7 years of age, according to Piaget, children enter the stage of ______________________, when they can think logically about the here and now but not yet about abstractions.

5. The ability to recognize that two equal quantities of matter remain equal--in substance, weight, or volume--so long as nothing is added or taken away--is called __________.

6. Children's inability to transfer what they have learned about one type of conservation to another was called ____________________ by Piaget.

7. Children in Piaget's first moral stage, ______________________, see everything in black and white, and they cannot conceive of more than one way of looking at a moral question.

8. The attainment of the stage of moral development that Piaget called morality of cooperation depends on a decrease in the child's _________________ thinking.

9. In response to "Heinz's" dilemma as posed by Lawrence Kohlberg, a child says, "He should steal the drug. If Heinz did nothing he'd be letting his wife die. You can't blame him for acting out of love to save her." This child is probably operating at the ______________________ level of moral reasoning, according to Kohlberg's theory.

10. Kohlberg's belief that children are "moral philosophers" who work out their moral systems by independent discovery is questionable. More recent studies show that moral judgments are strongly influenced by __________________.

11. Mnemonic strategies include these four techniques to aid memory: ______________, ____________________, __________________, and ________________.

12. Older children are more conscious of how memory works, and this knowledge called _________________________ develops in middle childhood.

13. The most widely used individual IQ tests for school children is the _________________________________.

14. One of the major issues concerning IQ tests is ______________, the tendency to include test elements that are more familiar to people of certain cultures.

15. The function of intelligence tests is not just to measure intelligence but to find out how to ___________________.

16. Knowledge of the processes of communication is called ______________________.

17. Mr. Ellsworth believes that his math class is of less than average ability (even though the children are really above average), and it is likely that his students will be negatively affected by his belief. This phenomenon is called the _________________________________.

18. _________________ involvement improves children's grades and their scores on IQ and achievement tests, as well as their behavior and attitude in school.

19. Most retarded children can benefit from __________________, at least up to the sixth grade level.

20. Behavioral modification techniques, techniques for improving basic skills, using cognitive strategies, and encouragement of progress are among the most successful aids in treating ________________________________.

21. The syndrome known as _________________________________ is marked by inattention, impulsivity, low tolerance of frustration, temper tantrums, and a great deal of activity at the wrong time and in the wrong place, like the classroom.

22. The integration of students with disabilities and nondisabled students is called ___________________________.

23. Superior general intellect, superiority in a single domain (like mathematics or science), talent in the arts, leadership, or creative thinking is a broad definition of __________.

24. Guilford distinguished between two kinds of thought: ________________, which seeks a single "right" answer (usually the traditional one); and ________________, which comes up with fresh, unusual possibilities.

25. Fluency in two languages is called ______________________.

ANSWERS FOR SELF-TESTS **CHAPTER 8**

Multiple-Choice

		Page				Page	
1.	c	272	factual	21.	c	286	conceptual
2.	c	273	conceptual	22.	a	286	factual
3.	d	273	factual	23.	d	287	conceptual
4.	a	274	factual	24.	c	288	conceptual
5.	d	274	factual	25.	d	288	factual
6.	d	275	conceptual	26.	d	289	factual
7.	b	276	factual	27.	a	290	conceptual
8.	d	277	factual	28.	b	292	conceptual
9.	a	278	factual	29.	b	293	factual
10.	d	278	factual	30.	d	293	conceptual
11.	c	279	conceptual	31.	a	294	factual
12.	a	279	conceptual	32.	d	294	conceptual
13.	d	279	factual	33.	c	295	factual
14.	c	280	factual	34.	b	296	factual
15.	b	280	factual	35.	c	296	conceptual
16.	c	281	conceptual	36.	c	297	conceptual
17.	d	282	factual	37.	d	297	factual
18.	d	282	factual	38.	c	298	factual
19.	a	285	conceptual	39.	b	300	conceptual
20.	a	285	factual	40.	d	300	factual

Completion

		Page			Page
1.	cavities	276	14.	cultural bias	288
2.	boys; girls	277	15.	improve it	289
3.	boys and girls	278	16.	metacommunication	292
4.	concrete operations	279	17.	self-fulfilling prophecy	294
5.	conservation	279			
6.	horizontal decalage	280	18.	Parents'	295
7.	morality of constraint	280	19.	schooling	296
8.	egocentric	281	20.	learning disabilities	297
9.	conventional morality	282	21.	attention deficit hyperactivity disorder (ADHD)	298
10.	education	284			
11.	rehearsal; organization elaboration, external aids	285	22.	mainstreaming	298
12.	metamemory	286	23.	giftedness	299
13.	Wechsler Intelligence Scale for Children (WISC-IV)	286	24.	convergent thinking; divergent thinking	300
			25.	bilingualism	301

CHAPTER 9

Personality and Social Development in Middle Childhood

INTRODUCTION

Cognitive changes of middle childhood were described in Chapter 8. As Chapter 9 explains, these are accompanied by personality and social changes. From the ages of 6 to 12, children's lives expand socially through greater interaction with peers, friends, neighbors, and families. Personal awareness of individual capabilities also expands as children enter school and other activities. Through these interactions, children can explore and develop their attitudes, values, and skills.

- Three major accomplishments during this stage are development of the self-concept, a centering of control from outside the child to within the child, and the development of self-esteem. Even though the family remains a vital influence, children during this stage become more independent of their parents.

- The peer group is an important arena for the building of self-concept and self-esteem. Both positive and negative effects of the peer group are discussed. Popularity also influences self-esteem. Children who are ignored and rejected by their peers are at risk of emotional and behavioral problems. Guidelines for helping unpopular children are provided.

- Because family structures have changed considerably over the past few generations (there are more divorces, more single parents, more working mothers, more children in day care, etc.), some children fail to develop healthy self-esteem and may be more susceptible to stress, child abuse, depression, and emotional disorders.

- Middle-aged children often develop emotional disturbances. These include acting-out behavior, anxiety disorders, and depression. A variety of ways to treat these emotional problems are discussed.

- Some psychologists are concerned about the "hurried" child of our society. Yet some "resilient" children are able to cope with stress. A variety of techniques are described to help children develop a healthy self-concept before entering the next stage of development, adolescence.

CHAPTER OUTLINE

I. The Self-Concept

- A. Developing a Self-Concept
  - 1. Beginnings: Self-Recognition and Self-Definition
  - 2. Coordination of Self-Regulation and Social-Regulation
- B. Self-Esteem
  - 1. Industry and Self-Esteem
  - 2. Sources of Self-Esteem

II. Aspects of Personality Development in Middle Childhood

- A. Everyday Life
  - 1. How do Children Spend Their Time?
  - 2. With Whom Do Children Spend Their Time?
- B. The Child in the Peer Group
  - 1. Functions and Influence of the Peer Group
    - a. Positive effects
    - b. Negative effects--conformity
  - 2. Makeup of the Peer Group
  - 3. Friendship
  - 4. Popularity
    - a. The Popular Child
    - b. The Unpopular Child
    - c. Family Influences on Popularity
    - d. How Can Unpopular Children be Helped?
- C. The Child in the Family
  - 1. Parent-Child Relationships
    - a. Issues Between Parents and Children
    - b. Discipline
    - c. Control and Coregulation
  - 2. Parents' Work: How it Affects Their Children
    - a. Mothers' Work
      - (1) The mother's psychological state
      - (2) Interactions in working-mother families
      - (3) Working mothers and children's values
      - (4) Children's reactions to mothers' work
    - b. Fathers' Work
  - 3. Children of Divorce
    - a. Children's Adjustment to Divorce
      - (1) Tasks of adjustment
    - b. Influences on Children's Adjustment to Divorce
      - (1) Parenting styles and parents' satisfaction
      - (2) Remarriage of the mother
      - (3) Remarriage of the father
      - (4) Accessibility of both parents
    - c. Long-term Effects of Divorce on Children
    - d. The One-Parent Family
      - (1) Current trends
      - (2) Effects on children
      - (3) Effects on schooling
      - (4) Long-term effects
      - (5) Stepfamilies
    - e. Sibling Relationships

III. Childhood Emotional Disturbances

A. Types of Emotional Problems
   1. Acting-Out Behavior
      a. Anxiety Disorders
         (1) Separation anxiety disorder
      b. School phobia
   2. Childhood Depression
B. Treatment for Emotional Problems
   1. Therapies
   2. Effectiveness of Therapy

IV. Stress and Resilience

A. Sources of Stress: Life Events, Fears, and the "Hurried" Child
B. Coping with Stress: The Resilient Child

KEY TERMS

---

acting-out behavior (page 331)

affective disorder (332)

behavior therapy (333)

childhood depression (332)

coregulation (320)

discipline (319)

drug therapy (333)

family therapy (333)

global self-worth (310)

ideal self (309)

individual psychotherapy (333)

industry versus inferiority (310)

prejudice (315)

psychological maltreatment (334)

real self (309)

school phobia (331)

self-care children (323)

self-concept (308)

self-definition (308)

self-esteem (309)

separation anxiety disorder (331)

LEARNING OBJECTIVES

After finishing Chapter 9, you should be able to:

1. Explain what is meant by a person's sense of self, or *self-concept*, which begins to develop during middle childhood. (pp. 308-309)

2. List some of the tasks children must fulfill toward the development of self-concept, as they strive to become functioning members of society. (p. 309)

3. Describe the development and importance of healthy *self-esteem*. (pp. 309-310)

4. Describe Erikson's middle childhood crisis of *industry vs. inferiority* and its successful resolution. (p. 310)

5. Explain the term *global self-worth*, and list some of the sources of *self-esteem*. (pp. 310-311)

6. Briefly discuss how, and with whom, middle-aged children spend their time. (pp. 311-313)

7. Explain some positive and negative effects of the peer group. (pp. 313-314)

8. Define *prejudice* and its effect on the peer group. (p. 315)

9. Differentiate between how a young child views a friend and how a child in the middle years views a friend. (pp. 315-316)

10. Explain some personality characteristics of popular children and unpopular children. (pp. 316-317)

11. List some ways in which adults can help unpopular children. (pp. 317-318)

12. Briefly describe the kinds of issues that arise between children in middle childhood and their parents concerning the following: (pp. 319-320)
    a. discipline

    b. control and coregulation

13. Explain some research findings concerning mothers' work and its effects on the following: (pp. 321-322)
    a. the mother's psychological state

    b. the father's involvement with the children

    c. the children's development

14. Discuss the topic of *self-care* children, and explain how parents can tell when a child is ready for *self-care*. (p. 323)

15. Briefly describe the research on how men's work (or unemployment) affects their families. (p. 322)

16. Describe some common reactions of children to parent's divorce. (pp. 322, 324)

17. List 5 suggestions for helping children adjust to divorce: (pp. 330)
    a.

    b.

    c.

    d.

    e.

18. Identify how each of the following factors influence a child's adjustment to divorce (based on research findings): (pp. 324-325)
    a. parenting styles

    b. the mother's remarriage

    c. relationship with the father

    d. accessibility of both parents

19. List some of the long-term effects of divorce on children. (pp. 325-326)

20. Briefly explain the current trend of one-parent families in the U.S., and list some of the common stressors for children from these families: (pp. 326-327)

21. Describe some research findings concerning stepfamilies. (p. 328)

22. Explain some research findings concerning sibling relationships. (pp. 328-329)

23. Describe the following nonphysical disturbances and list some possible treatments: (pp. 331-332)
    a. acting-out behavior
    b. separation anxiety disorder
    c. school phobia
    d. childhood depression

24. Name and explain the treatment techniques for these emotional disturbances: (p. 333)
    a. psychological therapies (3 forms)
    b. drug therapy

25. Explain the term psychological maltreatment and its relationship to child abuse. (p. 334)

26. Explain what David Elkind and other psychologists mean by the term "hurried" child. (p. 334)

27. List some ways that help a child cope with and become more resilient to stress. (pp. 334, 336)

SUPPLEMENTAL READING

The following article is reprinted with permission from Parents Magazine, ©April, 1994, Gruner + Jahr USA Publishing. Nancy Samalin is the author of Loving Your Child Is Not Enough and Love and Anger: The Parental Dilemma. Patricia McCormick is a contributing editor of Parents magazine.

Who, Me? Honesty Comes Easy When It's Safe to Tell the Truth

Nancy Samalin and Patricia McCormick

"Who left this mess in the kitchen?" Tina said angrily.

"I didn't do it!" protested her 9-year-old daughter, Sally.

"Well, somebody drank a glass of chocolate milk and left the milk, the syrup, and the dirty glass on the counter, and it wasn't Rover," said her mother.

"So?" retorted Sally. "Why do you always blame me?"

Her mother sighed. "Maybe it's because you have a milk mustache on your upper lip, for one thing. Sally, why do you have to tell a lie? Why don't you just admit that you did it?"

Although you may have found it amusing when your child was a preschooler and made statements such as "The vase breaked itself," you probably have very little tolerance for her guilty denials now that she is older. That is because we know that "lies" by young children are really more like wishful thinking. Lying by older children bothers us because they now know the difference between fantasy and reality.

Although it's true that older children can distinguish fact from fancy, there is still an element of wishful thinking in their lies. An older child may cling to the hope that if she doesn't fess up, she won't get caught, even if it's obvious that she is guilty. And if she doesn't get caught, she thinks, she won't be punished. Not a rational line of thought by our adult standards, but a basis for hope if you're 8 years old and very worried about being identified as the culprit for a stain on the new living-room rug.

One of the main reasons children lie is to protect themselves. They assume, often with good reason, that telling the truth is going to get them in trouble. And we may inadvertently encourage a child to lie by asking accusing questions that back her into a corner. Keep in mind that it is very difficult for a child to admit her guilt when she has done something that she knows will make you angry or disappointed.

So how do you discourage lying? By making it safe to tell the truth. That does not mean that you have to spare your child the consequences of her misdeed; it simply means that you create an atmosphere in which fear doesn't get in the way of telling the truth.

Here are some strategies to encourage your child to tell the truth:

Describe the scene instead of asking, "Did you do it?"

Confronted with the evidence of a crime--such as a wet towel on a bed--most parents ask pointed questions such as, "Tommy, did you leave this soggy towel on my bed?" But few children are going to step forward eagerly and admit, "Yes, I did it, Mom."

To make it easier for your child to own up to his misbehavior, describe what you see, and ask your child to help solve the problem. "A wet towel was left on my bed, and now my sheets and blanket are damp. Will you help me strip the bed and get some dry sheets?" (When you describe the scene, be sure to watch your tone of voice. Even if you're not directly accusing your child, if your voice sounds sarcastic or angry, it will sound as if you are blaming him.) This approach short-circuits the frustrating process of trying to pin the blame on the guilty party and moves both of you forward into the realm of working together to solve problems. It also leaves the door open for the child to say he is sorry.

Tone down your initial reaction to a lie.

You can offer your child a chance to recant by showing her that you're not going to blow up at the misdeed or the subsequent cover-up. Offer a cooling-off period by saying something such as, "Okay, I'm almost certain that you didn't empty the litter box even though you said you did. I'm not going to make a big deal about it. So let's not make matters worse by not telling the truth."

Ask your child what he's afraid of.

If your child continues to deny his obvious guilt, ask him what he thinks will happen if he tells the truth. He may be relieved to find that the consequences aren't as dreadful as he imagined. One mother whose 7-year-old daughter stoutly denied taking a package of stickers from the store said, "Something tells me you are really afraid of telling the truth. What do you think will happen if you admit that you took them?"

Her daughter answered, "You'll make me take them back, right?" The mother replied yes, she would have to return the stickers because they had not been paid for. When the girl said she was embarrassed to go back, her mother said she would go with her. "And you won't be mad at me anymore?" she asked.

"No," said her mother. "The case is closed as soon as you've done the correct thing. What's important is that you told the truth."

Avoid "Fifth Amendment" questions.

A Fifth Amendment question is one in which you are setting up a trap. If, for example, your child's teacher has called and told you that she has not been turning in her math homework, your casually asking, "So, how are you doing in math?" is unfair. Chances are your child will say, "Fine." You'll be angry because she has not only fallen down on her responsibilities but has also lied about it. Your child, meanwhile, will feel trapped and defensive. And neither of you will be in the mood to tackle the real problem. Instead, tell your child what the teacher said, and ask her what's going on.

Don't insist on a confession.

Very often, parents don't feel satisfied until they receive an admission of guilt from their children. But this doesn't offer the child any way to save face in an embarrassing situation. Often it's best to simply let your child know that you're aware of what he has done. That way you don't need to argue about why he didn't tell the truth; you can get down to the business of solving the problem.

Apply the innocent-until-proved-guilty rule.

All too often, parents are tempted to assume that their child is at fault, especially if the accusation comes from another adult. Before you join in the accusation, give your child the benefit of the doubt. Present her with the information you've received, and ask her for her side of the story. If your child feels as though you are on her side, or at least willing to listen to her point of view, she won't feel the need to conceal the truth from you. And if she turns out to be innocent, you will have avoided a mistake that could have resulted in a serious breach of trust between the two of you.

Reinforce truthfulness.

When a child finally does tell the truth, what he wants to hear is, "I'm so glad you told me the truth," or "It took a lot of courage to tell me when you knew I would be upset." The last thing he wants to hear is, "Why didn't you just admit it right from the start?"

Forgive and forget.

An occasional lie does not make your child a habitual liar. It means that your child is having trouble telling the truth right now and needs your help. Making your child feel loved and understood will help her develop the control she needs to tell the truth the next time.

Recognize that chronic lying may indicate a problem.

If, despite all your efforts, your child continually lies, such behavior may indicate a self-esteem problem. In this case, you may want to consider seeking professional help.

<u>Questions</u>:

You suspect that your 10-year-old child has taken some money from your wallet. Briefly explain about how you would approach talking about this with your child <u>before</u> you talk with your child. Then ask yourself, "How would I feel if my parents spoke to me in this way?"

What types of feelings/emotions do you think are behind a child's need to lie or exaggerate about events in his/her life?

SELF-TEST

Multiple-Choice

Circle the letter of the response which best completes or answers each of the following statements and questions.

1. At age 3, Kindah thinks of herself mostly in terms of externals--her curly hair, her white house, her activities at day care. This ability to identify the characteristics Kindah considers important to describe herself is called
   a. self-definition
   b. self-awareness
   c. self-esteem
   d. the ideal self

2. Which of the following is *not* considered an important task of middle childhood?
   a. expanding understanding of self and society
   b. developing trust in significant others
   c. developing acceptable behavioral standards
   d. managing one's own behavior

3. Truman, who is 8 years old, has high self-esteem, whereas Raphael, also 8, has low self-esteem. We can most reasonably infer which of the following about the behavior of Truman and Raphael?
   a. Truman adjusts relatively easily to change and can handle criticism and teasing.
   b. Raphael gives up easily when frustrated and reacts immaturely to stress.
   c. Truman is more likely to be cheerful, whereas Raphael is more likely to be depressed.
   d. all of the above

4. The successful resolution of Erikson's fourth crisis, industry versus inferiority, is
   a. popularity
   b. competence
   c. love
   d. the virtue of purpose

5. Veronica, who is 9 years old, is asked to rate the importance of doing well in five domains of life in order to feel good about herself. According to Susan Harter's research, which of the following domains will Veronica rate as most significant?
   a. how well she does in school
   b. how good an athlete she is
   c. what she looks like
   d. how well she behaves

6. Which of the following children is most likely to feel a strong sense of self-worth?
   a. Luis, who believes it is important to be smart and a good athlete and considers himself both but does not feel valued by his parents because he is their youngest child
   b. Charlotte, whose family and friends shower her with praise and support, but does not believe she is pretty, an attribute she regards highly
   c. Angel, who believes it is important to be a good student and attractive and considers herself both and who feels valued by her parents and peers
   d. All of the above 3 children should feel an equal sense of self-worth

7. Which of the following statements about middle childhood is false?
   a. The two main things children choose to do are playing and watching television.
   b. Children who read every day are likely to watch less television.
   c. Children watch television more in middle childhood than during any other period of childhood.
   d. Children spend a great deal of their free time with parents.

8. In Furman and Buhrmester's study in which children rated the important people in their lives, it was found that
   a. children look to their friends for affection, guidance, and enhancement of worth
   b. children rated their parents as the most important people in their lives
   c. boys relied more on their best friend than girls did
   d. fathers got higher companionship ratings than mothers

9. Which of the following is a positive effect of the peer group?
   a. It helps children learn how to get along in society.
   b. It helps children learn and frees them to make judgments.
   c. It counterbalances the influence of parents.
   d. all of the above

10. Omar is an African-American sixth grader. From research on the peer group, we can reasonably infer that
    a. Omar prefers to play with classmates of his own race
    b. Omar feels very negatively toward classmates of other races
    c. Omar is least susceptible to pressure to conform at this age
    d. all of the above

11. According to Selman, which of the following statements regarding childhood friendship is the most accurate?
    a. Girls value depth of relationships, while boys value number of relationships.
    b. Friendship plays only a minor role in a child's development.
    c. From ages 9 to 15, children value friends for material or physical attributes.
    d. Middle-childhood friends are typically of the opposite sex.

12. Ethan is a very popular, well-liked fourth grader. Which of the following characteristics is Ethan most likely to possess?
    a. He is a "goodie-goodie" in school.
    b. He is very aggressive and likes to "bully" his peers.
    c. He is trustworthy and loyal to his peers.
    d. none of the above

13. Which of these factors would probably *not* account for a child's unpopularity?
    a. unattractive appearance
    b. authoritarian parents
    c. expecting to be well-liked
    d. a learning disorder

14. Chandra is an unpopular fifth grader. She gets along poorly with her peers and is rejected by most of them. It is likely that Chandra
    a. may develop emotional and behavioral difficulties later in life
    b. has supportive parents whose approach to childrearing is authoritative
    c. tends to seek out friends who are just as antisocial as she is
    d. both a and c

15. Which of the following statements most accurately reflects research on the family ecologies of children from ethnic minority groups?
    a. Social roles in minority families tend to be less flexible than in majority culture families.
    b. By and large, ethnic minority children are encouraged to cooperate, share, and develop an interdependence with others.
    c. In ethnic minority families, ties are weak among extended family members, who are less likely than white families to share living quarters.
    d. all of the above

16. Theo and Lisa's twin boys have entered middle childhood. From research on parent-child relationships, we can assume that
    a. Theo and Lisa are more concerned with their sons' progress in school
    b. Theo and Lisa are concerned with their sons' whereabouts and with whom they are spending their free time
    c. Theo and Lisa often disagree with their sons over issues such as household chores and allowance
    d. all of the above

17. Naimah's two children are 4 and 12 years old. As a good parent, she has the responsibility of disciplining her children. Naimah is most likely to
    a. go about disciplining her 4 and 12 year old in a similar manner
    b. tell her 12 year old how to dress for school
    c. maintain a fairly consistent approach to disciplining her children over time
    d. all of the above

18. In order for the transitional phase of coregulation to work, how should parents act toward children in middle childhood?
    a. Allow children to adopt their own standards and control their own behavior.
    b. Communicate clearly with children and provide support, guidance, and general supervisory control.
    c. Impose rigid rules and regulations on children and constantly scrutinize children's actions.
    d. Influence children to adopt values and standards like their own.

19. Deonza, the mother of two children, has recently been divorced from her husband. As a result, she has started a full-time job. How will Deonza's employment affect her and her family?
    a. Deonza's job will cause her to feel less competent and be more apt to abuse her children.
    b. Deonza's job will enable her to feel more satisfied and to be a more effective parent.
    c. Deonza will feel such guilt over being away from her children that she will eventually quit her job.
    d. Deonza will have lower self-esteem than she did as a homemaker.

20. One finding from studies on mothers' working outside the home is that
    a. daughters of working women have fewer stereotypes about gender roles than children in "traditional" families
    b. mothers' homes tend to be less structured, without clear-cut rules, and their children are usually less independent
    c. boys in single-parent, lower-income families are negatively affected when their mothers work; in particular, they achieve less in school
    d. none of the above

21. Jerome's father recently lost his job and has become very irritable and depressed. How might we expect Jerome's behavior to change as a result?
    a. Jerome will set high aspirations for himself and try to avoid the failure his father has suffered.
    b. Jerome may become a behavioral problem in school and grow depressed as well.
    c. Jerome's behavior will remain unaffected by his father's crisis.
    d. Jerome will develop into a well-behaved child in order to mask his family's turmoil.

22. Rashad, 11, comes home from school, unlocks the door, throws down his books, and then fixes himself a snack. Soon after, he phones his mother at work to check in. This is Rashad's daily routine. He cares for himself until his mother returns from her job at 5 p.m. Research on self-care children leads us to believe that
    a. Rashad is from a poor, single-parent family
    b. Rashad's achievement in school is far less than that of an 11-year-old boy who is cared for by his mother after school
    c. as society adjusts to the growing number of working mothers, Rashad is less likely to be viewed as the stereotypical "latchkey" child (neglected and lonely)
    d. both b and c

23. Twelve-year-old Linda's parents have recently separated. From research on children of divorce, we can most reasonably infer that
    a. Linda may become depressed, disruptive, lonely, or sad
    b. Linda may suffer from fatigue, loss of appetite, or inability to concentrate
    c. Linda may come through the painful experience of divorce with a basically intact ego, depending upon her own resilience as well as how her parents handle the separation
    d. all of the above

24. The children of divorcing parents face several special challenges or "tasks" which are crucial to their adjustment. These tasks include all of the following *except* which?
    a. acknowledging the reality of the marital break-up
    b. adjusting to the many losses of the divorce: of the parent they are not living with, familiar daily routines and family traditions, etc.
    c. resolving anger and self-blame related to the divorce
    d. holding on to the fantasy that their parents will be reunited

25. Which of the following scenarios is most common among remarried mothers?
    a. Daughters of remarried women often experience more problems coping than daughters of nondivorced mothers.
    b. Remarried mothers tend to be less happy and less satisfied with their lives.
    c. The daughters of remarried women usually never adjust to coexistence with their stepfathers.
    d. Sons of remarried women often experience more problems coping than these women's daughters.

26. Which of the following statements is most accurate regarding the long-term effects of divorce on children?
    a. Ten years after the divorce, girls are far more likely to be emotionally troubled, lonely, and to hold back in relationships with boys.
    b. When children of divorce reach adulthood, they are a great deal more depressed and have far more frequent marital problems than people who had grown up in intact families.
    c. Ten years after the divorce, boys are far more likely to be emotionally troubled, lonely, and to hold back in relationships with girls.
    d. Most children of divorce never completely adjust to their parents separation, leaving them disturbed and uncaring as adults.

27. Tyrene, 12, is from a poor, single-parent family. In addition to raising Tyrene, her mother works full-time. We can reasonably infer that
    a. Tyrene is likely to have problems in school
    b. Tyrene is more likely to require disciplinary action than children with two parents
    c. Tyrene is more likely to be poor herself as an adult and to become a single parent than children with two parents
    d. all of the above

28. Which of the following factors best accounts for the finding that children from one-parent homes achieve less in school than those with two parents?
    a. low family income
    b. lack of reading material in the home
    c. having only one parent
    d. having frequent babysitters

29. Research on stepfamilies reveals which of the following?
    a. A man has the best chance of being accepted by his stepson if he assumes an authoritative role immediately.
    b. Girls are less likely than boys to accept a stepfather as a parent.
    c. Stepfathers tend to be much more involved than stepmothers, taking their stepchildren to various activities and providing emotional support.
    d. all of the above

30. Jeremiah is 10 years old, and his little sister, Desiree, is 5 years old. Research on sibling relationships tells us that
    a. Desiree, because she is second born, tends to be bossy and is more likely to attack, ignore, or bribe her older brother
    b. Jerrie, because he is first-born, tends to be a negotiator; he compromises, pleads, and reasons with his younger sister
    c. Desiree and Jerrie get along better and squabble less than two same-sex siblings.
    d. Jeremiah is more apt to reason with his younger sister to get her to do something; he is rarely bossy

31. Research on childhood emotional disturbances has found which of the following?
    a. Boys, African-American children, and children from poor families are at especially high risk for psychiatric problems.
    b. Only about 1 out of 5 children affected by emotional disturbances receives proper treatment.
    c. At least 3 to 9 million children are affected by psychiatric problems.
    d. all of the above

32. Marianna and Santos are getting a divorce. To help their children, 4 and 11, adjust to the break up, experts on family relations recommend that Marianna and Santos
    a. tell the 11-year-old about the divorce and how it will affect his life, but refrain from explaining it to the 4-year-old
    b. tell their children why the divorce is happening; Marianna has a boyfriend
    c. encourage both of their children to openly show emotions such as fear, anger, and sadness which they may be feeling
    d. allow their children to behave poorly; disciplining them will only make the adjustment to divorce that much harder

33. Children's emotional problems often show up in the way they act: they fight, they lie, they steal, and they break rules to gain attention. These are common signs of
    a. separation-anxiety disorder
    b. acting out behavior
    c. affective disorder
    d. phobia

34. Rolando, 10, has been at sleep-away camp for the last 15 days. He has complained daily of stomachaches, headaches, and has thrown up three times. When Rolando returns home with his parents, though, his symptoms disappear. Rolando has been suffering from
    a. separation anxiety disorder
    b. acting-out behavior
    c. affective disorder
    d. phobia

35. Which of the following statements is true regarding school phobia?
    a. School phobia may be a form of separation anxiety disorder.
    b. School phobia seems to have more to do with a fear of leaving the mother.
    c. School-phobic children tend to be average or good students, whose parents are professionals.
    d. all of the above

36. Eugenia, 10, has difficulty concentrating and is unable to have fun. She is often tired or extremely active. In addition, Eugenia cries a great deal, suffers from school phobia, and thinks about death. A psychologist would classify Eugenia as suffering from
    a. the "hurried-child" syndrome
    b. acting-out behavior
    c. childhood depression
    d. resilience

37. Claudia's daughter, Candace, aged 10, refuses to pay attention in school. She disrupts her classes, refuses to do her homework, and dislikes her teacher. Claudia takes her daughter to a therapist who employs the following approach: Each time Candace behaves well in class or does her homework, her mother rewards her with toys, candy, clothes, etc. This type of therapy is referred to as
    a. family therapy
    b. behavior therapy (behavior modification)
    c. drug therapy
    d. supportive therapy

38. Christopher's parents emotionally abuse their son by rejecting, insulting, and degrading him. They use such phrases as "Why are you so stupid?" and "I wish you were never born!" These parents are inflicting
    a. psychological maltreatment
    b. anxiety disorder
    c. resilience disorder
    d. institutional maltreatment

39. The child psychologist, David Elkind, concerned about the pressures on children today, coined which of the following terms?
    a. resilient child
    b. depressed child
    c. abnormal child
    d. hurried child

40. Which of the following factors seem/seems to contribute to children's resilience to stress?
    a. good relationship with parents
    b. experience solving social problems
    c. a supportive school environment and successful experiences in sports, music, or with other children
    d. all of the above

Completion

Supply the term or terms needed to complete each of the following statements.

1. Our sense of self, including our self-understanding, self-control, or self-regulation, is known as our ____________________.

2. Erikson's crisis of middle childhood is ____________ versus ______________, and its successful resolution leads to ____________________.

3. Susan Harter's theory of ________________ suggests that self-esteem comes from two major sources: how competent children think they are in various aspects of life and how much social support they receive from other people.

4. The main things that children choose to do with their time are ____________ and ____________________.

5. Racial segregation in peer groups often results from ____________________: negative attitudes toward certain groups.

6. In general, during middle childhood girls value ________________ of relationships, while boys value ____________________ of relationships.

7. The children of ______________________ parents (who guide their children by suggesting, explaining, supporting, and encouraging) are more popular than children of ___________________ parents (who criticize, command, and prohibit more).

8. Every parent struggles with the constant decisions involved in bringing up human beings who will think well of themselves, fulfill their potential, and become happy, productive people. This struggle is what __________________ is all about.

9. Middle childhood is a transitional stage of __________________, in which parent and child share power; parents continue to supervise, while children begin to exercise self-regulation.

10. Many children come through the painful experience of divorce with a basically intact ego; the ability to do this seems to be related partly to a child's own ____________________.

11. The majority of ________________ are not closely involved with their children after a divorce, but, fortunately, there are exceptions.

12. ____________________ custody--shared custody by both parents, does not seem to improve a child's situation in an amicable divorce and may worsen it in a bitter divorce.

13. An Australian report comparing rates in the mid-1980s for eight industrialized countries found that _________________ has the highest percentage of single-parent families, with the lowest rate by far in _________________.

14. Among 18,000 students in 14 states, children from one-parent homes achieved less in school; interviews with parents found that the critical factor was ____________________.

15. Mothers tend to talk more, explain more, and give more feedback to children with older _______________ than to children with older ______________, maybe because of________________ greater effectiveness with younger siblings.

16. A condition involving excessive anxiety for at least two weeks, concerning separation from people to whom the child is attached is known as _____________________.

17. An unrealistic fear that keeps children away from school which seems to have more to do with a fear of leaving the mother than a fear of the school itself is known as ___________________________.

18. In ___________________________ counseling, a therapist sees a child one-on-one to help the child gain insights into his or her personality and relationships and interpret feelings and behavior.

19. ______________________ has been broadly defined as action (or failure to act) that damages children's behavioral, cognitive, emotional, or physical functioning.

20. Children who bounce back from circumstances that would stunt the emotional development of most children are called ______________________.

ANSWERS FOR SELF-TESTS — CHAPTER 9

Multiple-Choice

		Page				Page	
1.	a	308	conceptual	21.	b	322	conceptual
2.	b	309	factual	22.	c	323	conceptual
3.	d	309	conceptual	23.	d	324	conceptual
4.	b	310	factual	24.	d	324	factual
5.	c	311	conceptual	25.	a	325	factual
6.	c	311	conceptual	26.	c	325	factual
7.	d	311	factual	27.	d	326	conceptual
8.	b	312	factual	28.	a	327	factual
9.	d	313	factual	29.	b	328	factual
10.	a	315	conceptual	30.	c	329	conceptual
11.	a	316	factual	31.	d	329	factual
12.	c	316	conceptual	32.	c	330	conceptual
13.	c	317	factual	33.	b	331	factual
14.	d	317	conceptual	34.	a	331	conceptual
15.	b	319	factual	35.	d	331	factual
16.	d	319	conceptual	36.	c	332	conceptual
17.	c	319	conceptual	37.	b	333	conceptual
18.	b	320	factual	38.	a	334	conceptual
19.	b	321	conceptual	39.	d	334	factual
20.	a	321	factual	40.	d	335	factual

Completion

		Page			Page
1.	self-concept	308	12.	joint	325
2.	industry, inferiority, competence	310	13.	the U.S.; Japan	326
3.	global self-worth	310	14.	family income	327
4.	playing, watching TV	312	15.	brothers, sisters, girls'	329
5.	prejudice	315	16.	separation anxiety disorder	331
6.	depth, number	316	17.	school phobia	331
7.	authoritative, authoritarian	317	18.	individual psycho-therapy	333
8.	discipline	319	19.	psychological maltreatment	334
9.	coregulation	320	20.	resilient	334
10.	resilience	324			
11.	fathers	325			

CHAPTER 10

Physical and Intellectual Development in Adolescence

INTRODUCTION

Chapter 10 examines the dramatic physical and intellectual development that occurs in adolescence. Physically, adolescence is a time of moving from pubescence to puberty, toward sexual and physical maturation; while intellectually this period is marked by the attainment of the ability to think abstractly.

- The chapter begins by examining the physiological changes of adolescence and the psychological impact of those changes.
- Health and nutrition are discussed, with special attention being paid to various nutrition and eating disorders.
- Current trends and various problems associated with drug use and abuse are discussed, as are sexually transmitted diseases, as they impact adolescents.
- Intellectual development is examined from the perspective of Piaget's theory, and adolescent egocentrism is discussed in detail.
- The development of moral reasoning is explored using Kohlberg's theory.
- The transition to secondary school is examined, including a discussion of some of the factors that influence that transition.
- The nature of the high school today is discussed, including an examination of home influences on high school achievement.
- The phenomenon of school drop outs is examined, culminating with a discussion of preventing dropping out.
- Finally, career planning in late adolescence is considered, with a description of the stages of vocational planning and a discussion of the influence of parents and gender on vocational planning.

CHAPTER OUTLINE

I. **Adolescence: A Developmental Transition**

PHYSICAL DEVELOPMENT

II. **Maturation in Adolescence**

A. Physical Changes
   1. Puberty and the Secular Trend
   2. The Adolescent Growth Spurt
   3. Primary Sex Characteristics
   4. Secondary Sex Characteristics
   5. Menarche

B. Psychological Impact of Physical Changes
   1. Effects of Early and Late Maturation
      a. Early and late maturation in boys
      b. Early and late maturation in girls
   2. The Relationship between Stress and the Timing of Puberty
   3. Reactions to Menarche and Menstruation
   4. Feelings about Physical Appearance

III. **Health Concerns of Adolescence**

A. Nutrition and Eating Disorders
   1. Nutritional Needs
   2. Obesity
   3. Anorexia Nervosa and Bulimia Nervosa
      a. Anorexia
      b. Bulimia
      c. Treatment for anorexia and bulimia

B. Use and Abuse of Drugs
   1. Current Trends
   2. Alcohol
   3. Marijuana
   4. Tobacco

C. Sexually Transmitted Diseases (STDs)
   1. What Are STDs?
   2. STDs and Adolescents

INTELLECTUAL DEVELOPMENT

IV. **Aspects of Intellectual Development in Adolescence**

A. Cognitive Development: Piaget's Stage of Formal Operations
   1. Cognitive Maturity: The Nature of Formal Operations
   2. Tracing Cognitive Development: The Pendulum Problem
   3. What Brings About Cognitive Maturity?
   4. Assessing Piaget's Theory

B. Adolescent Egocentrism
   1. Finding Fault with Authority Figures
   2. Argumentativeness
   3. Self-Consciousness
   4. Self-Centeredness
   5. Indecisiveness
   6. Apparent Hypocrisy
C. Moral Development: Kohlberg's Levels of Morality
   1. How Adolescents at Different Levels React to Kohlberg's Dilemmas
      a. Preconventional Level. Stage 1
      b. Stage 2
      c. Conventional Level. Stage 3
      d. Stage 4
      e. Postconventional Level. Stage 5
      f. Stage 6

V. Secondary School

A. The Transition to Junior High or High School
   1. Patterns of Transition
   2. Effects of the Transition
      a. Gender-related Causes
      b. School-related Causes
      c. Home-related Causes
B. High School Today
C. Home Influences on Achievement in High School
   1. Parent's Interest
   2. Parenting Styles
   3. Socioeconomic Status
D. Dropping Out of High School
   1. Who Drops Out?
   2. Why Do They Drop Out?
   3. What Happens to Drop Outs?
   4. How Can Dropping Out Be Prevented?

VI. Developing a Career

A. Stages in Vocational Planning
B. Influences on Vocational Planning
   1. Parents
   2. Gender

KEY TERMS

adolescence (page 342)

adolescent growth spurt (346)

anorexia nervosa (353)

bulimia nervosa (354)

ecological approach (367)

formal operations (360)

imaginary audience (363)

menarche (347)

obesity (352)

personal fable (363)

primary sex characteristics (347)

puberty (342)

secondary sex characteristics (347)

secular trend (346)

sexually transmitted diseases (STDs) (357)

LEARNING OBJECTIVES

After finishing Chapter 10, you should be able to:

1. Describe the process and characteristics of physical maturation in *adolescence*. (pp. 344-348)

2. List the *primary sex characteristics* and *secondary sex characteristics* of both boys and girls. (pp. 347)

3. Understand *menarche* and menstruation and their psychological effect. (pp. 347-348, pp. 349-350)

4. Discuss the psychological impact of physical changes and the effects of early and late maturation. (pp. 348-349)

5. Describe adolescents' concerns about physical appearance. (p. 350)

6. List the major health concerns during adolescence. (p. 351)

7. Explain the difference between various nutrition problems and eating disorders and describe their effect on teenagers. (pp. 352-354)

   a. *obesity*

   b. *anorexia nervosa*

   c. *bulimia nervosa*

8. List the drugs most commonly used by adolescents and discuss the problems of abuse for this age group. (pp. 354-357)

9. List the most common *sexually transmitted diseases* (STDs) and their effects, and describe how they are transmitted. (pp. 357-360)

10. From the list in item 9, identify which STDs are curable, which are not, and which are life-threatening. (pp. 357-360)

11. Discuss Piaget's stage of *formal operations* in cognitive development. (p. 360)

12. Describe how the solutions to the "pendulum problem" at different ages illustrate the changes in thinking associated with maturation. (pp. 360-361)

13. Describe egocentrism in the adolescent and give examples. (pp. 362-364)

14. List Kohlberg's levels of morality and provide a brief explanation of moral reasoning at each level. (pp. 364-365)

15. Describe the transition from elementary to secondary school and discuss some of the problems associated with that transition. (pp. 367-368)

16. Discuss the effects of high school on adolescents' development, and describe the influence of home and of socioeconomic status on achievement. (pp. 368-371)

17. Explain how different parenting styles may influence the school achievement of adolescents. (pp. 369-370)

18. Discuss the phenomenon of high school dropouts. (pp. 371-372)

19. Discuss career development, and the stages and influence of vocational planning. (pp. 372-375)

SUPPLEMENTAL READING

Richard M. Lerner, Ph.D., is director of the Institute for Children, Youth, and Families at Michigan State University, in East Lansing. Cheryl K. Olson, M.P.H., studies health behavior at the Harvard School of Public Health in Boston. This article is reprinted with permission from *Parents*, ©February 1994, Gruner + Jahr USA Publishing.

The Imaginary Audience: Why every preteen sees herself as the center of the world

Richard M. Lerner and Cheryl K. Olson

Thirteen-year-old Alexandra picks at her dinner, rolling the peas around her plate, not saying a word to anyone. Afterward, when her father invites her to join the rest of the family for a rental video and a bowl of popcorn, she instead barricades herself in her room.

There, overwhelmed by her feelings, she sulks and thinks about Sam, the guy who sits across from her in math class. How could he have ignored her sitting at the same table at lunch, especially when he *must* know how she feels about him? How could he *not* know? It doesn't occur to her that she has never said so much as "hello" to Sam.

Alexandra cannot imagine that anyone, ever, has felt so much or so deeply. Those who study adolescent behavior call this a "personal fable": the child's belief that she is, for better or worse, utterly different from everyone else. To a parent, such preteen--and even teenage--behavior appears self-centered, even grandiose. But it is absolutely normal and quite different from being selfish or putting on airs.

But how can you help your child get through this period of egocentrism, especially when it is frequently so difficult to communicate with her? You can start by maintaining your patience and empathy--and a good memory of your own adolescence.

By the preadolescent years, a child's emotional and mental sophistication has grown to the point that she is quite comfortable with thinking abstractly. She asks new questions: "What if I try acting like this instead?" "If I dress that way, what will happen?" Her sudden discovery of all these new alternatives is exhilarating, but with it comes profound uncertainty about making the right choices.

Within your family, your child often displays this uncertainty by questioning the house rules. Although being challenged by your preteen can be trying, remember that the question comes not out of disrespect but because, for the first time, your child envisions a range of alternatives.

At the same time that they are moving rapidly toward maturity, young teens are still in many ways children. They have a tendency to focus almost exclusively on their own ideas, feelings, and behavior. Assuming that they are as central in the thoughts of others as they are in their own, children this age often feel as if an imaginary audience is continually observing and judging everything they say, do, feel, and wear.

That's why 13-year-old Tom flushes with embarrassment and fury when his mother volunteers to chaperon a school dance. Even if he doesn't attend, he'll be humiliated because everyone will know that his mother is there. Reminded that there will be ten adult chaperons and, therefore, nine other classmates in the same boat, Tom responds, "Well, they don't care as much about what their parents do." As far as he is concerned, his own shame is uniquely awful.

Preteens tend to feel that their problems are more obvious and important than those of other people. Sally, 11, feels sure that everyone can tell she's wearing a tampon. And, 12-year-old Richard sits at his desk, head tucked into his arm, convinced that the new pimple on his cheek is the object of everyone's disgusted gaze.

The worst thing you can do when your child's outsize emotions are on display is to dismiss them. They may seem silly to you, but they are all too real to her. If she broods for days about whether she said the right thing to a boy she met at a party, or insists on a certain style of shirt, don't make fun of her or say that her worries aren't important. Doing so will only reinforce her sense that no one understands her.

Don't pooh-pooh a child's need to be accepted.

And be tolerant of the fact that, because your child feels so utterly different from everyone else, fitting in with his peers becomes a top priority in his life. Accept his need to be accepted. If he spurns your peck on his cheek as you're dropping him off at school and says, "You're embarrassing me in front of all my friends," it won't help for you to point out that no one can see inside the car.

Your wisest course of action in such cases is to talk about his concerns and to negotiate solutions that both of you can live with. For example, you might express your willingness not only to stop kissing him when you leave him at school but also to drop him off around the corner and out of sight--if he is willing to offer you a hug when he gets home. It should be added, however, that acknowledging your child's need to be part of the crowd does not require that you accept open rudeness or give in to demand for the most expensive sneakers in the shop.

You can't banish your preteen's self-consciousness, but you can help him see that although others think and care about him, they also have other things on their minds. One way to accomplish this is to share your own adolescence with him. (This is where a good memory--or a high school yearbook--can come in handy.)

Think back to your own adolescent crises. In describing to your child how embarrassed you were the time you had to take a shower after gym class or how hopelessly in love you were after your first date, you can help him understand that he is not alone in his feelings. Focus on how you felt at the time, not on how "everything worked out fine."

If your daughter is among the first girls in her class to start developing breasts, acknowledge how embarrassing that can be, and then talk about the ways that other kids in her class stand out. How might another girl feel about being the tallest or the only one with braces? Help your child see that all of her peers are different in some way, and that this difference is not necessarily bad.

Outside pursuits get kids outside themselves.

Another way that you can give your preteen a less egocentric perspective on the world is by encouraging her to be involved with a range of activities and people. Playing multiple roles in sports, joining arts groups, or even being with peers who share a hobby can shift your child's focus outside herself.

As your child gets older, she'll begin to realize that her thoughts and emotions are not as odd or unique as she once believed. Of course, most of us keep traces of our youthful egocentrism; we all feel that we're the ones who always get the parking ticket or pick the slowest line at the store. But adults have realized that their imaginary audience is just that--imaginary. Be patient; your preteen will realize it too.

Questions:

In what way is the adolescent sense of being unique associated with the willingness of many teenagers to take risks with their health and safety?

How is adolescent egocentrism, as exemplified by the imaginary audience, related to the young person's increasing reliance on peer, rather than family, influence?

SELF TESTS

Multiple-Choice

Circle the letter of the response which best completes or answers each of the following statements and questions.

1. The term puberty refers to the process that
   a. leads to sexual maturity
   b. follows the period of adolescence
   c. ends with the appearance of primary sex characteristics
   d. begins upon reaching age 13

2. Adolescence is generally considered as
   a. primarily a physical phenomenon
   b. primarily a psychological phenomenon
   c. ending with sexual maturity
   d. beginning with puberty

3. The age of the onset of puberty is most likely a result of
   a. some genetically determined limit
   b. a combination of genetic and environmental influences
   c. the influence of environmental factors
   d. an essentially random process

4. The lowering of the age when puberty begins and young people reach adult height and sexual maturity is known by the term
   a. maturational decline
   b. secular trend
   c. developmental regression
   d. sexual precocity

5. The adolescent growth spurt
   a. affects most muscles but few bones
   b. affects most bones but few muscles
   c. affects nearly all skeletal and muscular dimensions
   d. has almost no affect on skeletal or muscular dimensions

6. Characteristics directly related to reproduction are called
   a. secondary sex characteristics
   b. primary sex characteristics
   c. secular trend
   d. pubescence indicators

7. Which of these is not typically a characteristic of adolescence?
   a. spurt in physical growth
   b. tendency toward obesity
   c. appearance of pubic hair
   d. increasingly oily skin, often resulting in acne

8. Characteristics which are signs of sexual maturation, but which do not directly involve the sex organs, are called
   a. secondary sex characteristics
   b. primary sex characteristics
   c. secular trend
   d. pubescence indicators

9. On average, a girl's first menstruation--or menarche--occurs
   a. around the time that her breasts begin to develop
   b. as the first sign of the onset of puberty
   c. at the time of her first ovulation
   d. fairly late in the sequence of adolescent development

10. Which of the following statements regarding the timing of puberty is most accurate?
    a. Because of their focus on establishing an individual identity, adolescents tend to be unconcerned about late maturity.
    b. Most research concludes that boys who mature early enjoy definite advantages and few disadvantages.
    c. There are both advantages and disadvantages to early maturity for boys, as well as for boys who mature late.
    d. Girls who mature early almost always experience significant advantages over their later maturing counterparts.

11. Concern about early or late maturity and worries about weight both illustrate
    a. that the primary concern of adolescents tends to be with physical appearance
    b. the emotional instability that often accompanies adolescence
    c. the increasing importance of the secular trend
    d. the reversal of the secular trend since World War II

12. Adolescents' increasing tendency to take risks is reflected in the high death rate from
    a. sexually transmitted diseases (STDs)
    b. use of drugs, alcohol or both
    c. accidents, homicide, and suicide
    d. catastrophic illness

13. The most common health problems of adolescence include
    a. cardiovascular (i.e., heart and lung) disease
    b. cancer, especially leukemia, and blood disease
    c. hormonal abnormalities and endocrine and pituitary problems
    d. eating disorders, drug abuse, and sexually transmitted disease

14. Which of the following statements is most accurate?
    a. Most adolescents need not worry about diet and nutrition.
    b. Since they eat so much, adolescents usually receive all necessary nutrients and vitamins and minerals.
    c. The diet of many adolescents is deficient in iron, and many adolescents' diets are also deficient in calcium.
    d. Many adolescents' diets are deficient in the carbohydrates and fats needed to sustain their rapid physical growth.

15. Eating disorders tend to
    a. affect males more than females
    b. affect females more than males
    c. affect females and males in about equal proportions
    d. affect only a very small percentage of adolescents

16. Anorexia nervosa is characterized by
    a. being 20 percent over one's ideal body weight
    b. episodes of eating binges followed by self-induced vomiting
    c. compulsive and excessive eating to the point of illness
    d. obsessive dieting resulting in self-starvation

17. Bulimia is characterized by
    a. being 20 percent over one's ideal body weight
    b. episodes of eating binges followed by self-induced vomiting
    c. compulsive and excessive eating to the point of illness
    d. obsessive dieting resulting in self-starvation

18. The current use of drugs among adolescents is
    a. more prevalent than it was in the 1960s
    b. about the same as it was in the 1960s
    c. less prevalent than it was in the 1960s
    d. dramatically higher during the past decade

19. The drugs most popular with adolescents are
    a. alcohol, marijuana, and tobacco
    b. marijuana and crack
    c. cocaine and barbiturates
    d. stimulants

20. The percentage is highest for teenagers who use, or who have tried
    a. alcohol
    c. marijuana
    b. tobacco
    d. cocaine

21. Which of the following is most accurate?
    a. Girls are more likely than boys to drink every day.
    b. Most teenagers start to drink because it seems grownup.
    c. College bound teenagers drink more than those not planning to go to college.
    d. Most young people do not have their first drink until sometime after entering high school.

22. The most prevalent sexually transmitted disease is
    a. genital herpes
    c. syphilis
    b. AIDS
    d. chlamydia

23. Research evidence regarding AIDS education suggests that educating teens about sex
    a. makes them <u>more</u> sexually active
    b. makes them <u>less</u> sexually active
    c. has no effect on their sexual activity
    d. arouses their curiosity and promotes sexual experimentation

24. Worldwide, most HIV-infected adults are
    a. heterosexual
    c. bisexual
    b. homosexual
    d. hemophiliacs

25. Which of the following sexually transmitted diseases is not curable?
    a. genital herpes
    c. syphilis
    b. gonorrhea
    d. chlamydia

26. Because they are now able to think more abstractly, teenagers are more likely to
    a. accept the rules their parents establish
    b. rely more on personal experience than on possibilities in making decisions
    c. narrow the focus of their career planning
    d. think in broader terms about moral issues

27. The solutions to the "pendulum problem" at different ages illustrate that
    a. experience with an object is sufficient to allow learning to occur
    b. the level of cognitive functioning influences the problem-solving strategy
    c. learning to solve problems can occur as a result of trial and error
    d. repetition is a slow, but effective technique for solving problems

28. According to Piaget, cognitive maturity is brought about by
    a. maturation of brain structures
    b. widening social environments and hence broader experiences
    c. interaction of brain maturity and broader experiences
    d. hormonal changes that characterize adolescence

29. The highest Piagetian stage of cognitive development, often achieved in adolescence, is the __________ stage.
    a. sensorimotor
    b. preoperational
    c. concrete operations
    d. formal operations

30. Critics of Piaget's theory would point out that his ideas ignore
    a. aspects of intelligence other than mathematical/scientific reasoning
    b. the interaction between brain maturity and the widening social environment
    c. the emergence of hypothetical-deductive reasoning
    d. the adolescent's ability to think abstractly

31. Most adolescents are at which level of moral development, according to Kohlberg?
    a. morality of constraint
    b. conventional
    c. morality of cooperation
    d. postconventional

32. Which of the following statements about egocentric thinking in adolescence is most accurate?
    a. It takes the form of finding fault, argumentativeness, and self-consciousness.
    b. It takes the form of being unable to view a problem from more than one (i.e., one's own) perspective.
    c. It is almost nonexistent in adolescents, who are much more socially oriented and therefore aware of other perspectives.
    d. Although not completely absent, egocentrism is rapidly decreasing as the adolescent matures to adulthood.

33. A parent or teacher who wants to help a teenager move to a higher level of moral reasoning would be wise to
    a. provide tangible reinforcement for socially acceptable behavior
    b. set firm but fair standards for all aspects of behavior
    c. give ample opportunities to talk about, interpret, and enact moral dilemmas
    d. prohibit associations with peers who are judged to be bad influences

34. The central organizing experience of most teenagers' intellectual and social lives is
    a. the family, which provides them with adult role models
    b. their peer group
    c. their growing sense of personal identity
    d. high school

35. Teenagers who do well in school are those whose parents
    a. have allowed them complete freedom and independence
    b. who monitor their schoolwork but are uninvolved otherwise
    c. are involved with their lives, both in and outside of school
    d. who monitor their social activities but not their schoolwork

36. Which of the following statements most accurately describes the relationship between an adolescent's grades and his/her parent's level of interest?
    a. Grades are directly related to parental involvement in children's lives.
    b. Grades are inversely related to parental involvement in children's lives.
    c. Grades are minimally related to parental involvement in children's lives.
    d. Grades are not related to parental involvement in children's lives.

37. The parenting style of parents whose children get low grades is more likely to be
    a. authoritarian or permissive or one which waffles between styles
    b. authoritative, since this style offers the adolescent too much freedom
    c. consistent, since school success requires a high level of parental flexibility
    d. involved, since parental involvement removes responsibility from the teenager

38. Which of the following statements about high school dropouts is most accurate?
    a. Surprisingly, most dropouts tend to be gifted.
    b. Blacks have the highest dropout rate among ethnic groups.
    c. Most dropouts eventually reenter some educational program.
    d. Dropping out is more prevalent among young people whose parents are poorly educated.

39. With respect to the relationship between gender and career choice, which of the following statements is most accurate?
    a. Gender-typing in occupational choice is more prevalent today than ever before.
    b. Although many gender stereotypes have been broken down, gender still influences occupational choice.
    c. Gender still affects career choice, and this proves that there are innate intellectual differences between males and females.
    d. Gender stereotypes are as strong today as they ever were, but they do not seem to have any relationship to occupational choice.

40. Career planning for adolescents is
    a. primarily related to the experiences an adolescent has had and is largely unrelated to formal operational thinking
    b. mainly a matter of choosing a career that will financially support the hoped for lifestyle of the adolescent
    c. an outgrowth of high school job experiences and has little to do with the adolescent's search for identity
    d. related both to the ability to think broadly about one's future and the continuing effort to define one's self

Completion

Supply the term or terms needed to complete each of the following statements.

1. Puberty is defined as the process that leads to _____________ maturity.

2. Maturation during adolescence involves not only dramatic ____________ changes but also _______________ effects of those changes.

3. The period during which the reproductive functions mature, rapid growth occurs, the primary sex organs enlarge, and the secondary sex characteristics appear is known as _______________.

4. The tendency for the age when puberty begins to become lower over several generations is known as the ____________________ .

5. The dramatic increase in height and weight that typically occurs as an early sign of adolescent maturation is known as the __________________________ .

6. The primary sex characteristics are those that are directly related to _______________.

7. The secondary sex characteristics are physical signs of maturation that do not directly involve the ____________________.

8. In boys, the principal sign of sexual maturity is the presence of ______ in the _____.

9. A girl's first menstrual period is known as _______________.

10. Some studies have found that girls who grew up in settings characterized by family conflict tended to reach menarche ________ than those who lived in calmer settings.

11. The most common eating disorder in the United States is _______________.

12. The majority of adults, worldwide, who are HIV-infected are _____________ .

13. Piaget's highest level of intellectual development, formal operations, is characterized by the ability to think __________________.

14. Cognitive maturity emerges from the interaction between _______ maturation and the widening ________ environment.

15. The conviction that one is special and that one's own experience is unique is called the ______________________________ and is especially strong in adolescence.

16. Many adolescents behave self-consciously, as if they were being watched by a/an __________________________, an observer who exists only in their own minds and who is as concerned with their thoughts and behaviors as they are themselves.

17. Most adolescents are at Kohlberg's __________________________ level of moral development.

18. Kohlberg's theory of moral development has been criticized by some who feel that it focuses on the male-oriented dimension of morality, ____________________ and ignores the female-oriented dimension of morality, ____________________.

19. Bronfenbrenner's ________________________ approach emphasizes the interaction among the various environments in a child's life and can help us understand issues such as the transition from elementary to secondary school.

20. ______________________ is the central organizing experience in most adolescents' lives.

21. Children whose parents use a parenting style characterized as ____________ tend to do better in school than children of parents employing other styles.

22. More than half of the girls who drop out of school before graduating say they left because of ____________________________________.

23. Holding low-paying jobs, having higher risks of losing their jobs, and holding jobs requiring low-level skills are all typical of __________________.

24. Among various ethnic groups, ____________________________ have the lowest dropout rate.

25. Children's aspirations and achievement are influenced by the degree of their parents' __________________________ and _____________________ support.

26. At around the time of puberty, most adolescents are at the second stage of career development, called the ______________ period.

27. Recent studies of gender differences in mathematics performance suggest that the differences between the genders is ____________________ now than it was several decades ago.

28. Teenagers in high school who work at part-time jobs for more than 15 hours per week are ______________ likely to drop out of school than those who do not have part-time jobs.

29. Research indicates that the differences between boys and girls in ____________ ____________________ are virtually meaningless.

30. The choice of a career is closely tied with a central personality issue of adolescence: the continuing effort to define ________________.

ANSWERS FOR SELF-TESTS CHAPTER 10

Multiple-Choice

		Page				Page	
1.	a	342	factual	21.	b	356	factual
2.	d	342	factual	22.	c	357	factual
3.	b	345	cocceptual	23.	b	357	conceptual
4.	b	346	factual	24.	a	357	factual
5.	c	346	factual	25.	d	357	factual
6.	b	347	factual	26.	d	360	conceptual
7.	b	352	conceptual	27.	d	360	factual
8.	a	347	factual	28.	b	360-361	conceptual
9.	d	348	conceptual	29.	c	361	conceptual
10.	c	348-49	conceptual	30.	a	362	conceptual
11.	a	350	conceptual	31.	a	362-363	conceptual
12.	c	351	conceptual	32.	a	364	factual
13.	d	352	conceptual	33.	c	365	conceptual
14.	c	352	conceptual	34.	d	368	factual
15.	b	352	conceptual	35.	c	369	conceptual
16.	d	353	factual	36.	a	369-370	conceptual
17.	b	354	factual	37.	a	370	conceptual
18.	c	354	factual	38.	d	371	factual
19.	a	355	factual	39.	b	375	factual
20.	a	355	conceptual	40.	d	375	conceptual

Completion

		Page			Page
1.	sexual	342	16.	imaginary audience	363
2.	physical, psychological	344	17.	conventional	364
3.	puberty	344	18.	justice, care	366
4.	secular trend	346	19.	ecological	367
5.	adolescent growth spurt	346	20.	high school	368
6.	reproduction	347	21.	authoritative	370
7.	sex organs	347	22.	pregnancy or marriage	371
8.	sperm, urine	347	23.	dropouts	371
9.	menarche	347	24.	Asian Americans	372
10.	earlier	349	25.	encouragement, financial	373
11.	obesity	352	26.	tentative	373
12.	heterosexual	357	27.	smaller	375
13.	abstractly	360	28.	more	375
14.	brain, social	361	29.	verbal abilities	375
15.	personal fable	363	30.	self	375

CHAPTER 11

Personality and Social Development in Adolescence

INTRODUCTION

The search for one's identity is a major theme of adolescence, a time at which a person's physical, cognitive, emotional, and social development reach a peak. In Chapter 11 we learn that adolescence is a period of both struggle and triumph. During this eventful period, the young person's quest for individualism is influenced by several factors; in particular, the adolescent peer group and family play significant roles.

- The chapter begins with an examination of the major task of adolescence--the quest for identity, including sexual identity.
- The psychosocial task of defining identity is contrasted with the problem of identity (or role) confusion.
- The findings of recent research, which indicate that adolescence is a period during which people can be said to possess one of four identity states, are explained.
- The changing relationships between adolescents and their families and peers are described.
- Some current sexual practices and attitudes among adolescents are described, including a discussion of two persistent problems associated with adolescence: pregnancy and delinquency. Various preventive measures used by families affected by these problems are presented as well as how society, in general, tries to decrease the high rates of teenage pregnancy and juvenile delinquency.
- The chapter concludes with a discussion of the many special personality strengths possessed by adolescents. Three cohort studies are used to provide a positive view of adolescence.

CHAPTER OUTLINE

I. The Search for Identity

- A. Identity Versus Identity Confusion
- B. Research on Identity
  - 1. Identity Statuses: Crisis and Commitment
    - a. Identity achievement
    - b. Foreclosure
    - c. Identity confusion
    - d. Moratorium
  - 2. Gender Differences in Identity Formation
    - a. Research on female identity formation
    - b. Research on female self-esteem
  - 3. Ethnic Factors in Identity Formation
- C. Achieving Sexual Identity
  - 1. Studying Adolescents' Sexuality
  - 2. Sexual Attitudes and Behavior
    - a. Masturbation
    - b. Sexual orientation
      - (1) What determines sexual orientation?
      - (2) Homosexuality
      - (3) Attitudes, behavior, and the "sexual revolution"

II. Social Aspects of Personality Development in Adolescence

- A. Relationships with Parents
  - 1. An Ambivalent Relationship
  - 2. Conflict With Parents
  - 3. What Adolescents Need from Their Parents
  - 4. How Adolescents Are Affected by Their Parents' Life Situation
    - a. Parent's employment
    - b. "Self-care" adolescents
    - c. Adolescents with single parents
- B. Sibling Relationships
- C. Relationships with Peers
  - 1. How Adolescents Spend Their Time and with Whom
  - 2. Friendships in Adolescence
  - 3. Peer Pressure versus Parents' Influence
  - 4. Parents' Influence over Adolescents' Choice of Friends

III. Two Problems of Adolescence

- A. Teenage Pregnancy
  - 1. Consequences of Teenage Pregnancy
  - 2. Why Teenagers Get Pregnant?
  - 3. Who Is Likely to Get Pregnant?
  - 4. Preventing Teenage Pregnancy
  - 5. Helping Pregnant Teenagers and Teenage Parents

B. Juvenile Delinquency
   1. Personal Characteristics of Delinquents
   2. The Delinquent's Family
   3. The Influence of the Peer Group
   4. Dealing with Delinquency

IV. A Positive View of Adolescence: Three Cohort Studies

KEY TERMS

---

adolescent rebellion (page 390)

commitment (382)

crisis (382)

foreclosure (383)

heterosexual (386)

homosexual (386)

identity achievement (383)

identity diffusion (383)

identity versus identity confusion (380)

masturbation (385)

moratorium (383)

sexual orientation (386)

status offender (402)

LEARNING OBJECTIVES

After finishing Chapter 11, you should be able to:

1. Describe the psychosocial conflict of *identity versus identity confusion*. (pp. 380-381)

2. Discuss some of the ways that adolescents resolve the conflict of *identity versus identity confusion*. (pp. 380-381)

3. Describe the dangers of not being able to resolve the conflict of *identity versus identity confusion*. (p. 381)

4. Explain what is meant by the virtue of fidelity. (p. 381)

5. Name and explain the main characteristics of each of the 4 specific identity states described by James Marcia. (p. 383)

   a.
   c.
   b.
   d.

6. Describe some of the differences between males and females in the formation of identity. (pp. 383-384)

7. Describe how ethnic factors influence the formation of identity. (p. 385)

8. Discuss some of the current sexual practices and attitudes among adolescents. (pp. 385-389)

9. Briefly explain how adolescents' attitudes regarding sex differ from their actual sexual practices. (pp. 387-389)

10. Describe how the relationship between children and parents changes during adolescence. (pp. 390-391)

11. Explain how adolescents are affected by their parents' life situation. (pp. 392-394)

12. Discuss the changes in relationships with siblings during adolescence. (pp. 394-395)

13. Compare the importance of an adolescent's peer group to that of his/her family, and describe how each influences adolescents' attitudes and behaviors. (pp. 395-398)

14. Describe some of the reasons why teenagers become pregnant. (pp. 399-400)

15. Describe some of the consequences of teenage pregnancy. (p. 399)

16. Identify some of the disadvantages of being the child of a teenage parent? (p. 399)

17. Describe some of the factors that are related to the problem of juvenile delinquency. (pp. 402-404)

18. List some of the special personality strengths of adolescents. (pp. 404-405)

SUPPLEMENTAL READING

This article, reprinted with permission from the August 2, 1993 *Newsweek* magazine, was written by *Newsweek* reporter Connie Leslie with assistance from Nina Biddle, Debra Rosenberg, and Joe Wayne.

Girls Will Be Girls

Connie Leslie, with Nina Biddle, Debra Rosenberg, and Joe Wayne

It's not just boys. In San Antonio, Texas, recently, a 13-year-old girl allegedly beat and then held down another girl while police say several boys sexually assaulted her. In New Orleans, a 16-year-old schoolgirl pulled out a six-inch kitchen knife and plunged it into a classmate's back. On the streets of Los Angeles and New York, some girls carry small guns in their purses and razor blades in their mouths, in case they need to protect themselves--or find a victim ripe for the taking.

The plague of teen violence is an equal-opportunity scourge. Crime by girls is on the rise, or so various jurisdictions report. In Massachusetts, for instance, 15 percent of the crimes that girls were convicted of committing in 1987 were violent offenses. By 1991, that number had soared to 38 percent. In California, judges send the "hard core" girls to the Youth Authority's Ventura School. "You name the crime, we have it; you think about the worst scenarios and we have them here," says Edward Cue, a school official.

For some girls, the best defense is a good offense. "I've had fights with a lot of guys," say Laura Morales, a South End, Boston, youth. Years ago, she concedes, a girl might have to call a brother or a cousin to fight her battles. Today, says Morales, "If I have to take care of something, I'll do it by myself." A third-grade New Orleans girl recently took a .357 magnum to school to protect herself from a boy who was allegedly harassing her. After police confiscated the gun, she claimed that her complaints to the school officials had gone unheeded.

Girls are breaking into the traditionally male world of gangs, too. The Kings, one of San Antonio's largest gangs, recently started accepting young women. Where gang members used to refer to the girls as "hos and bitches," says Sgt. Kyle Coleman of the Bexar County Sheriff's Department Gang Unit, they're a little more reluctant now as those female gang members start to equal them in fights and drive-by shootings. Girls join gangs for a variety of reasons: protection, fun, because they like a particular boy, or for acceptance. The gangs also provide a makeshift family. Some teens will do anything to join. In one initiation rite in San Antonio, girls are kicked and beaten by half a dozen gang members.

In Boston, the two biggest female gangs are every bit as ruthless as the boys'. "They're shooting, stabbing, and they're into drug sales and stickups," says Tracy Litthcut, manager for the Boston Streetworkers violence-intervention program. In New York City, not only are packs of boys "whirlpooling," or surrounding girls in public swimming pools and molesting them, but groups of girls are attacking other female swimmers as well. "I've been amazed at the brutality of the beatings of girls by other girls," says Dr. Naftali Berrill, director of the New York Forensic Mental Health Group. The violence is a vicious, antisocial pack mentality aimed at a target who is incapable of fighting back, say Berrill. The pack smells weakness, and the situation turns into a free-for-all where no individual person feels responsible.

Social agencies haven't learned much about curbing violence among young women. The police and social workers know only how to worry about whether the girls are pregnant, says Franklin Tucker, director of the Barron Assessment Counseling Center, where students from Boston schools are sent if they are caught with a weapon on school grounds. "These young girls are very angry and very hostile," he says.

They have their reasons--some good, some not. Sheri Pasanen, a San Diego social worker, was caught short recently when she was showing the movie "Thelma and Louise" to a group of jailed young and older women. "When they shot the (attempted rapist), the whole class cheered," she says. The problem, says Pasanen, is that their reaction was reasonable. "Every single one of them in there has probably been abused." But if violence is learned behavior, it can also be unlearned. And these inmates now have some time to work on that lesson.

Questions:

How is the violent delinquency described in this article similar to and/or different from the violent behavior of male delinquents?

How is gang membership related to adolescents' search for identity?

SELF TESTS

Multiple-Choice

Circle the letter of the response which best completes or answers each of the following statements and questions.

1. The chief task of adolescence is to resolve the conflict of
   a. intimacy versus isolation
   b. industry versus inferiority
   c. generativity versus stagnation
   d. identity versus identity confusion

2. Erik Erikson characterizes the adolescent's effort to make sense of the world as a
   a. voyage begun during puberty and ending when the individual becomes an adult
   b. kind of maturational malaise
   c. vital process that contributes to adult ego strength
   d. temporary departure from the smooth process of psychosocial development

3. Fidelity, during adolescence, can be thought of as
   a. a dysfunctional sense of loyalty
   b. an expression of identity confusion which produces a fear of change
   c. an extensively developed sense of trust
   d. an expression of the emerging sense of generativity

4. According to Erikson the fundamental "virtue" that arises from the identity crisis is
   a. fidelity
   c. love
   b. empathy
   d. faith

5. The work of James Marcia related to identity is most accurately characterized as
   a. the basis for the main ideas embodied in Erikson's theory
   b. a refutation of Erikson's theory based on the work of Piaget
   c. an expansion and clarification of Erikson's theory
   d. a behavioristic challenge to most of Erikson's ideas

6. Most psychologists today would probably hold the view that
   a. most differences between males and females are a result of biology
   b. most differences between males and females are a result of socialization
   c. most differences between males and females are artifacts of researcher bias
   d. there are, in reality, no psychological differences between males and females

7. Carlos has resolved a fundamental identity crisis and is in the status of identity achievement. Which of the following is most likely to "resemble" Carlos?
   a. Sabrina, who is struggling with a crisis with her parents and appears headed for commitment
   b. Alicia, who has avoided commitments and not had any crises with her parents
   c. Renee, who has made commitments by accepting her parent's expectations
   d. Rhonda, who has not experienced a crisis nor has she made any commitments

8. People who exhibit commitments and a passive acceptance of other people's plan for their lives are said to be in which identity state?
   a. identity achievement
   b. foreclosure
   c. identity diffusion
   d. moratorium

9. A person in the status of identity diffusion exhibits which of the following elements?
   a. commitment based on crisis resolution
   b. commitment without having experienced a crisis
   c. no commitment but experiencing a crisis
   d. no commitment and no crisis

10. Research suggests that identity and intimacy
   a. develop sequentially for women, with identity developing first
   b. develop together for women
   c. are mutually exclusive for men
   d. develop similarly for both men and women

11. Which of the following statements is true?
   a. Intimacy appears to be more important for girls than for boys.
   b. Intimacy appears to be more important for boys than for girls.
   c. Intimacy is relatively unimportant for both boys and girls before age 16.
   d. Intimacy is of major importance for both boys and girls, even in childhood.

12. Research suggests that ethnic factors such as skin color and physical features
   a. are unrelated to adolescent identity formation
   b. are very important in the formation of a person's self-concept
   c. are more important for identity formation of girls than of boys
   d. have little or no bearing on the development of self-concept

13. Perceiving one's self as a sexual being is
   a. an important part of identity formation
   b. unrelated to identity formation
   c. a diversion from the pressures associated with identity formation
   d. an obstruction to the development of identity

14. Adolescents engage in sexual activity in order to
    a. keep up with their peers
    b. prove their maturity
    c. experience physical pleasure
    d. all of the above

15. Research studies of teenage sexual behavior
    a. demonstrate conclusively that teen sexual activity is increasing
    b. suggest that trends over time indicate changes in sexual mores.
    c. indicate that girls are more sexually active, but boys are becoming less so
    d. are largely useless due to the methodological problems of studying this topic

16. Although most educators stress that masturbation is normal and healthy,
    a. many psychologists and physicians argue that it retards sexual maturation
    b. it actually interferes with learning how to give pleasure to others
    c. new research indicates that it can cause long-lasting physical harm
    d. many teenagers regard it as shameful

17. Which view of the specific causes of homosexuality has received the most support?
    a. Interaction of biological and environmental events is crucial in determining a person's sexual preference.
    b. Homosexuality is a specific mental disorder.
    c. Genetic factors create homosexual tendencies.
    d. A chance homosexual encounter at a critical period determines homosexuality.

18. Research on attitudes towards sexual activity reveals that
    a. men hold no double standard, but women hold themselves to a higher standard regarding sexual activity than they hold men
    b. both men and women consider it more immoral for a woman to have many sexual partners than for a man to do so
    c. women hold no double standard, but men hold women to a higher standard regarding sexual activity than they hold men
    d. the so-called "double standard" for men and women is dead

19. The attitudes and values of most teenagers have been shown to be
    a. consistent with responsible sexual conduct
    b. incompatible with sexual responsibility
    c. consistent with the actual sexual behavior in which they engage
    d. reflective of the general erosion of moral and sexual responsibility

20. Compared to those who are afraid to talk about sex with their parents, teenagers who are comfortable discussing sexual matters with their parents
    a. have a better chance of achieving a mature sexual identity
    b. are just as likely to succumb to the influence of the media which promotes sexual promiscuity
    c. are more likely to accept the idea of premarital, unprotected sex
    d. are more likely to have multiple sexual partners

21. The belief that teenagers and their parents do not like each other and do not get along with each other is most accurately classified as
    a. an unfortunate fact
    b. a finding of an overwhelming body of research
    c. a pervasive myth
    d. a universal truth

22. Most conflicts between teenagers and their parents are about
    a. mundane matters like schoolwork, chores, and dating
    b. philosophical, social, and moral issues like war, social justice, and poverty
    c. economic issues
    d. religious and political values

23. The pattern of adolescent-parent conflict typically
    a. increases during early adolescence, decreases during middle adolescence, and increases again after age eighteen
    b. increases during early adolescence, stabilizes during middle adolescence, and decreases after about age eighteen
    c. increases steadily throughout adolescence, reaching a peak at around the end of high school
    d. starts at a high level early and then steadily decreases as the adolescent matures

24. According to research studies on the effect of their parent's life situation,
    a. adolescents are unaffected, since their search for identity leads them to respond to peer influences, rather than family influences
    b. divorce, both parents working outside of the home, and the death of a parent all increase the likelihood of adjustment problems among adolescents
    c. divorce, both parents working outside of the home, and the death of a parent all lead to increased independence and earlier maturity among adolescents
    d. the relationship between their parent's life situation and adolescents' adjustment is not clear and needs to be researched further

25. Adolescents' relationships with their siblings
    a. deteriorate noticeably as the adolescent is influenced by hormonal factors
    b. usually do not change from the basic patterns that were established earlier
    c. tend to change as they try to find an identity beyond their family
    d. improve noticeably as adolescents become more adult-like in their perspective

26. During adolescence, which of the following would probably be most important in forming a friendship?
    a. similarity
    b. dissimilarity
    c. egocentricity
    d. identity status

27. Adolescents who have close friendships
    a. are low in self-esteem
    b. consider themselves competent
    c. do poorly in school
    d. consider themselves not competent

28. Peers have more influence than parents on teenagers' decisions about
    a. moral dilemmas
    b. what job to take
    c. everyday social issues
    d. what education to pursue

29. Research indicates that parents of adolescents
    a. have lost any leverage they ever had over their children's choice of friends
    b. exert a "reverse" influence over their children's choice of friends
    c. actually gain in the influence they have over their children's choice of friends
    d. exert considerable indirect influence over their children's choice of friends

30. Teenage mothers are less likely to
    a. have repeat pregnancies
    b. have money troubles
    c. finish high school
    d. receive public assistance

31. What is the primary reason given when adolescents are asked why they do not use an effective method of birth control?
    a. They didn't expect to have intercourse.
    b. They lack information.
    c. Contraception makes sex less enjoyable.
    d. They want to get pregnant.

32. Which of the following characterizes girls who are likely to use effective birth control?
    a. low grades
    b. not active in sports
    c. not active in other activities
    d. have career aspirations

33. How did the babies of those mothers who received parental training differ from the infants whose mothers received no training?
    a. They weighed more.
    b. They had more advanced motor skills
    c. They were hyperactive.
    d. both a and b

34. Which of the following could result in the classification as a status offender?
    a. commit robbery
    b. being sexually active
    c. commit rape
    d. commit murder

35. Which of the following is most accurate?
    a. Teenagers commit proportionally fewer crimes against property.
    b. Girls are more likely to get into trouble than boys.
    c. Teenagers commit proportionally more crimes.
    d. Boys and girls are equally likely to commit crimes.

36. The strongest predictor of juvenile delinquency is
    a. the socioeconomic status of the family
    b. a history of physical and sexual abuse or neurological and psychiatric problems
    c. the level of the parents' education
    d. the family's supervision and discipline of children

37. Analysis of police and court records indicates that
    a. adolescent misbehavior is a good predictor of adult criminality
    b. few people report having engaged in adolescent misbehavior, but many commit crimes as adults
    c. most adolescent misbehavior is committed by the same relatively small group of individuals
    d. most people report having engaged in adolescent misbehavior, yet few ever commit crimes as adults

38. Studies of adolescents during the past three decades indicate that
    a. adolescence has become more difficult, and few adolescents "enjoy life"
    b. there has been a steady decline in the quality of life during adolescence
    c. most adolescents are happy and "enjoy life"
    d. adolescence is a period of great "storm and stress" for most teenagers

39. Research suggests that the idea that adolescence is a period of rebellion, disturbance, and alienation is
    a. actually understated
    b. generally accurate
    c. probably exaggerated
    d. increasingly true

40. Overall, what percentage of the teenage population experiences real problems during adolescence?
    a. 10 percent
    b. 20 percent
    c. 30 percent
    d. 40 percent

Completion

Supply the term or terms needed to complete each of the following statements.

1. According to Erikson, the chief task of adolescence is to resolve the conflict of ____________________ versus __________________________.

2. By ______________, James Marcia means a period of conscious decision making, and he defines ____________ as a personal investment in an occupation or a system of beliefs.

3. According to Marcia, a person who has gone through a crisis and has made sincere commitment to his or her beliefs would be categorized as __________________.

4. A person who has made a commitment without crisis is in the status of ______________________.

5. The status of __________________ is used in reference to people who are in a crisis without having made any serious commitments.

6. According to Gilligan, the female definition of self is less concerned with achieving a separate identity than establishing ______________ with other people.

7. Research shows that both boys and girls experience a drop in their sense of self-worth, but that the drop is more pronounced for __________.

8. In comparing the self-esteem of girls of different races, research indicates that ______ African American girls were confident in high school, compared to white and Hispanic girls.

9. ______________________ is the first sexual experience for most people, and is almost universal.

10. Being a homosexual or heterosexual is referred to as __________________.

11. A person who is affectionally interested in members of the other sex is a ________ ____________________.

12. A person who is affectionally interested in members of the same sex is a __________ ______________.

13. The prevailing view today is that sexual orientation is influenced by the interaction of both ________________ and _________________ events.

14. The code that gives males more sexual freedom than females is referred to as the _________________________.

15. Many adolescents hold attitudes and values consistent with __________________ sexual conduct.

16. The storm and stress often associated with the teenage years are called ____________ ______________________.

17. Discord between parents and adolescents generally ________________ during early adolescence, ________________ during middle adolescence, and ______________ after the young person is about 18 years of age.

18. The style of parenting that seems to provide the right balance between providing parental protectiveness and allowing teenagers independence is the ________________ ____________ style.

19. By and large, adolescents who do not live with their ____________ run a greater risk of giving into peer pressure and getting into trouble.

20. Research suggests that, as children grow older, their relationships with siblings become more __________________ and more ________________ .

21. Adolescents tend to choose friends who are ___________________________ .

22. Teenage mothers are twice as likely as older mothers to bear _____________ babies.

23. A leading cause of teenage pregnancy is not using ________________ .

24. In a teenage pregnancy, the ____________ is often left with the financial and emotional burden of child rearing.

25. The ________________________ is a young person who has been truant, has run away from home, has been sexually active, or has done something else that is ordinarily not considered criminal--except when done by a minor.

26. Stealing, lying, truancy, and __________________________ are all important predictors of delinquency.

27. __________________________ is the poorest predictor of delinquency.

28. The strongest predictor of delinquency is the family's supervision and ______________ of the children.

29. Most adolescents ______________ their "wild oats" as they become more mature.

30. According to research studies, the _____________ serves as adolescent's first line of psychological defense.

ANSWERS FOR SELF-TESTS — CHAPTER 11

Multiple-Choice

		Page	
1.	d	380	factual
2.	a	380	factual
3.	c	381	conceptual
4.	a	381	factual
5.	c	382	conceptual
6.	b	383	conceptual
7.	c	383	conceptual
8.	b	383	factual
9.	d	383	conceptual
10.	b	384	conceptual
11.	a	384	factual
12.	b	385	conceptual
13.	a	385	conceptual
14.	d	385	factual
15.	b	385	conceptual
16.	d	386	conceptual
17.	a	386	conceptual
18.	b	387	conceptual
19.	a	388	factual
20.	a	389	conceptual
21.	c	390	conceptual
22.	a	391	factual
23.	b	391	factual
24.	d	392	conceptual
25.	c	394	conceptual
26.	a	397	factual
27.	b	397	factual
28.	c	398	factual
29.	d	398	factual
30.	c	399	factual
31.	a	399	factual
32.	d	400	factual
33.	d	402	factual
34.	b	402	factual
35.	c	402	conceptual
36.	d	403	factual
37.	d	404	conceptual
38.	c	404	conceptual
39.	c	404	conceptual
40.	b	405	factual

Completion

		Page
1.	identity; identity confusion	380
2.	crisis; commitment	382
3.	identity achievement	383
4.	foreclosure	383
5.	moratorium	383
6.	relationships	383
7.	girls	384
8.	more	385
9.	masturbation	385
10.	sexual orientation	386
11.	heterosexual	386
12.	homosexual	386
13.	biological; environmental	386
14.	double standard	387
15.	responsible	388
16.	adolescent rebellion	389
17.	increases, stabilizes, decreases	391
18.	authoritative	392
19.	fathers	393
20.	egalitarian, distant	394
21.	already like them	397
22.	low birthweight	399
23.	contraception	399
24.	mother	400
25.	status offender	402
26.	poor achievement in school	402
27.	socioeconomic status	402
28.	discipline	403
29.	outgrow	404
30.	family	404

CHAPTER 12

Physical and Intellectual Development in Young Adulthood

INTRODUCTION

Chapter 12 examines the physical and intellectual development which occurs in young adulthood, from about 20 to 40 years of age.

- The chapter begins with a discussion of the general physical condition of young adults and how sensory and psychomotor functioning reach their peak in this period.
- Health issues especially pertinent to young adults are addressed, with emphasis on factors that influence the health and fitness of people in this age category.
- Aspects of intellectual development are reviewed, with an explanation of how intellectual functioning continues to develop into the adult years.
- Theoretical approaches useful in describing cognitive development during this period are discussed, and the development of morality during young adulthood is examined.
- The college experience as a part of the life of many young adults is considered and the relationship between college and career decisions and intellectual functioning are explored.
- The chapter concludes with an exploration of career development and how age and gender influence a person's satisfaction with work.

CHAPTER OUTLINE

PHYSICAL DEVELOPMENT

I. Sensory and Psychomotor Functioning

II. Health in Young Adulthood

- A. Health Status
- B. Influences on Health and Fitness
  - 1. Diet
    - a. Diet and weight
    - b. Diet and cholesterol
    - c. Diet and cancer
  - 2. Exercise
  - 3. Smoking
  - 4. Alcohol
  - 5. Indirect Influences on Health
    - a. Socioeconomic factors
    - b. Education
    - c. Gender
    - d. Biological differences
    - e. Behavioral and attitudinal differences
    - f. Marital status

INTELLECTUAL DEVELOPMENT

III. Adult Thought: Theoretical Approaches

- A. K. Warner Schaie: Stages of Cognitive Development
- B. Robert Sternberg: Three Aspects of Intelligence
- C. Beyond Jean Piaget: Postformal Thought

IV. Adult Moral Development

- A. How Does Experience Affect Moral Judgments?
- B. Are There Gender Differences in Moral Development?

V. College

- A. Who Goes to College?
- B. Intellectual Growth in College
- C. Gender Differences in Achievement in College
- D. Leaving College

VI. Starting a Career

- A. Work and Age
  - 1. How Young Adults Feel About Their Jobs
  - 2. How Young Adults Perform on the Job
- B. Work and Gender

KEY TERMS

achieving stage (page 420)

acquisitive stage (420)

componential element (421)

contextual element (421-422)

executive stage (420)

experiential element (421)

postformal thought (422-423)

premenstrual syndrome (419)

reintegrative stage (420)

responsible stage (420)

tacit knowledge (422)

LEARNING OBJECTIVES

After finishing Chapter 12, you should be able to:

1. Describe the sensory and psychomotor functioning of a typical young adult. (pp. 410-411)

2. Discuss health during young adulthood, including the factors that influence health and fitness. (pp. 411-420)

3. List some of the factors that indirectly influence young adult health. (pp. 417-420)

4. Describe the specific things an individual can do to improve his or her health. (pp. 411-420)

5. Describe the relationship between socioeconomic factors and health. (pp. 417-418)

6. Explain how good health is related to an individual's level of education. (p. 418)

7. Discuss some of the factors that account for health and death rate differences in men and women. (p. 418)

8. Describe the intellectual development and functioning of young adults. (pp. 420-423)

9. Describe Schaie's five stages of cognitive development. (pp. 420-421)

10. Describe the three aspects of intelligence formulated by Sternberg. (pp. 421-422)

11. Describe the characteristics of mature, or *postformal thought*. (pp. 422-423)

12. Describe Kohlberg's theory of moral development as it applies to young adults. (pp. 423-424)

13. Discuss the issue of possible gender differences in moral development. (pp. 424-425)

14. Explain who goes, and who does not go, to college. (p. 426)

15. Describe how the college experience affects intellectual growth. (pp. 426-427)

16. Discuss how the college experience differs for men and women. (p. 427)

17. Summarize some of the implications of leaving college, both permanently and temporarily. (p. 428)

18. Describe how a person's age, or stage of life, affects the way he or she thinks about work. (pp. 428-430)

19. Discuss the relationship between work and gender. (pp. 430-431)

SUPPLEMENTAL READING

"Baby buster" Brian Steinberg, who was recently hired as a clerk at the Washington, D.C. bureau of *The New York Times*, blasts his elders, who think he should just work harder. This article is reprinted with permission from the March 11, 1994 issue of *USA Weekend*.

Me and My Work Ethic

Brian Steinberg

Imagine my surprise during a recent job interview when I was told that my generation lacked any sort of work ethic. Wasn't my presence there evidence enough of my desire to join the working world, jump-start my career? Weren't my degrees from the top schools proof of my willingness to put my nose to the grindstone? Oh, what is to become of me and so many others facing the same situation?

Now, no doubt, is the time when many of you reading this will shake your noggins and respond with a sympathetic click of the tongue, or perhaps a hushed "That poor sap."

Others, however, will conclude that this is just another sad tale of woe from a member of that hip-but-oh-so-sorrowful Generation X. A real honest-to-goodness slacker! A twentynothing. Both responses stink, and I'll tell you why.

As for the first, sympathy and pity don't help me and thousands like me get the sort of job we're looking for--a job demanding education and enthusiasm, rather than the ability to warm a seat.

As for the second, there's no such thing as "Generation X." Although I'm 24, I don't consider myself a slacker, or a buster, or any of those terms used to pigeonhole so conveniently America's younger generation. Frankly, I prefer a hipper, more esoteric term: "unemployed."

That's right. Just like so many, I'm out of work. No crime in that. But I know many people think workers my age are a special case--unwilling to commit to a job, stay till it's done, start at the bottom. So I spoke with someone who knows all about the work habits of America's supposed "Lost Generation." Bruce Steinberg (no relation) is spokesman for the National Association of Temporary Services. He ought to know something about us; after all, dead-end temp jobs that utilize roughly a hundredth (if even that) of our college training basically are all we get.

More than half of temporary workers are twentysomethings, Steinberg told me; 28 percent are 16 to 24 years old. "The whole generation has been much maligned," he said. Companies are much more finicky about their full-time hires today. But younger workers have a better grasp of new office technology, he said. And he suggested that businesses value temp workers for their industriousness and flexibility.

You see, we're valued--and this in jobs we hate and take only to pay the monthly rent.

I think you'll find that my generation will work pretty darn hard--if it gets a chance. I decided to test my theory with a few former classmates of mine from Yale.

"Why would you assume that you can define an entire generation as aimless or just drifting?" asks Phil Cohen, 24, a third-year medical student in New Jersey who seriously considered taking time off before pursuing higher education. He didn't. "[Our generation often] doesn't want to invest too much energy down one path, because it ends up being a brick wall."

Twenty-five-year-old Donna Tiburzi is another example of a hard worker. She works in a woman's shelter 48 hours a week and puts in more hours at a bookstore.

"I'm loaded with skills, a veritable bounty for any employer. Yet here I am, pounding the pavement," says 24-year-old Brad Peniston, who is fluent in Russian and proficient in all sorts of computer technology. He's working temp jobs until he can land the job he wants in foreign policy or journalism.

"A slacker is someone who hasn't done anything, and I've accomplished things," says Mark Santangelo, 25, who just moved to Washington, D.C., after working as director of constituent services for a New York City councilman.

All of these people are college graduates; all of them hope to make a difference with what they do. Does "slacker' still apply?

Look, this whole mistake isn't necessarily your fault. You gathered round the media campfire like everyone else and listened to all those scary tales of youth gone wrong. All you ever hear about are kids who don't want to work or seem to lack direction.

The "slacker" really turns out to be over-educated, hungry and filled to the brim with cynicism after being shut out for so long.

It's going to be generational warfare out there, folks, because there are no "slackers." Instead, there is a legion of smart, driven workers-to-be with ambitions that know no end. And guess what: They won't pay your Social Security next decade. And they will gladly take your job--and do it better, to boot.

<u>Questions</u>:

Explain how the attitudes reflected in this article are consistent with, or not consistent with the attitudes of typical young adults toward work, as described in the textbook.

How are the attitudes expressed in this article likely to affect the author's job performance and attitudes toward work?

SELF TESTS

Multiple-Choice

Circle the letter of the response which best completes or answers each of the following statements and questions.

1. The peak of muscular strength occurs sometime around
   a. 18 to 24 years of age
   b. 25 to 30 years of age
   c. 30 to 35 years of age
   d. 36 to 40 years of age

2. Which of the following statements is most accurate?
   a. The senses are still improving during young adulthood.
   b. The senses have begun imperceptibly to decline during young adulthood.
   c. The senses are at their sharpest during young adulthood.
   d. Most people notice a decline in sensory functioning during young adulthood.

3. In general, in the United States,
   a. young adulthood is the healthiest age category
   b. young adulthood is a health risky period because of the many career and other life changes that typically occur at this time
   c. young adulthood is characterized by a noticeable deterioration in health status
   d. young adulthood is when the poor health consequences of adolescent risky behaviors become evident

4. Gender, race, and ethnicity have been shown to be
   a. unrelated to death rates of young adults, who are uniformly healthy
   b. only marginally related to health risks and death rates of young adults
   c. related to the causes of death, but unrelated to death rates of young adults
   d. significantly related to death rates and causes of death among young adults

5. Health is defined by the World Health Organization as
   a. the extent to which a person feels physically able to perform everyday tasks
   b. the extent to which a person is free from disease or infirmity
   c. a state of complete physical, mental, and social well-being
   d. the ability of a person to recover from disease or injury

6. The risk of becoming overweight is
   a. relatively low during young adulthood because young adults are so active
   b. highest from ages 25 to 34, making young adults a prime target for prevention
   c. highest after age 35 as most young adults adopt a more sedentary lifestyle
   d. lowest during young adulthood since the metabolism of young adults is so high

7. The link between heart disease and cholesterol levels in the blood
   a. has been definitively established
   b. has been suggested, but is not generally accepted in the medical community
   c. has been minimized by the discovery of new medicines
   d. is indirect and only weakly supported by research

8. The most important determinant of blood cholesterol levels seems to be
   a. heredity and the genetic predisposition of some people to produce cholesterol
   b. the ability of the body to produce certain cholesterol blocking enzymes
   c. the kind and amount of food that a person eats
   d. the amount of exercise that a person gets

9. Research on the effect of exercise reveals that
   a. regular exercise produces a wide variety of health benefits
   b. moderate exercise produces little benefit, but strenuous exercise is beneficial
   c. exercise makes people feel better, but has little effect on death rates
   d. those who exercise strenuously as adults actually increase their health risk

10. Passive smoke
    a. may be annoying to some people, but is generally not a threat to health
    b. is a leading preventable cause of death in the United States today
    c. is harmful to children, but the risk diminishes completely by adulthood
    d. is thought to be harmful, but there is no research evidence to support that view

11. Which of the following statements is the most accurate, regarding factors that indirectly influence the health of young adults?
    a. The apparent relationship between education and health is really just further evidence of the relationship between income and health.
    b. The general availability of medical resources for treatment of people of low income has virtually eliminated any relationship between income and health.
    c. People with low income, if they are well educated, are every bit as healthy as people with high income.
    d. Income and education are positively related to health; the higher a person's income and level of education, the healthier that person tends to be.

12. Research on the relationship between gender and health
    a. suggests that women are healthier and tend to live longer than men
    b. is not clear, since much of the research did not include women in the studies
    c. indicates that although men tend to live longer than women, they have more health problems during their lifespans
    d. concludes that there are no health differences between men and women

13. Premenstrual syndrome (PMS) is a disorder characterized by
    a. emotional instability and physical weakness
    b. mental confusion and physical lethargy
    c. physical discomfort and emotional tension
    d. emotional instability without any physical symptoms

14. Research about PMS indicates that the cause for this condition is
    a. primarily psychological, and can be effectively treated by counseling
    b. mostly related to diet, and can be treated by limiting protein in the diet
    c. unknown, but may be related to hormonal and biochemical changes
    d. *dysmenorrhea*, the contractions of the uterus which cause menstrual cramping

15. Gender differences in health and longevity
    a. provide clear evidence for the primacy of biological factors in influencing the health of young adults
    b. are most likely due to the considerable hormonal and biochemical differences between adult women and men
    c. offer convincing counter-arguments to those who claim that environmental and lifestyle factors are significant influences on health
    d. are, to some extent, probably influenced by differences between men and women in their attitudes toward health and health issues

16. Recent research about adult patterns and styles of thinking
    a. indicates that adult thinking is no different from adolescent thinking, other than that adults have had more experiences than adolescents
    b. supports the commonly held view that adults think differently from children and adolescents
    c. suggests that adult thinking is remarkably similar to the thinking style of children who are in the early and middle elementary school years
    d. contradicts the commonly held view that adults think differently from children and adolescents

17. In which of K. Warner Schaie's stages are information and skills learned for their own sake, without regard to context?
    a. reintegrative
    b. executive
    c. acquisitive
    d. responsible

18. In which of Schaie's stages are people more selective about the tasks on which they choose to expend time and more concerned about the purpose of what they do?
    a. reintegrative
    b. executive
    c. acquisitive
    d. responsible

19. In which of K. Warner Schaie's stages do people need to integrate complex information on a number of levels?
    a. reintegrative
    b. executive
    c. acquisitive
    d. responsible

20. In which of K. Warner Schaie's stages are people concerned with long-range goals and practical problems?
    a. reintegrative
    b. executive
    c. acquisitive
    d. responsible

21. Which of Sternberg's aspects of intelligence refers to how people approach novel and familiar tasks?
    a. achieving
    b. experiential
    c. contextual
    d. componential

22. Which of Sternberg's aspects of intelligence refers to how efficiently people process and analyze information?
    a. achieving
    b. experiential
    c. contextual
    d. componential

23. Which of Sternberg's aspects of intelligence refers to how people deal with their environment?
    a. achieving
    b. experiential
    c. contextual
    d. componential

24. The kind of intelligence that is typically measured on psychometric tests is known as
    a. theoretical
    b. componential
    c. experiential
    d. contextual

25. A component of practical intelligence that involves such things as knowing how to win a promotion or cut through red tape is called
    a. tacit knowledge
    b. academic knowledge
    c. intuitive knowledge
    d. concrete knowledge

26. The kind of intelligence that relies on subjectivity and intuition is called
    a. formal thought
    b. postformal thought
    c. concrete operational thought
    d. sensorimotor thought

27. Moral judgments in adulthood are often based on
    a. theory
    b. experience
    c. research
    d. intuition

28. Which of the following statements about the relationship between the stage of cognitive development and the stage of moral development is more accurate?
    a. The moral stage sets the upper limit for the cognitive stage.
    b. The moral stage sets the lower limit for the cognitive stage.
    c. The cognitive stage sets the upper limit for the moral stage.
    d. The cognitive stage sets the lower limit for the moral stage.

29. Findings from research studies on moral decision making among adults suggest that
    a. there are differences in the levels of moral development achieved by men and women, and these differences generally favor women
    b. men tend to compromise their moral values more readily than do women at a comparable stage of cognitive and moral development
    c. women tend to compromise their moral values more readily than do men at a comparable stage of cognitive and moral development
    d. men and women seem to look at moral issues in different ways, to define morality differently, and to base their moral decisions on different values

30. Carol Gilligan, arguing that Kohlberg's theory does not address the way women think about moral issues, holds that, with respect to reasoning about moral issues,
    a. men think more in terms of fairness while women consider responsibility to specific people
    b. women think more in terms of fairness while men consider responsibility to specific people
    c. men think more in concrete, specific terms while women think in more general, abstract terms
    d. men seem to advance through the stages of moral development at a slightly slower rate than women of equal cognitive ability

31. Research on intellectual development during college found that students showed
    a. improvement in reasoning from the first to the fourth year of college
    b. initial improvement in reasoning, with the gains being lost by graduation
    c. a gradual decrease in reasoning from the first to the fourth year of college
    d. no change in reasoning ability during the college years

32. Interviews of Harvard and Radcliffe students during their undergraduate years found that students' thinking changed from
    a. rigidity to flexibility, and ultimately back to a more rigid style
    b. flexibility to rigidity, and ultimately to conformity to parents' values
    c. flexibility to rigidity, and ultimately back to a more flexible style
    d. rigidity to flexibility, and ultimately to freely chosen commitments

33. Studies of women in college showed that
    a. girls--who outshone boys in elementary and high school--often slipped behind the boys academically in college
    b. girls--who outshone boys in elementary and high school--continued to outshine them academically in college
    c. although women no longer performed better than men in college, their self-esteem and career aspirations were higher
    d. there were no noticeable differences between women and men by the time they had completed the first year of college

34. The reasons people give for leaving, or dropping out of college are
    a. usually the same as those given for dropping out of high school
    b. typically related to lack of confidence in their ability to do the work
    c. varied, including: marriage, dissatisfaction, and a change in occupational status
    d. usually attempts to hide the fact that their school work was unsatisfactory

35. Studies show that younger workers (those under age 40) are
    a. more satisfied with their jobs than any other age group
    b. more committed to their employers than they will be later
    c. less likely than older workers to change jobs
    d. less satisfied with their jobs than they will be later

36. The relationship between work and other aspects of development can best be characterized by stating that work
    a. is affected by intellectual, physical, social and emotional factors; and work can affect every other area of a person's life
    b. is clearly affected by intellectual, physical, social and emotional factors; but work seems to have little effect on other areas of a person's life
    c. is rarely affected by intellectual, physical, social and emotional factors; but work can have a significant affect on other areas of a person's life
    d. can easily be separated from other aspects of a person's life, especially if the person is well adjusted to begin with

37. Younger workers, compared to older workers, are more concerned with
    a. the friendliness of supervisors
    b. the friendliness of coworkers
    c. receiving help with their work
    d. how interesting their work is

38. Findings from studies investigating any possible relationships between age and job performance have found that
    a. there are no differences between younger workers and older workers in terms of their job performance
    b. younger workers perform their jobs better than their older counterparts, probably because of their greater enthusiasm and energy
    c. older workers are less productive than their younger counterparts, probably because of their becoming "burned out" over time
    d. younger workers tend to have more avoidable absences, whereas older workers tend to have more unavoidable absences

39. Gender, as it relates to vocational choice, is
    a. becoming more important in recent years, reversing a twenty-five year trend of declining importance
    b. more of a factor now than it was several decades ago
    c. less of a factor now than it was several decades ago
    d. unchanged in importance during the past several decades

40. The number of women working outside of their homes for pay
    a. has increased to the point where there are more women in the labor force now, than ever before
    b. stabilized in the late 1980s, and has begun to decline
    c. has been matched by a corresponding increase in the number of men who are homemakers
    d. has resulted in virtual equality of pay for comparable work in the labor force

Completion

Supply the term or terms needed to complete each of the following statements.

1. The typical young adult is a healthy physical specimen. ___________, ___________, and ___________ are at their peak.

2. The senses are at their sharpest during ___________.

3. Given the healthy state of most young adults, it is not surprising that ___________ is/are the leading cause of death at this age.

4. ___________ is the leading cause of death for young African American men.

5. "A state of complete physical, mental, and social well-being and not merely the absence of disease and infirmity" is the definition of ___________ according to the World Health Organization.

6. The risk of becoming ___________ is highest from ages 25 to 34.

7. High levels of a fatty substance called ___________ in the bloodstream results in an increased risk of heart disease.

8. There is a clear-cut relationship between a high-fat diet and the risk of ___________ .

9. Research on the relationship between health/fitness and exercise found that those who were the least fit led the most ___________ lives.

10. Nonsmokers are at risk of health problems because of ___________; that is, inhaling smoke when smoking by others is taking place around them.

11. ___________ abuse is a major cause of death from automobile accidents.

12. Although death rates have declined overall in the United States since 1960, death rates for _______ and ___________ people continue to be higher than for others.

13. A problem in determining the comparative health of men and women is that _______ have not been included in many of the major health studies.

14. _______________ is sometimes confused with dysmenorrhea, or menstrual cramping.

15. For the most part, __________ tend to be more health conscious than their counterparts.

16. Schaie's stage of cognitive development where individuals use what they know to become competent and independent is called the _________ stage.

17. According to Schaie, people in the responsible stage are concerned with __________ goals and practical real-life problems.

18. People who need to integrate complex relationships on several levels are said by Schaie to be at the ____________ stage of cognitive development.

19. According to Sternberg, the degree of efficiency in processing and analyzing information is called the __________________ element.

20. Sternberg calls practical, "real-world" intelligence the ___________ element.

21. Psychometric tests of intelligence concentrate on the aspect that Sternberg called ______________ intelligence.

22. Practical knowledge, such as knowing how to cut through bureaucratic red tape is known as _______________ knowledge.

23. Mature thinking, or _______________________ , relies on subjectivity and intuition as well as on pure logic.

24. A woman's central moral dilemma, according to Gilligan, is the conflict between ____________________.

25. Kohlberg's theory focuses on a morality of _____________ , whereas Gilligan's theory focuses on a morality of ________________ .

26. Studies show that student's thinking changes in definable stages while they are in college. The last stage is characterized by freely chosen ______________________.

27. Studies of men and women in college reveal that women tended to avoid __________ ______________________.

28. Although most college dropouts have lower average aptitude scores than people who stay in school, they are usually doing ___________ work.

29. About _________ of all people who enter college never receive a degree.

30. Younger workers tend to have more ___________ absences from work than older workers.

ANSWERS FOR SELF-TESTS — CHAPTER 12

Multiple-Choice

		Page				Page	
1.	b	410	factual	21.	b	421	conceptual
2.	c	411	factual	22.	d	421	conceptual
3.	a	411	conceptual	23.	c	421-422	conceptual
4.	d	411	conceptual	24.	b	421	factual
5.	c	412	factual	25.	a	422	factual
6.	b	414	conceptual	26.	b	422-423	factual
7.	a	414	conceptual	27.	b	423	factual
8.	c	414	conceptual	28.	c	423-424	conceptual
9.	a	415	conceptual	29.	d	424	conceptual
10.	b	416	factual	30.	a	425	conceptual
11.	d	418	conceptual	31.	a	426	factual
12.	b	418	conceptual	32.	d	426	conceptual
13.	c	419	factual	33.	a	427	conceptual
14.	c	419	factual	34.	c	428	factual
15.	d	419	conceptual	35.	d	428	factual
16.	b	420	conceptual	36.	a	428	conceptual
17.	c	420	factual	37.	d	430	factual
18.	a	420	factual	38.	d	430	conceptual
19.	b	420	factual	39.	c	430	factual
20.	d	420	factual	40.	a	430	factual

Completion

		Page			Page
1.	strength, energy, endurance	410	16.	achieving	420
2.	young adulthood	411	17.	long range	420
3.	accidents	411	18.	executive	420
4.	murder	412	19.	componential	421
5.	health	412	20.	contextual	421
6.	overweight	414	21.	componential	421
7.	cholesterol	414	22.	tacit	422
8.	colon cancer	415	23.	postformal thought	422
9.	sedentary	415	24.	herself and others	425
10.	passive smoking	416	25.	rights, responsibility	425
11.	alcohol	417	26.	commitments	426
12.	poor, poorly educated	418	27.	academic risks	427
13.	women	418	28.	satisfactory	428
14.	premenstrual syndrome	419	29.	half	428
15.	women	419			
			30.	avoidable	430

CHAPTER 13

Personality and Social Development in Young Adulthood

INTRODUCTION

Following the critical period of adolescence, during which all aspects of development proceed at an alarming rate, most young adults have reached the point where physical growth has stabilized. However, development of the adult personality continues throughout life. Young adults are at the stage where they are just learning to maximize their physical and intellectual capabilities and realize that social and emotional development is a life-long process. Chapter 13 looks specifically at how the major events of young adulthood influence an individual's personality and social development.

- Two models of personality development in young adulthood are discussed: the normative-crisis model and the timing-of-events model. The normative-crisis model describes human development in terms of a predictable sequence of chronological changes. The timing-of-events model suggests that adult development proceeds according to individual experiences in relation to the time in a person's life when they occur.

- The chapter then focuses on the desire of young adults to form intimate, sexual relationships with each other. This need to develop intimate relationships is discussed from the perspective of the influence it will have on future social and emotional development.

- The advantages and disadvantages of various specific lifestyles (marriage, divorce, cohabitation, or single) are discussed.

- The text discusses parenthood as a developmental experience for both the parent and the child. The alternative of remaining childless is also examined.

- The chapter concludes with a discussion of the characteristics of friendships in young adulthood.

CHAPTER OUTLINE

I. Personality Development In Young Adulthood: Two Models

- A. Normative-Crisis Model
  - 1. Erik Erikson: Crisis--Intimacy versus Isolation
  - 2. George Vaillant: Adaptation to Life
    - a. Vaillant's adaptive mechanisms
    - b. Career consolidation and stages of development
  - 3. Daniel Levinson: Life Structure
    - a. Levinson's life eras
    - b. Women and Levinson's theory
      - (1) The dream
      - (2) The love relationship
      - (3) The mentor
      - (4) Forming an occupation
  - 4. Evaluation of the Normative-Crisis Approach
- B. Timing-of-Events Model
  - 1. Types and Timing of Life Events
    - a. Normative versus nonnormative events
    - b. Individual versus cultural events
    - c. The decline of age consciousness
  - 2. Responding to Life Events

II. Intimate Relationships and Personal Lifestyles

- A. Love
- B. Marriage
  - 1. Benefits of Marriage
  - 2. Marriage and Happiness
  - 3. Marriage and Health
  - 4. Predicting Success in Marriage
  - 5. Domestic Violence
- C. Divorce
  - 1. Why Divorce Has Increased
  - 2. Reactions to Divorce
  - 3. Remarriage after Divorce
- D. Single Life
- E. Cohabitation
- F. Sexuality
  - 1. Sexual Activity among Unmarried People
  - 2. Sexual Activity in Marriage
  - 3. Extramarital Sex
- G. Parenthood
  - 1. Why People Have Children
  - 2. When People Have Children

3. Finding Alternative Ways to Parenthood
   a. Infertility
      (1) Psychological effects of infertility
      (2) Causes of infertility
   b. Adoption
   c. New methods of becoming a parent
      (1) Artificial insemination
      (2) In vitro fertilization
      (3) Ovum transfer
      (4) Surrogate motherhood
      (5) Technology and conception: Ethical issues
4. The Transition to Parenthood
5. Parenthood as a Developmental Experience
6. Blended Families

H. Remaining Childless

I. Friendship
1. Characteristics of Adult Friendship
2. Benefits of Friendship

KEY TERMS

adaptive mechanisms (page 438)

artificial insemination (458)

cohabitation (453)

in vitro fertilization (459)

infertility (456)

intimacy versus isolation (436)

life structure (439)

nonnormative life events (442)

normative life events (442)

normative-crisis model (436)

ovum transfer (459)

surrogate motherhood (459)

timing-of-events model (442)

triangular theory of love (444)

LEARNING OBJECTIVES

After finishing Chapter 13, you should be able to:

1. Describe personality development in young adulthood according to the *normative-crisis model* and the *timing-of-events* model. (pp. 436-443)

2. Describe the crisis of young adulthood according to Erikson. (pp. 436-438)

3. Explain Vaillant's formulation of the mechanisms by which people adapt to life circumstances. (pp. 438-439)

4. Discuss the developmental changes that occur during each phase of young adulthood, according to Levinson. (pp. 439-441)

5. Explain how the adult development of women is different from that of men, according to Levinson's theory. (pp. 441-442)

6. Evaluate the *normative-crisis* approach to adult development. (p. 442)

7. Explain the differences between *normative life events* and *nonnormative life events*, and give an example of each. (pp. 442-443)

8. Distinguish between individual and cultural events. (p. 443)

9. Explain the *triangular theory of love*. (pp. 444-445)

10. List some of the advantages of married life. (p. 446)

11. Discuss the relationship between marriage and each of the following:

    a. happiness (p. 446)

    b. health (pp. 446-448)

12. List some of the factors related to success in marriage. (pp. 448-449)

13. Discuss the problem of domestic violence. (p. 449)

14. Discuss the phenomenon of divorce, including its causes and consequences. (pp. 449-452)

15. Discuss being single and *cohabitation* as alternatives to marriage. (pp. 452-453)

16. Discuss sexuality and sexual activity during young adulthood. (pp. 453-455)

17. List the reasons why people become parents. (p. 455)

18. Discuss the trend toward delayed parenthood and identify the advantages and disadvantages of this trend. (pp. 455-456)

60 percent of couples whose infertility is due to sperm-penetration problems.

Miraculous as microtechniques are, they're just a refinement of in vitro fertilization (IVF), the grandmommy of today's high-tech fertility treatments. Introduced in 1978 (and made famous with the birth of Louise Brown, the world's first "test tube baby"), IVF brings egg and sperm together in a laboratory dish. Two days later the fertilized eggs (embryos) are transferred through the vagina into the uterus, where, with luck, at least one will implant and develop.

Even women without ovaries or who are past menopause can use IVF to become pregnant if they're willing to "adopt" eggs donated by another woman. Donors are generally younger, since research has shown that success rates for IVF drop starting when a woman is over 34 (and then dramatically when she's over 41), explains Zev Rosenwaks, M.D., of New York Hospital-Cornell Medical Center in New York City.

In hopes of boosting the success rates of IVF, doctors have developed two other variations--known as ZIFT (for zygote intrafallopian transfer) and GIFT (gamete intrafallopian transfer)--that each allow nature to take over at an earlier stage. With ZIFT, egg and sperm unite in the lab, as they do in IVF, but are transferred at an earlier developmental stage (the "zygote" stage) to the fallopian tubes. With GIFT, eggs and sperm (aka "gametes") are surgically placed in a woman's fallopian tubes to meet and mate. For either of these procedures to work, a woman's tubes must be in good working order.

When a couple is undergoing any of these procedures, they're likely to produce more embryos than can safely be implanted. The "leftovers" can be frozen, to be used in the future if implantation fails of if the couple wants another child. The advantage: The woman is spared another round of drugs, testing, ultrasound, and egg removal.

Low-Tech Success

Such high-tech miracles have not replaced older treatments such as fertility drugs or surgery, which, in fact, remain more effective. Ovulation failures, for example, can often be overcome with drugs. "With four to six months of treatment with the drug Clomid, between forty and sixty percent of all women will become pregnant," says reproductive specialist Richard Marrs, M.D., of The Hospital of the Good Samaritan in Los Angeles. If Clomid doesn't work, injections of Pergonal may do the trick. The treatment with estrogen can change the chemistry of hostile cervical mucus. (Recent reports have linked fertility drugs to a risk of ovarian cancer. A national study is under way, but for now, doctors say women can continue to take these drugs, as long as they have careful follow-up exams).

Doctors may also recommend bypassing the mucus entirely via intrauterine insemination (IUI), a spin-off of artificial insemination in which

19. Define infertility, discuss the psychological effects of infertility, and explain some of the common causes of infertility. (pp. 456-458)

20. List and describe the various alternative methods for becoming a parent. (pp. 458-459)

21. Discuss some of the ethical issues related to the alternative methods for becoming a parent. (p. 459)

22. Describe the transition to parenthood and explain the process of becoming a parent in developmental terms. (pp. 459-461)

23. Explain what is meant by a blended family and discuss the various strategies for coping with the stress associated with blended families. (pp. 461-464)

24. Discuss various aspects of the choice to remain childless. (p. 464)

25. Explain some of the characteristics and benefits of friendship during young adulthood. (pp. 464-465)

SUPPLEMENTAL READING

This article, which first appeared in the A
about 90% of the time, the specific cause
are able to be successfully treated. Paula
You? This article is reprinted by permissi

New Hope for Co

Pa

Whether at a dinner party or on the news, no doub
you've heard about today's infertility "epidemic."
As couples talk despairingly of temperature cycles
or low sperm counts, or as medical reports serve
up another round of frightening statistics, you may
start to worry about yourself. Perhaps you're still
waiting for the "perfect" time to start a family or
have your second child. Or you may be thinking
of your just-married sister or your best friend.
Exactly how anxious should you be?

First, the reality: "Epidemic" is actually a misnomer, since there hasn't been a rise in the percentage of women unable to become pregnant; the ratio remains 1 in 12 couples. But doctors are seeing a greater number of cases, due to the fact that many more baby boomers have hit the 35-44-year-old range and have been seeking treatment in droves, explains William Mosher, Ph.D., of the National Center for Health Statistics. This is why, experts say, a couple might want to start planning their pregnancy sooner rather than later, given that a woman's chances of becoming pregnant naturally begin to wane in her midthirties, when treatment may also be far less effective.

For those who seek treatment early enough, there's reason to be optimistic: Specific causes of infertility can now be pinpointed about 90 percent of the time. And at least half of the one million couples a year who are treated will take a healthy baby home from the hospital.

What Goes Wrong

About 40 percent of the time, a couple's problem can be traced to some glitch in a woman's reproductive system.

First, and most common, are ovulation abnormalities. Without a ripe egg being produced each month, the odds for conception are drastically reduced. Irregular or absent ovulation is generally due to hormonal imbalances of various kinds, age, or a delayed return to ovulation after using birth control pills.

Even if a woman is ovulating normally, hormonal miscues may prevent fertilization. Again, blood or urine testing can be revealing, according to John J. Stangel, M.D., medical director of IVF America--an in vitro fertilization program in Port Chester, New York.

Last is a category doctors refer to as

SELF TESTS

Multiple-Choice

Circle the letter of the response which best completes or answers each of the following statements and questions.

1. Erikson's crisis during early adulthood is intimacy versus
   a. stagnation
   b. isolation
   c. self-absorption
   d. despair

2. According to the normative-crisis model, human development can be described as
   a. following a definite sequence
   b. depending on a person's gender
   c. unpredictable
   d. both b and c

3. According to Erikson, what is the ultimate goal for young adults involved in heterosexual relationships?
   a. total intimacy
   b. independence from their parents
   c. satisfactory development for their own children
   d. marriage

4. The "virtue" that develops in young adulthood, according to Erikson's theory, is
   a. the virtue of intimacy or mutuality of attraction
   b. the virtue of attraction or mutuality of identification
   c. the virtue of mutual intimacy and exclusiveness
   d. the virtue of love or mutuality of devotion

5. Critics of Erikson's theory, regarding young adults, would most likely argue that
   a. Erikson's theory does not pay sufficient attention to homosexual relationships, or to celibate, childless, and single lifestyles
   b. Erikson's theory does not sufficiently emphasize the importance of the young adult's desire to procreate
   c. young adults' need to form intimate relationships is only addressed superficially by Erikson's theory
   d. the normative-crisis model is a more realistic and practical explanation for social and personality aspects of young adult development

6. Which is a major criticism of Erikson's sixth crisis?
   a. He extends healthy development to homosexual relationships.
   b. He places too much emphasis on the male pattern of development.
   c. He asserts that the search for identity continues through adulthood.
   d. He neglects the importance of producing children.

7. According to Vaillant, what determines the level of an individual's mental health?
   a. number of traumatic events in a person's life
   b. number of satisfactory relationships in a person's life
   c. development of the "virtue" of love
   d. person's adaptation mechanisms for dealing with their life circumstances

8. Which characteristic best describes a person who, according to Vaillant, uses immature mechanisms to adjust to life situations?
   a. enjoys helping others
   b. develops aches and pains with no physical basis
   c. distorts reality
   d. develops irrational fears

9. Vaillant concluded that the most well-adjusted men possessed which type of ego defense mechanisms?
   a. immature
   b. psychotic
   c. mature
   d. realistic

10. Career consolidation, according to Vaillant, is a phenomenon that is
    a. characteristic of men, up until around middle age
    b. not relevant to women, since they are more domestically oriented
    c. a substitute for the failure to achieve intimacy
    d. a manifestation of inadequately developed identity during adolescence

11. A life structure is the underlying design of a person's life, including
    a. the people, places, and things a person considers important
    b. the subconscious aspirations for autonomy and intimacy
    c. the ego defense mechanisms of projection and sublimation
    d. the adaptation mechanisms for dealing with life circumstances

12. According to Levinson, a man seeks independence from his parents
    a. during the novice phase of early adulthood
    b. during the preadulthood period
    c. during the culminating phase of young adulthood
    d. during adolescence

13. According to Levinson, the divorce rate for men is likely to peak
    a. prior to the novice phase of early adulthood
    b. during the preadulthood period
    c. during the culminating phase of young adulthood
    d. shortly after adolescence

14. Studies show that men's dreams were mostly concerned with achievement, while women's dreams were more likely to be concerned with
    a. relationships
    b. achievement
    c. separating from families
    d. achievement and relationships

15. Some research suggests that young adult women develop identity
    a. by breaking away from authority and influence
    b. by establishing independence in career and family situations
    c. through the establishment of autonomy and competence
    d. through responsibility and attachment in relationships

16. The women who found the age-30 transition most stressful were those who were unsatisfied with their
    a. personal relationships
    b. occupational achievement
    c. both a and b
    d. physical appearance

17. The development of adult females
    a. has been shown to be essentially the same as that of adult males
    b. has been studied more extensively than that of males
    c. is more stable and less stressful than that of males
    d. has been studied less extensively than that of males

18. Which of the following statements is most accurate?
    a. Individual differences in personality and life history are better indicators of adult development than age.
    b. Most adults in a society experience significant events at or around the same time, therefore age is an excellent indicator of adult development.
    c. Research indicates that, like child development, adult development occurs in a series of definite, discrete stages.
    d. Studies of adult development in other cultures suggest that there are universal patterns to the process of adult development.

19. Which model suggests that people develop in response to the specific events in their lives and the specific times when they occur?
    a. normative-crisis model
    b. nonnormative-crisis model
    c. life-structure model
    d. timing-of-events model

20. Which one of the following theorists is a supporter of the timing-of-events model?
    a. Erikson
    b. Levinson
    c. Vaillant
    d. Neugarten

21. The timing-of-events model suggests that unexpected life events may result in
    a. relief
    b. stress
    c. confusion
    d. pleasure

22. Which of the following is not a factor related to the ability of a person to respond to life events?
    a. physical health
    b. social support
    c. life history
    d. all of the above are factors

23. The idea that there is a "right time" to do certain things has become less widespread,
    a. and thus social expectations of age appropriate events have been eliminated
    b. but there are still societal expectations about appropriate ages for some events
    c. and research shows this has led to stress from confusion about societal norms
    d. but there has been a corresponding increase in cultural expectations

24. The key issue regarding the effect of life events on adult development is
    a. the timing of those events with respect to a person's stage of development
    b. how a person responds to those events
    c. whether or not those events are judged age appropriate by society
    d. whether or not a person is sufficiently intellectually mature for the event

25. For most young adults today
    a. societal norms for getting married and having children are as strong as ever
    b. the social rules for acceptable family behavior are more rigid than ever
    c. the establishment of a loving relationship is a pivotal factor in their lives
    d. loving relationships are less important than satisfying careers

26. According to Robert Sternberg, love is comprised of
    a. the single essential element of absolute trust
    b. three elements; intimacy, passion, and commitment
    c. two interrelated aspects; physical attraction and intellectual interest
    d. three attractions: physical, social/intellectual, and moral

27. Which of the following statements about love is most accurate?
    a. Married love is not different in kind from unmarried love.
    b. Physical intimacy becomes steadily less important from late adolescence on.
    c. Love is primarily a phenomenon of the young, decreasing with age.
    d. Married love is more realistic and more mature than unmarried love.

28. Marriage, as an institution, ideally
    a. offers economic and social benefits, but at the expense of personal growth
    b. provides personal benefits, but often at an economic or emotional cost
    c. provides economic, personal, emotional, and social benefits
    d. should not be examined from a "benefits" perspective, since it is based on love

29. Research suggests that today, compared to past years, never married people (especially men) are ________, and married people (especially women) are ________.
    a. happier, also happier
    b. happier, less happy
    c. less happy, happier
    d. less happy, also less happy

30. According to a survey, which group experiences the fewest health problems?
    a. married couples
    b. the widowed
    c. never married people
    d. divorced or separated couples

31. According to a study, which of the following strategies for dealing with conflict seemed to be good for a marriage?
    a. arguing and showing anger
    b. withdrawing by walking away
    c. not talking about a problem
    d. none of the above are good

32. Men who abuse women tend to
    a. have higher than normal self-esteem
    b. be sexually inadequate
    c. be socially engaged and involved
    d. have no sense of jealousy or envy

33. People married to spouses who abuse them often stay with that person because
    a. they believe that their mate did not intend to hurt them
    b. they feel that they deserve to be beaten
    c. they are financially dependent on their spouse
    d. all of the above are correct

34. The divorce rate in the United States is
    a. one of the lowest in the world
    b. one of the highest in the world
    c. rising more rapidly than ever before
    d. lowest among young adults

35. Cohabitation, the arrangement where a couple in a romantic and sexual relationship live together without being married, has been shown to
    a. result in problems similar to those experienced by newlyweds
    b. result in happier and longer lasting marriages, once the couples marry
    c. lead inevitably to marital problems if the couples subsequently marry
    d. be a long-lasting arrangement, enduring longer than most marriages

36. Parents today, compared to the previous generation, tend to have
    a. fewer children and have them earlier in life
    b. the same number of children but tend to have them earlier in life
    c. the same number of children but tend to have them later in life
    d. fewer children and have them later in life

37. Which is the most accurate statement about the effects of adoption on children?
    a. They saw their adoptive parents as less nurturing than the nonadoptive children did in a control group.
    b. They got into trouble more than the nonadopted children.
    c. They were generally more confident and felt in better control of their lives than the nonadopted children.
    d. both a and b

38. Compared to people with children, people who choose childlessness
    a. have non-typical family backgrounds
    b. report less marital satisfaction
    c. spend less time in enjoyable activities as a couple
    d. have less traditional attitudes toward women

39. Which group of individuals has the greatest number of friendships?
    a. elderly
    b. newlyweds
    c. adolescents
    d. middle-aged

40. Which of the following statements is most accurate?
    a. Most people's best friends are of the opposite sex.
    b. Romantic bonds have little in common with friendships.
    c. "Best friendships" are often seen as more stable than ties to a spouse or lover.
    d. Isolation from friends and family is related to better health.

Completion

Supply the term or terms needed to complete each of the following statements.

1. Erik Erikson's theory is an example of the ______________________________, which describes human development in terms of a definite sequence of age-related social and emotional changes.

2. The sixth of Erikson's eight crises--and what he considers to be the major issue of young adulthood--is ______________________________________.

3. The "virtue" that develops in young adulthood, according to Erikson's theory, is the ______________________ or ______________________ .

4. Vaillant identified four types of ______________________________, or characteristic ways in which people adapt to life situations.

5. The stage of ____________________________ is characterized by preoccupation with strengthening one's career.

6. The underlying pattern or design of a person's life at a given time is his/her ____________________________.

7. Men often enter adulthood with a _______________ of the future, couched in terms of a career.

8. A ___________________ offers guidance and inspiration and passes on wisdom, moral support, and practical help in both career and personal matters.

9. Women's dreams, in contrast to those of men, were split between ______________ and _________________ .

10. The ______________________________ model views development as a result of the times in people's lives when important events take place.

11. Expected life events are called __________________ life events, and unexpected life events are known as _________________________ life events.

12. A(n) ___________________ event, such as a pregnancy or a promotion, happens to one person or one family.

13. A(n) ________________ event, such as an economic depression or a war, shapes the context in which individuals develop.

14. The idea that love consists of three elements; intimacy, passion, and commitment is central to the ____________________________ .

15. Women tend to see marriage as a place to express and talk about ___________, whereas men tend to express love through ___________ and giving practical help.

16. Men who are _______________ for family violence are less likely to continue to abuse their families.

17. ______________ initiate divorce more often than _________ .

18. An increasingly common living arrangement is ______________________, in which an unrelated man and woman live together.

19. Moral or religious scruples, concern about how it will affect a future marriage, fear of pregnancy or sexually transmitted diseases, and public opinion are all reasons that young adults give for not ______________________________ .

20. By and large, today's couples have ________ children and have them __________ in life.

21. Ten to 15 percent of American couples experience the disappointment of ______________, the inability to conceive after trying for 12 to 18 months.

22. The most common cause of infertility in men is the ____________________________ .

23. Some couples are able to produce children through means of ____________, injection of a man's sperm directly into the woman's cervix.

24. ____________________, fertilization that takes place outside the body, is becoming increasingly common for women whose Fallopian tubes are blocked or damaged.

25. Women who cannot produce normal ova may be able to bear children through the use of __________, ova donated from fertile women--the female counterpart of AID.

26. ___________________ motherhood occurs when a woman who is not married to a man bears his baby and agrees to give the child to the biological father and his wife.

27. A ___________ family is one comprised of a husband and wife and children from prior marriages, as well as former spouses, former in-laws, and aunts, uncles, and cousins on both sides.

28. In a study comparing couples who had chosen either parenthood or childlessness, the childless couples tended to have ________________ attitudes toward women.

29. In comparing adolescents, newlyweds, the middle-aged, and the elderly, __________ had more friends than the other groups.

30. In a research study, respondents saw "best friendships" as _______________ than ties to a spouse or lover.

ANSWERS FOR SELF-TESTS **CHAPTER 13**

Multiple-Choice

		Page				Page	
1.	b	436	factual	21.	b	443	factual
2.	a	436	factual	22.	d	443	factual
3.	c	436	conceptual	23.	b	443	conceptual
4.	d	438	factual	24.	b	443	conceptual
5.	a	438	conceptual	25.	c	443	conceptual
6.	b	438	conceptual	26.	b	444	conceptual
7.	d	438	conceptual	27.	a	445	factual
8.	b	438	factual	28.	c	446	conceptual
9.	c	438	factual	29.	b	446	factual
10.	a	438	conceptual	30.	a	446-448	factual
11.	a	439	conceptual	31.	a	449	conceptual
12.	a	441	factual	32.	b	449	factual
13.	c	441	conceptual	33.	d	449	conceptual
14.	d	441	conceptual	34.	b	449	factual
15.	d	441	conceptual	35.	a	453	conceptual
16.	c	442	factual	36.	d	455	factual
17.	d	442	factual	37.	c	458	conceptual
18.	a	442	conceptual	38.	d	464	conceptual
19.	d	442	factual	39.	b	465	factual
20.	d	442	factual	40.	c	465	factual

Completion

		Page			Page
1.	normative-crisis model	435	16.	arrested	449
2.	intimacy versus isolation	436	17.	women; men	451
3.	virtue of love; mutuality of devotion	438	18.	cohabitation	453
4.	adaptive mechanisms	438	19.	engaging in premarital sex	454
5.	career consolidation	438	20.	fewer; later	455
6.	life structure	439	21.	infertility	456
7.	dream	441	22.	production of too few sperm	456
8.	mentor	441	23.	artificial insemination	458
9.	achievement; relationships	441	24.	in vitro fertilization	459
10.	timing-of-events model	442	25.	donor eggs	459
11.	normative; nonnormative	442	26.	surrogate	459
12.	individual	443	27.	blended	463
13.	cultural	443	28.	less traditional	464
14.	triangular theory of love	444	29.	newlyweds	465
15.	emotions; sex	446	30.	more stable	465

CHAPTER 14

Physical and Intellectual Development in Middle Adulthood

INTRODUCTION

Chapter 14 examines physical and intellectual development in middle adulthood, the period between the ages of 40 and 65 years.

- The physical changes which occur during this period are discussed, including: changes in reproductive and sexual capacity, appearance, and loss of reserve capacity.

- The general status of health of middle adults is described, and various health concerns and problems of this age group are also discussed.

- In the area of intellectual development, the chapter examines intelligence and cognition in adults and discusses various aspects of the adult learner.

- Occupational patterns are described and factors related to work in middle adulthood, such as occupational stress and career changes, are considered.

CHAPTER OUTLINE

PHYSICAL DEVELOPMENT

I. Physical Changes of Middle Age

A. Sensory and Psychomotor Functioning
   1. Vision, Hearing, Taste, and Smell
   2. Strength, Coordination, and Reaction Time
   3. Physiological Changes
B. Sexuality
   1. Sexual Activity
   2. Reproductive and Sexual Capacity
      a. Menopause
         (1) Physical effects of menopause
         (2) Psychological effects of menopause
      b. The male climacteric
C. Appearance: The Double Standard of Aging

II. Health in Middle Age

A. Health Status
B. Health Problems
   1. Diseases and Disorders
   2. The Impact of Stress on Health
      a. Can stressful life events lead to illness?
      b. Why does stress affect some people more than others?
         (1) Control and stress
         (2) Personality and stress: Behavioral patterns and heart disease
   3. Death Rates and Causes of Death
C. The Impact of Race and Socioeconomics on Health

INTELLECTUAL DEVELOPMENT

III. Aspects of Intellectual Development in Middle Adulthood

A. Intelligence and Cognition
   1. Psychometrics: Does Intelligence Change in Adulthood
   2. Mature Thinkers: Does Cognition Change in Adulthood
      a. Integrative thinking
      b. Practical problem solving
B. The Adult Learner

IV. Work in Middle Adulthood

A. Occupational Patterns
   1. Pattern 1: Stable Careers
   2. Pattern 2: Changing Careers
B. Occupational Stress
C. Unemployment
D. Work and Intellectual Growth

KEY TERMS

burnout (page 492)

climacteric (475)

crystallized intelligence (485)

fluid intelligence (485)

hypertension (480)

male climacteric (478)

menopause (475)

osteoporosis (475)

presbycusis (473)

presbyopia (473)

stress (480)

substantive complexity (493)

LEARNING OBJECTIVES

After finishing Chapter 14, you should be able to:

1. Identify the period known as middle age and the markers that denote it. (p. 472)

2. List some common physical abilities which decline in middle adulthood. (pp. 473-474)

3. Describe the compensations that can be made for the changes listed in item 2. (pp. 473-474)

4. Discuss sexuality in midlife. (pp. 474-475)

5. Describe *menopause* and its effects, both physical and psychological. (pp. 475-477)

6. Describe the *male climacteric* and its effects, both physical and psychological. (pp. 477-478)

7. Describe the "double standard of aging" in the United States. (pp. 478-479)

8. List the major health problems of middle age. (pp. 479-480)

9. Describe the impact of stress on health. (pp. 480-482)

10. Discuss the impact of race and socioeconomics on health. (pp. 482-484)

11. Discuss the results and appropriateness of standardized intelligence testing on middle-aged adults. (pp. 484-486)

12. Explain the term "fluid intelligence." (p. 485)

13. Explain the term "crystallized intelligence." (p. 485)

14. Compare and contrast fluid intelligence and crystallized intelligence. (pp. 485-486)

15. Describe the processes of integrative thinking and problem solving in middle age. (pp. 486-489)

16. Identify the characteristics and attitudes of adults who attend school. (p. 489)

17. Describe different occupational patterns of middle-aged people. (pp. 490-491)

18. Describe how occupational stress can affect physical and emotional well-being. (pp. 491-492)

19. Discuss the effects of unemployment on middle-aged people. (pp. 492-493)

20. Discuss how the work people do affects their intellectual growth. (pp. 493-495)

SUPPLEMENTAL READING

While the economy is growing steadily again, more than nine million Americans remain jobless, victims of changes they cannot control. This article, reprinted with permission from the March 8, 1993 issue of *Fortune*, describes why their lives will never be the same.

The New Unemployed

Kenneth Labich

Tom Brown, 44, had been working as New York regional comptroller for McKesson, the big wholesale drug distributor, when he got the news that he no longer had a job. He knew that layoffs were inevitable, but he still thinks he should have been treated better after 13 years with the company. "Management didn't want to talk to me after my position had been eliminated," he says. "They basically didn't want to know that I existed."

Terry Cantine, 49, was product marketing manager for a Sun Valley, California company called AVX Filters when she got the ax last September. She's been brushing up on her computer skills, and she tells prospective employers she's willing to take a big pay cut, but nothing has turned up yet. Says Cantine: "My life was my job, but now I'm finding out how wrong that is."

James Kmetz was laid off last April after four years as a trust specialist at Now West Corp. in Minneapolis. He received a one-minute outplacement interview and no severance, and he has grown weary of hearing that his education and experience make him overqualified for the menial jobs he applies for. Says Kmetz, 46: "I have no career aspirations. I don't want to move up. At my age, I'm not very hopeful about finding another good job. For me, the American Dream is dead."

You cannot miss the pain in these voices as a new generation of unemployed Americans describes the savage realities of today's job market. Pain compounded by shock--for these are typically the kinds of people who didn't lose jobs in past recessions. And the economy they've been thrown into is something their experience never prepared them for. Any way you look at it, unemployment just isn't what it used to be.

In particular, this downturn has been much tougher than past ones on older workers, who often have a harder time finding a new job, and on white-collar workers, who have long considered themselves immune to the harsh effects of business cycles. Compared with the recessions of the 1970s, this one has hit with layoffs about double the proportion of workers ages 35 to 54 and of white-collar types.

Jobs have usually come back strong after past recessions. But this time unemployment remains stubbornly high, at over nine million people, or more than 7% of the work force, even after some signs of strengthening job growth in January. A startling number of recent layoffs appear to be permanent. Only 15% of workers recently laid off expect to return to the same job, says the Bureau of Labor Statistics (BLS). During the previous four recessions, an average of 44% of laid-off workers expected to be recalled.

The real employment picture is probably darker than these figures suggest. More than six million people are working part time because they can't find a full-time job, figures the BLS, and another million or so have simply given up looking for work. That means nearly 17 million people, or almost 12% of the labor force, are unemployed or underemployed.

Unaccustomed to joblessness, many of the new unemployed believe that retraining will land them a new position. It might, but often they train for jobs that aren't out there. The new jobless reasonably look to small companies for employment--these enterprises were the main engine of job growth in the Eighties--only to find the engine largely shut down since the recession.

The few jobs available are often a disappointment to the displaced managers competing for them. Most of the action lately has been in low-pay, low-perk service jobs; during a recent month an astounding 118,000 of the 126,000 jobs created were in the retail and service sectors. Only about half the laid-off workers who have found new jobs during this recovery are matching their previous pay.

The near future looks pretty grim as well. Big corporations have been whacking away big time over the past few weeks: Sears has cut 50,000 jobs, IBM has lopped off another 25,000, Boeing announced a 20,000 cut, United Technologies called for 10,500 new firings, McDonnell Douglas announced another 8,700, and Eastman Kodak fired 2,000.

The bloodletting will likely continue. A survey by management consulting firm Kepner-Tregoe finds that downsizing has become a kind of "management addiction" at many big companies. Top brass at more than a third of the corporations that had downsized in the previous five years expected to lop heads again within 12 months. Defense cutbacks will add to the losses for years to come; the total of jobs eliminated in that sector could be as high as 2.6 million by 1997.

Adding fuel to the firings is the familiar trend away from hierarchical, vertically integrated corporations to leaner, more flexible organizations that outsource many functions and add temporary employees for particular projects--the so-called modular corporations. Multiplied thousands of time, this phenomenon adds up to a profound structural change in the U.S. labor market

One hears that being fired has lost its stigma, since most people are beginning to recognize the change--it happens to everybody nowadays, right? Perhaps, but it still packs a wallop. Mike Meyers, 55, was a department head at Electrospace Systems, a division of Chrysler Technologies in Crystal City, Virginia, until he was laid off last June. He had been on the job for 11 years, since shortly after he retired from the Navy, and he's still trying to cope with the wrenching change in his life. "I'm pretty discouraged at the moment," he says. "Even the physical act of getting a resume together has been tougher than I anticipated." Meyers concedes that defense contractors like the one he worked for are in tough shape, but he's still bitter about the way he was treated. Says Meyers: "I asked for outplacement, and they didn't even respond to my request. I network, I call everyone I once knew as a business contact. I tell you, friendly people are not that friendly when you're out of a job."

For many of the newly unemployed, the loss of a job also means a diminished sense of self-worth and the loss of support and stimulus provided by colleagues. Ronald Spangler, 42, was laid off from a managerial job in Philadelphia city government just before Christmas. He recalls, with venom, feeling like an outsider when he attended holiday parties. "If you tell people you've been laid off, they start to pity you," he says. "You get treated like a nonperson, a nonentity. One of the gauges of who you are is your job."

Personal problems such as alcoholism and depression are common among the newly unemployed, and marriages are often strained. "Being unemployed is a full-time job," says Edoardo Leoncavallo, 56, a hotel architect formerly employed by Walt Disney Imagineering in Glendale, California. "There's a lot of stress to deal with, including family stress. I think my wife initially felt resentment. I think she felt, Why can't you bring home the bacon?"

Many of the new unemployed are experienced workers and practically novice job seekers. The first time Spangler hit the unemployment office, the place shut down for lunch after he had waited hours to get his claim processed. Bill Thompson, 55, has been looking for work for nearly two years, ever since he lost his electrical engineering job with Control Data in Minneapolis. He has come to loathe the seemingly endless minuet he must dance with prospective employers. "What's lacking is the mechanism for finding a job," he says. "I mean, the job interview is something short of a farce--all they are doing is hiring the better actor."

For many workers the shock of unemployment is compounded by the realization that no employer wants the skills they have developed over the years. Sometimes the problem is advancing technology. John Mazur, a 50-year-old sheet metal worker from Queens, New York, saw his work hours recede steadily last year because machines have replaced most men in the plants that turn out ductwork. Says he: "Now ten men can produce as much as 60 to 100 men did 30 years ago, when I got into the business."

Millions of other workers find that their job experience has made them too specialized to entice a new employer. Nick Nguyen, 26, was laid off from his job in computer support at United Way in Alexander, Virginia, last year after a much-ballyhooed management scandal sliced into the revenues at the charity. Since he had been using specially designed software for highly specific tasks, his skills are not easily transferable. Nguyen has been trying to retrain by learning big software packages like Windows and Lotus, but he has been stumped on the job trail. Says he: "I'd rather not relocate, but I will if I have to . . . I'm starting to think I'll take anything I can get."

The growing army of so-called discouraged workers, those who have simply given up after looking months or years for decent work, illustrates an important way the job market has changed. At this stage in past economic recoveries, the number of such dropouts would usually have declined sharply as they reconnected with the system. But this time the official number of discouraged workers has held steady at slightly over one million--and few experts doubt that the true number could be considerably higher.

The ranks of the discouraged are loaded with older workers, especially those past 55. According to a survey conducted by the Commonwealth Fund, a New York research group, at least two million older workers are ready and able to work but cannot find jobs. Many were swept up in the early-retirement programs in vogue at major corporations; a recent Conference Board survey of 400 big companies found about 40% offering packages to early retirees as part of downsizing efforts.

The big problem, say human-resources experts who counsel older workers, is that many of these folks were financially and psychologically unprepared for retirement. Say Michael C. Barth, senior vice president at ICF Inc., a Washington, D.C., human-resources consulting firm: "Somewhere about 18 to 24 months down the line, they often discover two things. First, they need money. Second, they are bored out of their skulls."

Yet, many see no way back into the work force because companies have shut their doors to older workers. Gregory Genco, 54, of New York City has worked as an office manager and head administrator at several law firms, yet he has all but lost hope of finding another job. "Why should they hire me when they can get someone in their 20s for half the price?", he asks. "At my age I'd say my chances are pretty close to nil." Rosaleen Fettig, 55, lost her production line job at Briggs & Stratton in Milwaukee last April and ran right into apparent age discrimination. She was filling out a job application at a prospective employer's plant when the boss spotted her. The receptionist went into his office to arrange an interview for her. Recalls Fettig: "When she came out, her face was just red. And she said, 'Oh, I'm sorry, I didn't know the job has already been filled.'"

Advocates for older workers say that attitude is not just cruel but also downright stupid. The Conference Board study found that companies continue to lay off and package out senior workers even though they are more reliable than younger employees, have better work attitudes, have better job skills, are absent less often, and are less likely to quit. About 70% of the companies surveyed also said older workers were at least as cost effective as their younger colleagues. Concludes the Conference Board: "The effect of current practices and trends may be eroding a valued resource to a degree that is unintended and imprudent."

Two other recent studies conducted by the Commonwealth Fund dramatically point up just how unwise it may be to shun employees who show a bit of gray hair. The first, which compared older and younger employees working as telephone reservation clerks for Days Inn from 1987 through 1990, found that the older workers were just as efficient as their younger colleagues, cost less to recruit and train, and were far more likely to put up with the demands of the job. After the first year only 29.9% of the youngsters were still around vs. 87.3% of the employees over 50. Even the seniors' health care costs were about the same as the younger workers. The authors of the study suggest that's because older workers still on the job rank above average in health and tend to have fewer dependents.

In the second study, from 1988 to 1991, a large hardware chain staffed one of its stores solely with employees over 50 and compared its results with those of five stores with younger employees. Again, the older workers were far more likely to stay on the job; the turnover rate was five times higher at the comparison stores. In productivity measured by sales vs. labor costs, the post-50s soundly thrashed two of the other stores and held their own with the other three. Overall, the store staffed by the over-50 employees was about 18% more profitable than the other five and nearly 9% more profitable than the companywide average. Top managers at the chain were so impressed with the results of the experiment that they plan to staff two more stores solely with over-50 workers and step up recruitment of older workers for the chain.

As months pass and rejections mount, many of the new unemployed cast about for fresh ways to plug back into the system. One popular strategy is to take courses to sharpen business skills or retrain for a new career. In a survey of 376 unemployed executives conducted by the New York City outplacement firm Lee Hecht Harrison, 90% said they needed to upgrade their abilities--particularly communication skills--before hitting the interview circuit. Ex-accountants are looking into the health care field. Bankers are taking education courses in the hope of becoming teachers. After he was laid off from an administrative job in technical support at Alliant Techsystems in Minneapolis, Harold Smith, 50, took a job-placement test that indicated he might be suited for sales. Now he is an independent sales rep, offering financial products for Primerica. Says he: "I don't ever want to get laid off again. I want to control my own destiny." Lori Bielinski, a 30-year-old data specialist from Seattle slated for a layoff next June, is using retraining money from US West, her current employer, to become a massage therapist.

The problem with this flurry of education and retraining is that it is too seldom geared to the needs of a specific employer or job, so workers may not be gathering the skills companies are looking for. As Janet Norwood, a senior research fellow at the Urban Institute, puts it, "We simply have not done a very good job in focusing on relevant training. There is a lack of connectedness between business and the education process."

Like past recessions, this one has not beaten up on each part of the country with equal ferocity, so many thousands of workers each month pull up stakes and relocate on the theory that the employment will be greener somewhere else. Over 1.3 million unemployed people in search of work moved to another state during the 1980s, says the BLS, and the trend seems to have accelerated recently.

The tactic improves the odds a little: About 17% more relocated workers land jobs than those who stay home. The problem is that many of the jobs now to be had are mere stopgaps. Job hunters, white collar and blue collar, increasingly face options far inferior to the situations they have left--low pay, no benefits, temporary or part-time work.

Leslie Goldberg, 45, of Los Angeles considered herself lucky to find a new job in her field, employee training and human resources, after a year of looking, but she had to swallow a $10,000 pay cut. Shirley Martin, 52, of Maryville, Tennessee, had been working at a Levi Strauss plant for 11 years when her shop was shut down. "They said that workers' comp was costing too much, and that's why they closed the plant," she says. "In reality, they moved to work overseas." Martin found a job in a smaller sewing factory after about two years, but her pay dropped from $8 an hour to $4.25. She was recently laid off from that job as well. Says Martin: "It seems like you're always starting over, from the bottom."

This sort of experience has become so common among the new unemployed that labor experts have begun to suggest that rethinking the nation's job-creation machinery may be necessary. Studies in the 1980's acclaimed small businesses as the mighty generators of job growth. Declared President Reagan in 1985: "We have lived through the age of industry and the age of the giant corporation. But I believe that this is the age of the entrepreneur." A year later U.S. Chamber of Commerce President Richard Lesher asserted, "Small business is America's ace in the hole."

But for employees this golden age of entrepreneurship is not an unalloyed blessing. James L. Medoff, a professor of economics at Harvard, points out that small businesses, those with 500 or fewer employees, have such a high failure rate that the new jobs they create may not last long. His research shows that 40% of 80 million jobs in the Small Business Administration database in 1980 had disappeared six years later.

Small companies usually don't pay as well; big ones beat them by about 30% on average. A few factors account for most of that difference. Larger companies tend to hire more skilled and experienced workers, who can demand a higher wage. More big companies are unionized, and others pay better than small companies to avoid unionization. But after adjusting for these factors, you still come up with a 10% differential based on sheer size, and it applies across industries and regions.

The disparity between big and small companies is even greater when it comes to benefits. A study conducted for the Small Business Administration found that every large company surveyed offered a health insurance plan: only 55% of the small businesses did. About 94% of the biggies offered life insurance vs. just 29% of the small guys. Three out of four of the large companies offered a benefits package that included paid vacation, sick leave, and some kind of pension or retirement plan, while a measly 7% of the smaller firms had comparable packages. This is one area of business where economies of scale still operate: Big companies can offer more benefits for less cost per employee.

Other studies show that employees at larger companies receive considerably more training than those at smaller companies, that big-company workers are less likely to quit their jobs voluntarily, and that they are more likely to have received varied work experiences on the job. Because of the political power small businesses wield in Washington, they are often exempt from federal regulations regarding treatment of workers. For example, at least half the people employed in the U.S.--those at smaller companies--will not benefit from the recently enacted family leave bill.

All this reflects the hard fact that jobs are not a product of the economy but a byproduct. They derive from the process of wealth creation, and when a company is creating lots of wealth, as many of today's giants were in the Sixties and Seventies, it can ladle out pay and benefits to its workers, as those companies did. But when outfits like GM and IBM are using up wealth rather than creating it, and when they are based on business models of previous decades, rich jobs look like relics. They aren't. The relics are those companies and their ways of operating, which will be changed or be replaced by companies that have figured out new ways to create lots of wealth.

That is cold comfort to the new unemployed, many of whom have skills and attitudes formed in an earlier era. Yet some labor experts have spotted a semblance of a silver lining in the current gloom. Audrey Freedman, president of the New York consulting firm Manpower Plus, says that with so many businesses looking for temporary, or "contingent," employees, workers have far more opportunity to try on different hats and find the best match for their skills and interests. Once they have looked beyond the narrow boundaries of their former roles, says Freedman, a lot of folks may find they are much happier doing something entirely different. The advertising executive who spent every spare moment puttering around the house may wind up more fulfilled as a general contractor. The human-resources executive may discover she has a natural talent for sales. The group vice president who was a weekend gourmand may find he was born to run a restaurant. Says Freedman: "People have hobbies and skills they don't yet realize can be channeled into productive work."

At least some of the unemployed report unexpected insights from stepping off the corporate carousel. They have learned the folly of blind loyalty to an employer and the importance of self-reliance, they say. They vow they approach their next job as an opportunity for personal development.

Matching skills and interests. Self-realization. Personal development. It all sounds so exciting, and may even be so. But how many of the new unemployed would happily have foregone such opportunities?

Questions:

How is being unemployed in middle age different from being unemployed in young adulthood?

How does unemployment in middle adulthood affect other aspects of development?

SELF TESTS

Multiple-Choice

Circle the letter of the response which best completes or answers each of the following statements and questions.

1. The changes in sensory and motor capabilities during midlife are usually
   a. substantial, and cause adjustment problems for most middle-aged people
   b. substantial, but most middle-aged people compensate well for them
   c. fairly small, but cause adjustment problems for most middle-aged people
   d. fairly small, and most middle-aged people compensate well for them

2. The farsightedness associated with aging is known as
   a. presbycusis
   b. presbyteria
   c. presbyopia
   d. myopia

3. The hearing loss, especially for high-pitched sounds, associated with aging is called
   a. presbycusis
   b. presbyteria
   c. presbyopia
   d. myopia

4. Which of the following statements about middle age is true?
   a. Strength declines but coordination improves.
   b. Coordination declines but strength improves.
   c. Both strength and coordination decline.
   d. Both strength and coordination improve.

5. Which of the following statements about sensory functioning in middle age is correct?
   a. As the eye's lens softens, many people become nearsighted.
   b. Sensitivity to smell declines.
   c. Taste sensation is more acute, resulting in greater appetite.
   d. Hearing becomes sharper, especially for lower frequency sounds.

6. Which of the following would be consistent with sensory changes associated with middle age?
   a. Finding foods that had been bland now tasting more flavorful.
   b. Using more spices to make foods, which now taste bland, more flavorful.
   c. Reducing the use of spices in foods because of increased taste sensitivity.
   d. Rejecting foods that were previously enjoyed because they now taste overpowering.

7. Middle aged people are engaged in sexual activity
   a. less often and in less varied ways than ever before
   b. less often but in more varied ways than ever before
   c. more often and in more varied ways than ever before
   d. more often but in less varied ways than ever before

8. Factors that can enhance sexuality in midlife include
   a. increased estrogen production in women and improved libido in men
   b. decreased estrogen production in women and more regular menstrual cycles
   c. increased testosterone production in men and improved libido in women
   d. freedom from worry about pregnancy and more time to spend with a partner

9. Which of the following statements about reproductive capacity in middle age is most accurate?
   a. Women's ability to bear children comes to an end.
   b. Men's ability to father children comes to an end.
   c. Although women are still fertile, their interest in sex declines.
   d. Although men are now infertile, their interest in sex increases.

10. The cessation of ovulation and menstruation is known as
    a. menarche
    b. menorrhea
    c. menopause
    d. menorrhagia

11. In a research study of middle-aged women, most reported that their sex life was
    a. better than earlier
    b. less satisfactory than earlier
    c. no different than it was earlier
    d. less important than earlier

12. The 2- to 5-year period during which the changes resulting in menopause occur is called the
    a. premenopausal period
    b. hormone depletion stage
    c. menarche
    d. climacteric

13. Preceding menopause, the body reduces its production of
    a. estrogen
    b. progesterone
    c. testosterone
    d. adrenaline

14. Thinning of the bones, increasing the risk of fractures, is called
    a. osteomyelitis
    b. osteoporosis
    c. decalcification
    d. calcium deficiency syndrome

15. Estrogen replacement therapy for treating symptoms associated with menopause
    a. has been found to be almost universally helpful with few harmful side effects
    b. may help some women, but may also be related to serious side effects
    c. is usually of little benefit, but does no harm either
    d. is of no benefit, but can cause serious side effects

16. Women's psychological problems during midlife are
    a. a direct consequence of physical changes related to menopause
    b. more likely due to a woman's attitude than to physical changes
    c. are virtually non-existent for women who receive estrogen replacement therapy
    d. are a result of decreased progesterone production

17. <u>Male climacteric</u> refers to the
    a. cessation of sperm production
    b. inability to father children
    c. period of change in the male's reproductive system
    d. male's adjustment to reproductive changes in his female peers

18. The double standard of aging means that
    a. men appear to age at double the rate for women
    b. women appear to age at double the rate for men
    c. women are affected more adversely than men by society's standards of physical attractiveness
    d. men are affected more adversely than women by society's standards of physical attractiveness

19. Male climacteric brings
    a. decline in fertility
    b. increase of impotence
    c. lower libido
    d. all of the above

20. The phenomenon of a midlife crisis is produced by
    a. reduction in hormone production during the climacteric for both men and women
    b. psychological responses to societal expectations for men, and reduction in hormones in women
    c. the inability of men and women to cope adequately with the double standard of aging
    d. societal pressures to look and act young combined with real physical losses that accompany aging

21. The majority of middle-aged Americans reported that their health was
    a. poor to fair
    b. poor, fair, or satisfactory
    c. fair to good
    d. good, very good, or excellent

22. Which of the following is <u>not</u> a common physical ailment associated with middle age?
    a. skin disorders such as hives, rashes, and eczema
    b. impaired sight and hearing
    c. malfunction of the digestive system
    d. respiratory ailments such as asthma or bronchitis

23. Hypertension is
    a. high blood pressure
    b. excessive response to stress
    c. excessive worrying
    d. tightening of muscles, especially in the face and neck

24. Heart or blood vessel disease is
    a. more prevalent among men than women
    b. more prevalent among women than men
    c. equally prevalent among men and women
    d. more prevalent among men earlier, but more prevalent among women later in middle-age

25. Estrogen replacement therapy has been linked to
    a. decreased risk for breast cancer, but increased risk for heart disease
    b. decreased risk for heart disease, but increased risk for breast cancer
    c. decreased risk for both heart disease and breast cancer
    d. increased risk for both heart disease and breast cancer

26. The finding that an event may be stressful to some people, but not to others, may be explained by
    a. the relationship between measured hormone levels and reported stress levels
    b. an individual's genetic predisposition to stress induced illness
    c. the different levels of control that people feel they have over stressful events
    d. different levels of certain brain chemicals and reported stress levels

27. Death in middle age is most likely to occur as a result of
    a. accidents
    b. violent crime
    c. natural causes
    d. suicide

28. Which of the following statements about mortality in middle age is accurate?
    a. Despite medical advances, there has been no decline in midlife mortality.
    b. As a result of medical advances and changing lifestyles, midlife mortality is the same as mortality in young adulthood.
    c. Midlife mortality decreased immediately after World War II, but there has been no change since 1950.
    d. There has been a significant decrease in midlife mortality since the late 1970s.

29. The largest single factor that accounts for the high death rate and overall poor health status of inner-city African-Americans is
    a. heredity
    b. poverty
    c. lack of health insurance
    d. pollution

30. Research has shown that middle-age people have a distinct advantage in
    a. recall of factual information
    b. solving problems of everyday life
    c. mental games
    d. using logic to solve abstract mental problems

31. Regarding adult intelligence, which of the following statements is most accurate?
    a. Research shows that intelligence, like many physical capabilities, begins to decline noticeably during middle-age.
    b. Studies indicate that there are no changes, either in the level of intelligence or the nature of intelligence, as a function of aging.
    c. Studies show that as adults age, all aspects of intelligence decline steadily.
    d. Research indicates that the intelligence of adults in midlife is different from, but not necessarily lower than the intelligence of younger people.

32. Adults tend to think in a/an
    a. logical way
    b. methodical way
    c. integrative way
    d. none of the above

33. The reasons given by most adult students for returning to school were related to
    a. their job
    b. personal fulfillment
    c. boredom with other aspects of their lives
    d. the need to make new acquaintances

34. Compared with younger students, mature learners tend to be
    a. more motivated
    b. less anxious
    c. more self-confident
    d. less interested

35. During middle adulthood, the typical worker is likely to be
    a. at the peak of a career chosen in younger adulthood
    b. on the threshold of a new vocation
    c. frustrated by occupational stagnation
    d. either a or b

36. A major cause of daily stress on the job is
    a. difficulty in performing menial tasks
    b. dissatisfaction with work conditions
    c. conflicts with supervisors, subordinates, co-workers
    d. either a or b

37. Emotional exhaustion and a feeling that one can no longer accomplish anything on the job are commonly known as
    a. midlife occupational stagnation
    b. burnout
    c. vocational menopause
    d. midlife crisis

38. Two major sources of stress associated with unemployment are
    a. financial hardship and feelings of lowered self-worth
    b. burnout and midlife crisis
    c. decreased intellectual stimulation and increased weight gain
    d. difficulty in filling increased leisure time and more contact with spouse

39. The degree to which work, by its very substance, requires thought and independent judgement is called
    a. occupational stimulation
    b. substantive complexity
    c. occupational complexity
    d. occupational substance

40. Research indicates that complex work
    a. causes intellectual burnout, resulting in lethargy and illness
    b. overburdens people to a greater degree as they become older
    c. produces more rigid thinkers, who in turn seek comfort from routine activities
    d. produces more flexible thinkers, who in turn seek more stimulating activities

Completion

Supply the term or terms needed to complete each of the following statements.

1. Farsightedness associated with aging is called ____________________.

2. The gradual hearing loss that often occurs during middle age, especially for high-frequency sounds, is called ___________________.

3. People who lead sedentary lives lose ______________ and ___________ and therefore become even less able to exert themselves physically.

4. The 2 to 5 year period during which a woman's body undergoes the various physiological changes that bring on menopause is known as the ____________ .

5. The cessation of ovulation and menstruation is called ______________ and indicates that a woman can no longer bear children.

6. During the climacteric, a woman's body reduces its production of the hormone ___________________.

7. ______________ is the condition in which the bones become thinner and more susceptible to fracture.

8. Osteoporosis can be prevented by increasing the daily intake of _________________.

9. The __________________ is the period of physiological, emotional, and psychological change involving a man's reproductive system and other body systems.

10. The male climacteric generally begins about ______ years later than the woman's climacteric period.

11. The societal premium on youth, which adversely affects women more severely than men is referred to as the ____________________ .

12. High blood pressure, or ____________________, is strongly related to risk of heart attacks or strokes.

13. ____________________ is a controversial treatment to prevent heart disease in postmenopausal women.

14. ____________ is the organism's physiological and psychological reaction to the demands made on it.

15. People are less likely to get sick as a result of a stressful event if they feel that they can ______________ the stressful event.

16. People who are impatient, competitive, aggressive, and hostile show the _________ behavior pattern.

17. The __________ behavior pattern is exhibited by people who are relaxed, easygoing, and unhurried.

18. As in young adulthood, death rates in middle age are ____________ for men than for women and ___________ for white people than for black people.

19. The capacity to apply intellectual ability in new situations is called ____________ .

20. ____________________ is the ability to remember and use learned information.

21. According to Shaie's model of adult development, adults in middle age use their intelligence to focus on ______________ problems.

22. The tendency for middle-aged people to interpret what they read, see, or hear in terms of its personal and psychological meaning reflects __________ thinking.

23. Most adults who go to school do so for ____________ reasons.

24. Mature learners tend to be more ___________ than younger learners.

25. Most business, academic, and political leaders tend to be in their ____________ years.

26. Middle-aged men with stable careers tend to be either ____________ or ___________

27. ______________ is a reaction to work-related stress that involves emotional exhaustion, a feeling of being unable to accomplish anything on the job, and a sense of helplessness and loss of control.

28. The greatest work-related stressor is sudden, unexpected ______________ .

29. The single occupational factor having the strongest impact on psychological functioning was found to be the _______________ of the work itself.

30. An accurate summary of midlife is that it is a time of ____________.

Multiple-Choice

		Page	
1.	d	473	conceptual
2.	c	473	factual
3.	a	473	factual
4.	c	473	conceptual
5.	b	473	factual
6.	b	473	conceptual
7.	c	474	conceptual
8.	d	474-475	conceptual
9.	a	475	factual
10.	c	475	factual
11.	a	475	conceptual
12.	d	475	factual
13.	a	475	factual
14.	b	475	factual
15.	b	475-477	conceptual
16.	b	477	conceptual
17.	c	478	factual
18.	c	478	conceptual
19.	d	478	factual
20.	d	479	conceptual
21.	d	479	factual
22.	a	479-480	factual
23.	a	480	factual
24.	a	480	conceptual
25.	b	480	conceptual
26.	c	481	conceptual
27.	c	482	factual
28.	d	482	factual
29.	b	483	conceptual
30.	b	484	conceptual
31.	d	484-489	conceptual
32.	c	486	conceptual
33.	a	489	factual
34.	a	489	factual
35.	d	490	conceptual
36.	c	492	factual
37.	b	492	factual
38.	a	493	conceptual
39.	b	493	factual
40.	d	493	conceptual

Completion

		Page
1.	presbyopia	473
2.	presbycusis	473
3.	muscle tone; energy	473
4.	climacteric	475
5.	menopause	475
6.	estrogen	475
7.	osteoporosis	475
8.	calcium	476
9.	male climacteric	478
10.	10	478
11.	double standard of aging	478
12.	hypertension	480
13.	estrogen replacement therapy	480
14.	stress	480
15.	control	481
16.	Type A	482
17.	Type B	482
18.	higher; lower	482
19.	fluid intelligence	485
20.	crystallized intelligence	485
21.	real-life	486
22.	integrative	486
23.	job-related	489
24.	motivated	489
25.	middle	490
26.	workaholics; mellowed	490
27.	burnout	492
28.	loss of job	492
29.	substantive complexity	493
30.	reevaluation	495

CHAPTER 15

Personality and Social Development in Middle Adulthood

INTRODUCTION

Midlife is a time to search for meaning in one's life with respect to the achievement of earlier goals and ambitions (particularly in the areas of careers and intimate relationships) often with recognition that if there are changes to be made, one will need to act quickly.

- Chapter 15 begins with a discussion of the stressful period during the early to middle forties which supposedly accounts for the common changes in personality and lifestyle during middle adulthood. This period is referred to as the midlife crisis.

- The chapter then examines middle adulthood (ages 40 to 65) from several theoretical perspectives: those of Carl Jung, Erik Erikson, and Robert Peck.

- Men's development in middle adulthood is discussed in light of the research of George Vaillant and Daniel Levinson, and women's development is discussed from the viewpoint of research on a variety of themes.

- A discussion of pervasiveness of the midlife crisis forms the basis for an evaluation of the normative-crisis model for development in middle adulthood.

- The text discusses several important relationships from the perspective of the timing of events model, including a variety of important events such as changes in: marriages (which often end in divorce at this time), sexual relationships, relationships with siblings, friendships, relationships with one's own maturing children, and relationships with parents.

- The chapter concludes with a discussion of the changes brought about as a result of the strain that accompanies the demands of caring for aging and often infirm parents.

CHAPTER OUTLINE

I. Midlife: The Normative-Crisis Approach

- A. The "Midlife Crisis"
- B. Theories and Research
  - 1. Carl Jung: Balancing the Personality
  - 2. Erik Erikson: Crisis 7--Generativity versus Stagnation
  - 3. Robert Peck: Four Adjustments of Middle Age
    - a. Valuing wisdom versus valuing physical power
    - b. Socializing versus sexualizing in human relationships
    - c. Emotional flexibility versus emotional impoverishment
    - d. Mental flexibility versus mental rigidity
  - 4. Men's Development in Middle Adulthood
    - a. George Vaillant: Introspection and transition
    - b. Daniel Levinson: Changing life structures
  - 5. Women's Development in Middle Adulthood
    - a. Mastery, pleasure, and women's adjustment
    - b. "Rewriting of the life story": The struggle for an independent identity
    - c. Typical crisis themes
    - d. Ego identity status
    - e. "The prime of life"
- C. Evaluating the Normative-Crisis Model
  - 1. Can the Findings of Normative-Crisis Research Be Generalized to Other Populations?
  - 2. How Typical is the "Midlife Crisis"?
  - 3. Is Adult Development Age-Linked?
  - 4. How Healthy Is the Male Model?

II. Personal Relationships and Timing of Events in Midlife

- A. Marriage and Divorce
  - 1. Marital Satisfaction in Midlife
  - 2. What Makes Middle-Aged Couples Divorce or Stay Together?
- B. Relationships with Siblings
- C. Friendships
- D. Relationships with Maturing Children
  - 1. Adolescent Children: Issues for Parents
  - 2. When Children Leave: The "Empty Nest"
  - 3. When Children Stay or Return: The Not-So-Empty Nest
  - 4. Lifelong Parenting
- E. Relationships with Aging Parents
  - 1. Contact with Parents
  - 2. Mutual Help
  - 3. Caring for Parents

KEY TERMS

emotional flexibility versus emotional impoverishment (page 503)

"empty nest" (515)

generativity versus stagnation (503)

interiority (504)

mental flexibility versus mental rigidity (503)

midlife crisis (500)

socializing versus sexualizing in human relationships (503)

valuing wisdom versus valuing physical powers (503)

LEARNING OBJECTIVES

After finishing Chapter 15, you should be able to:

1. Describe the characteristics of what is known as the *midlife crisis*. (p. 500)

2. Summarize the major elements of development in middle adulthood according to Carl Jung's theory. (p. 501)

3. Explain Jung's notion of balancing the personality in midlife. (p. 501)

4. Summarize the major elements of development in middle adulthood according to Erik Erikson's theory. (p. 503)

5. Explain Erikson's seventh crisis--*generativity versus stagnation*. (p. 503)

6. Identify the virtue of Erikson's seventh stage. (p. 503)

7. Summarize the major elements of development in middle adulthood according to Robert Peck's theory. (pp. 503-504)

8. Describe the four psychological developments that Peck views as critical to successful adjustment to middle age. (p. 503)
   a.
   b.
   c.
   d.

9. Describe the findings relevant to middle adulthood of Vaillant's longitudinal Grant Study. (p. 504)

10. Describe the changes in life structures that characterize midlife according to the view of Levinson. (p. 504)

11. Describe how mastery and pleasure combine to influence women's adjustment in the middle adult years. (pp. 504-506)

12. Identify and describe the typical crisis themes that characterize women's development in the middle years. (pp. 506-508)

13. Discuss the proposition that middle age is the "prime of life" for women. (p. 508)

14. Identify and discuss the major criticisms of the research on middle age, particularly of the normative-crisis model. (pp. 508-510)

15. Describe the pattern of marital satisfaction through adulthood. (pp. 511-512)

16. Discuss the factors that influence whether a couple remains married or gets divorced. (pp. 512-513)

17. Describe the status of relationships with siblings in middle age. (pp. 513-514)

18. Discuss friendship in middle age. (p. 514)

19. Explain some of the research findings about relationships between maturing children and their middle-aged parent(s). (pp. 514-517)

20. Explain what is meant by the terms:

    a. *"empty nest"* (p. 515)

    b. "not-so-empty nest" (pp. 515-516)

21. Explain the phenomenon of lifelong parenting. (pp. 516-517)

22. Describe how relationships with older parents often change during middle age, and how those changes affect the development of the middle aged adult. (pp. 517-519)

23. Discuss how the relationship between aging parents and middle aged children is affected when a parent becomes infirm. (pp. 518-519)

SUPPLEMENTAL READING

Jane Adams is the author of *I'M STILL YOUR MOTHER: How to Get Along with Your Grown-Up Children for the Rest of Your Life*, and a mother who's been there. This article, which is based on that book, is reprinted with permission from the February 1994 issue of *Good Housekeeping*.

Whose Life Is It, Anyway?

Jane Adams

I tossed restlessly as the wind whistled through the trees outside my bedroom window, surprised by my sleeplessness. I thought of my son and daughter, finally settled in college dormitories on opposite ends of the continent. It had been a long, wearying journey getting them this far, so why couldn't I sleep?

I got up and went into their rooms, banishing the silence with a flurry of shaking, dusting, and sweeping, stopping now and then to examine the discards of their childhood--outgrown clothes, old term papers, even, in a corner, a tattered teddy bear. It had always comforted me, that annual autumn rite, as if by changing the linen on their beds and lining their bureau drawers I was making a fresh start for them. But that night the familiar task seemed futile. I was troubled by the idea that there was some essential parental task I had neglected, like taking them to the dentist or teaching them to say "please" and "thank you." But their teeth and their manners were sound, so it could not be that. And it occurred to me that I was refurbishing and repairing a past they had already put behind them--that although they would be returning to this house, to these rooms, they would not be living in them again, merely passing through. And that whatever I forgot to do for them--to teach, show, notice, praise, give, or honor--they must do for themselves, or else do without. And that was why I could not sleep.

Virginia tells me about Tina, her 20-year-old, who is spending a year traveling in South America. To date she has contracted dengue fever in Bolivia, had her pocket picked in Bogota, fallen in love with several guys Virginia has never met, wired home for money, lost her passport . . . and Virginia is exhausted. "You raise them to be independent, self-reliant, and to think for themselves," she says with a sigh, "and then you spend the rest of your life worrying while they do it."

Well, yes. And no. A certain amount of apprehension is inevitable and even reasonable--the kind that started the first day your child crossed the street alone. But just as most of us eventually stop telling our kids to look both ways, we finally understand that they are beyond our protection. As Virginia adds, "All I guess I can do now is be there with a safety net."

What constitutes a safety net for an adult child? Most parents who can, don't hesitate to help out in a crisis, especially if we perceive it as not a direct result of our offspring's actions. But even that judgment is fluid, to say the least:

"Jonathan lost his job as a result of a company merger and had to borrow money from us. Yes, he should have seen it coming and not blown his savings on a Porsche, but it wasn't his fault."

"Heather left her husband and came home with the baby. She doesn't want to leave him with a sitter, and I have a job, so we've been supporting her. It's not her fault."

"Pete broke his leg skiing. I was shocked to learn he had no medical insurance, so I paid the bills. Of course it wasn't his fault."

Of course it wasn't. Although we have internalized for ourselves the values of our parents' generation about prudence, self-reliance, and independence, we judge our children's behavior according to a less stringent credo, nurtured by the "Me Decade" of the Seventies and the "victim culture" of the Eighties. For them we want fulfillment, gratification, self-realization.

Still, now that the chickens hatched by a generation of permissive, indulgent, process-oriented parents are coming home to roost, many of us, like Carrie, are beginning to run out of patience. "There are three things my grown kids can count on: a hot meal, a bed for a night, and my ear. Beyond that, I'm not making any promises," she says.

Love Means Never Saying I Told You So

Sarah never made a decision her mother didn't make for her until she married a man her mother warned her against and moved across the country with him. Things turned out exactly as her mother predicted, but Sarah, who brought the baby home once, won't come back, because her mother can't help rubbing Sarah's mistake in her face, or bad-mouthing her ex-son-in-law. When Sarah talks about the decisions she has to make now--where to live, what kind of work to do, what to do about day care--her mother undermines her confidence by harping on the one bad decision she made before and by finding flaws in Sarah's new plans: "She's just so unrealistic. She goes for the wrong kind of guys--she's seeing one now who makes the first one look like Mr. Wonderful by comparison, and he was pretty terrible. And now she's going to move into a house with two other single women and their children because she can't afford to stay in that house I told her not to buy."

Elliott quit a secure job and started a business with his savings and money borrowed from his friends. Since the venture failed, Elliott has been trying to pick up the pieces of his life and start again, with his father coaching from the sidelines. But his father's business experience occurred in a different economic climate, in an earlier time, and in a totally unrelated field. And unlike his father, who was a company man, Elliott is an entrepreneur. So parental advice on what he should do next is aggravating, even without the I told you so's.

Few people get everything right the first time, and no matter how mature or competent our children are, they're bound to suffer disappointments and failures. We pointed out the pitfalls, the consequences, and when they ensued, we told them we saw it coming.

Actually we couldn't have. Because what we predicted was based on remembering our own past and the feelings stirred up by our failures. That's how we learned not to stay out all night and party just before a final exam, not to let ourselves be exploited by people, not to get into debt--by experience, the hard way. And that's how they have to.

When They Can't Learn from Our Mistakes

We think we are closer to our children in attitude, beliefs, and life-style than our parents were to us. And in some ways we are, simply because we've lived through a cultural and societal adolescence together, rebelling against authority, questioning our institutions, liberating ourselves from outdated notions about what our proper roles should be--all that Sixties and Seventies stuff.

My daughter and I seem contemporaneous in a way my mother and I never were; after all, my mother was a wife nearly all her life, and all her other roles and pursuits were secondary. I am single, as Jenny was until last fall; we nourish careers and consciousness with equal devotion. My mother loved and lived with one man; my daughter and I have lived through a wider array of sexual choices. Our politics, values, and life-styles are remarkably similar, despite the 26 years between us. And it has taken me that long to face up to the truth that despite how contemporaneous with her I sometimes feel, she and I are not peers. Economically, socially, sexually, and professionally, Jenny's world--the one she grew up in and the one she lives in today--is as different from mine as mine was from my mother's. My daughter and I are both the New Woman, but she is newer than I am, and that makes all the difference. And when, as an adult, she makes decisions that will have major life consequences--about career, marriage, children, health--I am galled to discover that it's just as hard to let her make them herself, particularly if I think they're the wrong ones, as it must have been for my mother. The generation gap is real; only by standing on our own sides, seeing the distance between us, and acknowledging it can we bridge it.

Boomerang Kids

I couldn't wait to get my first apartment, and neither could any of my friends. So why, we all wonder, won't our kids get out of the house? Or once they do, why won't they stay out?

One reason is that we've accustomed them to a standard of living most of them won't be able to afford for years, if ever. But there are other factors contributing to the boomerang phenomenon, all of which point out the differences between their generation and ours. They're marrying later than we did, divorcing faster, spending more of their income on nonessentials, staying in school longer, competing for jobs in a retrenching economy, and being priced out of the real-estate market. This "Postponed Generation" has extended its coming-of-age by at least half a decade, if by that phrase we mean transiting the rituals that spelled adulthood to us and functioning independently. And between young adulthood and functioning independence, some of them are coming home to roost, to rest, and--so it sometimes seems--to ruin our lives.

The person who moves back in with

you is not the one who left. He has stumbled on the way to adulthood--but he has not failed at it, whatever the circumstances that brought him home. He is disillusioned, disenchanted, and disappointed, which naturally stirs your sympathy. He wants to be taken care of, and he wants to take care of himself. He may not have broken his attachment to you, although he knows by now he should have. And he feels entitled to whatever you have, which makes you angry when you give it to him or guilty when you don't. In fact he may be genuinely confused that you aren't welcoming him with open arms, refrigerator, and purse--when have you ever denied him?

Many of us have always given them not only what they need but what they want; it's time now to define the difference, to supply only some, not all, of the former, and to give the latter sparingly, even if we can afford it.

Jean Okimoto and Phyllis Stegall, in their excellent book *Boomerang Kids: How to Live with Adult Children Who Return Home* (Pocket Books), say that what adult children who return home need from their parents is empathy; a new viewpoint; encouragement to develop confidence and competence; respect for their autonomy; and acceptance of their emotional responses. Here's what we need when they're under our roof: acceptance of the conditions necessary for our comfort, which reinforces the reality that it's our house, not theirs; a way to express our feelings without taking their recrimination or anger; agreement on our personal and territorial boundaries; and an estimated date of departure.

If at First They Don't Succeed

People grow in different ways at different ages. Your daughter has her personal life together--she's in a good relationship with a decent guy--but she can't seem to hold a job. Your son knows everything about particle physics and is a rising star in his field, but he can't make a commitment to a woman or balance his checkbook. Your youngest is a psychiatric social worker with a successful practice, but at family celebrations she still picks a fight with her elder sister.

The twenties are the tryout years, and what motivates young people are two contradictory impulses: the urge to create a structure that will serve their needs into the (barely) foreseeable future and the fear of being locked into a pattern that will ultimately prove unsatisfying.

A 28-year-old who has tried three different education tracks and still hasn't finished or focused on one is driving his parents to distraction--and near bankruptcy. A 32-year-old middle manager who has hit the glass ceiling just informed her parents that she's planning to have a child on her own; her father, in turn, hits the roof. When one young man went to Israel to live in an Orthodox, fundamentalist community, his parents, mildly observant Conservative Jews, were aghast.

The truth is that our sons and daughters follow their own timetables, and when we don't agree with their priorities or validate that their needs are their own and not ours, we rob them of the chance to shape their own lives.

Maybe our spiritual wanderers will find their way home again. Maybe our children's first, youthful marriages will be their only ones. Maybe our can't-decides will find something they can stick with--someone must want a smart nearly-30-year-old with two years of med school, a third of a law degree, and all but a thesis in Renaissance history. If our unmarried daughter chooses to have a child, it won't be because it just happened, the way it did for many of us--so maybe she'll approach it with more seriousness and forethought.

According to an old Yiddish proverb, "Little children disturb your sleep, big ones, your life." You can let go of your children only when there are no conditions attached to your love for them and when you truly accept that their rights and responsibilities are the same as your own. Otherwise, you will never be more than a parent, and your child will never be more than your child.

Once, that was enough. But if you want a lifelong connection with that person, you must set aside those labels long enough to discover another way of relating to him or her--as a friend.

<u>Questions</u>:

How would being a "boomerang" child affect the development of the returning child?

How does having a "boomerang" child affect friendships and relationships with aging parents?

SELF TESTS

Multiple-Choice

Circle the letter of the response which best completes or answers each of the following statements and questions.

1. It has been suggested that midlife crisis, which may be a potentially stressful period in early to mid 40s, is brought on by
   a. living with teenagers
   b. dissatisfaction with one's career
   c. dissatisfaction with one's marriage
   d. review and reevaluation of one's past

2. The idea of a midlife crisis springs from the ________ model of adult development.
   a. normative-crisis
   b. timing-of-events
   c. developmental-crisis
   d. transitionary disturbance

3. According to Carl Jung, after about age 40 men and women are
   a. concentrating on their obligations to their families
   b. free to balance their personalities
   c. concentrating on their obligations to society
   d. free to upset the balance in their lives

4. Jung's theory of personality development emphasized the
   a. early development of self-esteem
   b. search for identity in mid-life
   c. elimination of egocentrism in mid-life
   d. quest for meaning in life

5. The virtue resulting from successful resolution of Erikson's seventh crisis--generativity versus stagnation--is
   a. love
   b. trust
   c. self-control
   d. care

6. Which aspect of Erikson's view of generativity is most likely to be rejected today?
   a. People usually seek a mentor.
   b. People are concerned about their mortality.
   c. People who have not been parents do not easily achieve generativity.
   d. People value wisdom over physical power.

7. Generativity corresponds to Schaie's ____________ and __________ stages of cognitive development.
   a. productive; purposeful
   b. industry; achievement
   c. commitment; attachment
   d. responsible; executive

8. _______________, defined by Peck as the ability to make the best choices in life, appears to depend largely on sheer life experience and the opportunities of encountering a wide range of relationships and situation.
   a. emotional flexibility
   b. wisdom
   c. mental flexibility
   d. stagnation

9. According to Peck, various psychological developments must take place
   a. prior to middle age or the person will regress to an earlier stage
   b. during middle age for optimal developmental maturity
   c. by midlife or the person will not make a successful emotional adjustment
   d. after midlife to first allow the successful resolution of the midlife crisis

10. Vaillant found that the Harvard male graduates he studied had a tendency toward
    a. depression
    b. introspection
    c. crisis
    d. happiness

11. Erikson's theory was supported by Vaillant's finding that
    a. the best-adjusted men were also the most generative
    b. most men reported a disturbance in midlife that approached a crisis
    c. generativity was more work related for men and more home-related for women
    d. the midlife crisis was typically related to generativity issues

12. An important task for men in midlife, according to Levinson's studies, is to deal with
    a. reevaluation and change
    b. career disappointments
    c. financial demands
    d. mental inflexibility

13. A criticism of the normative-crisis models of Erikson, Vaillant, and Levinson is that
    a. they lack longitudinal studies
    b. none have been based on current trends
    c. they have all been male-oriented
    d. the samples were too small

14. Barnett, Baruch and Rivers studied almost 300 women between the ages of 35 and 55 and found that two elements which appear to influence a woman's mental health are
    a. mastery of and pleasure from her life
    b. nurturance and freedom
    c. freedom and pleasure
    d. individuality and sexuality

15. Based on research studies, a woman's well-being generally
    a. flourishes when the demands on her are low
    b. is highest when she must deal with multiple roles
    c. deteriorates when she must deal with multiple roles
    d. is lowest when she must deal with the stress of too much to do

16. Women generally reported the period of middle age, especially around age 50, as
    a. no different from any other age
    b. the most stressful age
    c. a time of extreme turmoil
    d. the prime of life

17. All of the following, except which statement, are cited criticisms of the normative-crisis model of adult development?
    a. The subjects of most studies have been privileged white men, or women born in the 1920s or 1930s.
    b. Studies have been too limited to support a definite age-linked sequence of development.
    c. The midlife crisis, which is virtually both inevitable and universal, is not given sufficient consideration.
    d. Because the men in these models are characterized as emotionally constricted, the models are inappropriate, not only to women, but also to healthy men.

18. Research best supports the conclusion that adult development is
    a. the product of a definite age-linked sequence
    b. influenced by culture and gender as well as age
    c. a result of gender roles and unrelated to age
    d. strictly a cultural phenomenon with no age-related aspects

19. Based on a variety of research studies, midlife is best characterized as a period of
    a. tranquility c. turmoil
    b. crisis d. transition

20. Proponents of the self-in-relation theory suggest that
    a. women are oriented more to connections and men more to independence
    b. men need to be "trained" to connect whereas women are natural connectors
    c. both men and women have a primary desire for connection with others
    d. happiness for men is self-oriented and for women is relation-oriented

21. The view that adult development hinges on the events in people's lives is called the
    a. life-event developmental model c. life-event crisis model
    b. normative-crisis model d. timing-of-events model

22. Which of the following statements best characterizes marital satisfaction in a long-term marriage?
    a. From an early high point, it declines until late middle age and then rises again through the first part of late adulthood.
    b. From its early starting point, it increases until late middle age and then declines through the first part of late adulthood.
    c. From an early low point, it increases until late middle age and remains stable until the first part of late adulthood.
    d. From its early starting point, it remains stable until late middle age and then rises again through the first part of late adulthood.

23. A recent finding about marital satisfaction suggests that
    a. the happiest time is during the child rearing years
    b. the least happy time is old age
    c. the years immediately after children leave home may bring as much contentment as the early years of the marriage
    d. the happiest time is when people are heavily involved in their careers

24. A criticism of the research on marital satisfaction is that
    a. samples have been too large
    b. samples have been cross-sectional rather than longitudinal
    c. samples were not randomly assigned to groups
    d. samples have been longitudinal rather than cross-sectional

25. A strong marriage, which fits Sternberg's definition of consummate love, embodies
    a. stability, attachment, and comfort
    b. intense physical attraction with emotional ups and downs
    c. passion, intimacy, and commitment
    d. mutual admiration and compatibility of interests

26. The reason/reasons most frequently given for lasting marriages is/are
    a. a positive attitude toward the spouse as a friend and a person
    b. a commitment to marriage
    c. agreement on aims and goals in life
    d. all of the above

27. Divorces among middle-aged married couples
    a. are rare once the children are grown and leave home
    b. occur for many of the same reasons that younger couples divorce
    c. have occurred at a decreasing rate since about 1980
    d. occur at the lowest rate of any age group of married couples

28. On a survey by Lauer and Lauer, happily married couples responded that
    a. they were happy despite disagreements over aims and goals in life
    b. sex was the primary reason for their happiness
    c. they spent much time apart pursuing separate interests
    d. they spent much time together and shared many activities

29. In midlife, relationships with siblings
    a. usually deteriorate with only infrequent and sporadic contacts
    b. are usually damaged by events like divorces, widowhood, or death
    c. are often the longest-lasting relationships in people's lives
    d. are generally not close, especially for sisters who become intense rivals

30. Which of the following statements about friendships in middle age is false?
    a. Age is more a factor in making friends than similarity of life events.
    b. Friendships do persist through life and are a strong source of emotional support.
    c. Middle-aged people seem to have less time or energy for friendship than people in other stages of life.
    d. Similarity of life events is more important in making friends than age.

31. Middle-aged people tend to have
    a. fewer friends than newlyweds, but more than older people
    b. fewer friends than either newlyweds or people about to retire
    c. more friends than newlyweds, but fewer than people near retirement
    d. more friends than any other age group

32. Which of the following statements about relationships with maturing children is most accurate?
    a. The most frequent area of disagreement among middle-aged couples was about adult children returning to live at home.
    b. Children often overidentify with their parents' ambitions.
    c. Children must realize that their parents have total control over them.
    d. An important task for parents is to accept their children as they are.

33. The "empty-nest" crisis is particularly difficult for
    a. fathers
    b. parents whose children do not become independent
    c. women who have not prepared for their children's leaving
    d. all of the above

34. Most women report that, after the children leave home, they
    a. experience severe depression
    b. feel emotionally conflicted
    c. feel liberated
    d. miss the "chronic emergency of parenthood"

35. If children do not leave home when the parents expect them to, there may be psychological conflict because
    a. adult children living with parents may fall into dependent habits while parents continue as caregivers.
    b. young adults are likely to feel isolated from peers and not develop intimacy
    c. parents may be deprived of freedom to renew intimacy and to resolve marital issues
    d. all of the above

36. The return of a child to live at home works best when
    a. it is temporary
    b. the children are over 25 years old
    c. the child is unemployed
    d. the child socializes primarily with the parents' friends

37. Generally speaking, middle-aged parents and their adult children
    a. are resentful and are adversaries on many issues
    b. get along well and enjoy each others company
    c. get along at a distance, with minimal contacts
    d. reverse the roles that each had filled previously

38. Which of the following statements about caring for elderly parents is false?
    a. Many older people feel it would be easy to live with their children.
    b. The strain of caring for elderly parents most often shows up in physical and emotional exhaustion.
    c. Somehow, most people do not expect to have to take care of their parents and rarely plan ahead for it.
    d. Relationships between middle-aged adults and their parents are usually characterized by a strong bond of affection.

39. The "sandwich generation" refers to
    a. adolescent children of middle-aged parents who feel torn between loyalty to their parents and the need to associate with their peers
    b. middle-aged parents torn between obligations to their parents and the need to help launch their own children
    c. adolescent children of middle-aged parents who feel squeezed between adults and younger siblings
    d. middle-aged adults who feel anguish over their lost youth and who also fear the infirmities associated with aging

40. The death of a parent often results in mid-life adults
    a. seeking new relationships with elderly people
    b. abandoning relationships with other elderly people
    c. reviewing and evaluating their own lives and goals
    d. regressing to an earlier developmental stage

Completion

Supply the term or terms needed to complete the following statements.

1. A potentially stressful period during the early to mid forties precipitated by an evaluation of one's life is called __________.

2. The __________ approach to human development, popularized by Vaillant and Levinson (and Erikson) is that human personality goes through a universal sequence of critical changes at certain ages.

3. Carl Jung's theory emphasized the quest for ___________ in life.

4. Erikson's seventh crisis in development, which occurs at midlife, is _____________ versus _______________.

5. _________ is the concern of mature adults for establishing and guiding the next generation (or for productivity or creativity), because people feel a need to participate in the continuation of life.

6. If this crisis is not met or resolved successfully, Erikson says that people will become ___________________.

7. A mutually fulfilling relationship that satisfies a younger protégé's need for guidance as well as an older person's need for generativity is often found in ___________ .

8. The virtue in Erikson's seventh stage is ________ .

9. Peck's four critical psychological developments related to successful adjustment in middle age are: valuing wisdom versus _________ powers; socializing versus _________; emotional flexibility versus emotional _________; and mental flexibility versus mental _________.

10. Vaillant's Grant Study, which was a longitudinal study into middle age, found that the best-adjusted men in the study saw the years from 35 to 49 as the ________________.

11. Neugarten's term for people's concern with introspection (their "inner" life) is _________.

12. Levinson describes midlife for men as a time when life structures _________ change appreciably.

13. The most influential normative-crisis theories of adult development have been based primarily on ____________________ subjects.

14. Two main factors influence middle aged women's mental health; ___________ and ______________.

15. Women's well being during middle adulthood seems to flourish in _____________.

16. The _________ model suggests that personality development is influenced less by age than by what events people experience and when they occur.

17. Marital satisfaction usually starts high, then _____________ until middle age and then ______________ through the first part of late adulthood.

18. A strong marriage that embodies passion, intimacy, and commitment seems to fit Sternberg's definition of __________________ .

19. Relationships with siblings are the _________________ in most people's lives.

20. The time of transition for a couple when the last child leaves home is popularly called the _____________________, which may be a time of personal or marital crisis.

21. The ______________________ refers to the phenomenon of adult children returning home to live with their parents.

22. Most parents of children 16 or over express ____________ with their role as parent.

23. _________________ refers to the adult child's sense of duty to help aging parents.

24. Often during middle age, people are able to look at their parents ____________ for the first time.

25. The strong mother-daughter bond may be partly explained by the fact that adult children are most likely to help the ____________ parent.

26. The person who is most likely to care for elderly parents is a ________________.

27. Elderly parents tend to be somewhat selective focusing their attention and aid on the child who ______________________.

28. The text refers to the "sandwich generation" as adults who are torn between obligations to their ______________ and ______________ .

29. The stress associated with caring for elderly parents was _________ for African American daughters than for white women.

30. Parents and children both feel better when the care children give aging parents comes more from a sense of ______________ than a sense of _________ .

Multiple-Choice

		Page				Page	
1.	d	500	conceptual	21.	d	511	factual
2.	a	500	conceptual	22.	d	511	factual
3.	b	501	factual	23.	c	511	factual
4.	d	501	factual	24.	b	512	factual
5.	d	503	factual	25.	c	513	factual
6.	c	503	factual	26.	d	513	factual
7.	d	503	factual	27.	b	513	conceptual
8.	b	503	factual	28.	d	513	factual
9.	c	504	conceptual	29.	c	513	conceptual
10.	b	504	conceptual	30.	a	514	conceptual
11.	a	504	conceptual	31.	b	514	factual
12.	a	504	conceptual	32.	d	515	conceptual
13.	c	504	factual	33.	d	515	conceptual
14.	a	506	conceptual	34.	c	515	factual
15.	b	506	conceptual	35.	d	516	conceptual
16.	d	508, 515	conceptual	36.	a	516	factual
17.	c	508-511	conceptual	37.	b	516	factual
18.	b	508-511	conceptual	38.	a	518-519	conceptual
19.	d	510	conceptual	39.	b	519	factual
20.	c	510	conceptual	40.	c	520	conceptual

Completion

		Page			Page
1.	midlife crisis	500	16.	timing-of-events	511
2.	normative crisis	501	17.	declines; rises	511
3.	meaning	501	18.	consummate love	513
4.	generativity; stagnation	503	19.	longest lasting	513
5.	generativity	503	20.	empty nest	515
6.	stagnant	503	21.	not-so-empty-nest	515
7.	mentorship	503	22.	satisfaction	516
8.	care	503	23.	filial responsibility	517
9.	physical; sexualizing; impoverishment; rigidity	503	24.	objectively	517
			25.	same-sex	518
10.	happiest	504	26.	daughter	518
11.	interiority	504	27.	needs them most	518
12.	always	504	28.	parents; children	519
13.	male	504	29.	less	519
14.	mastery; pleasure	506	30.	attachment; duty	519
15.	multiple roles	506			

CHAPTER 16

Physical and Intellectual Development in Late Adulthood

INTRODUCTION

Many developmental changes and challenges still lie ahead for people after the age of 65. Chapter 16 examines physical and intellectual development in late adulthood, the last age-defined group discussed in the text.

- The chapter begins with an examination of some common myths about aging and a discussion of how people can make the most of their later years.
- Longevity and the aging process are discussed from two theoretical perspectives, and the physical changes in late adulthood and health problems and concerns of older adults are described.
- Changes in intelligence and intellectual functioning in late adulthood are discussed, as are changes in the functioning of memory.
- The relationship between intellectual activity and intellectual functioning are discussed in the context of lifelong learning.
- Finally, the chapter closes with an examination of the influence of work and the transition to retirement.

CHAPTER OUTLINE

I. **Old Age Today**

- A. What is our Attitude toward Old Age?
- B. Who are the Elderly?
  - 1. "Young Old" and "Old Old"
  - 2. The Graying of the Population
  - 3. The Oldest Old
    - a. Gender differences
    - b. Health
    - c. Life circumstances
- C. How Can We Make the Most of the Later Years?

PHYSICAL DEVELOPMENT

II. **Longevity and the Aging Process**

- A. Life Expectancy
  - 1. Trends in Life Expectancy
  - 2. Death Rates and Causes of Death
  - 3. Race, Gender, and Life Expectancy
    - a. Racial differences
    - b. Gender differences
- B. Why People Age: Two Theories
  - 1. Programmed Aging
  - 2. Aging as Wear and Tear

III. **Physical Changes of Old Age**

- A. Sensory and Psychomotor Functioning
  - 1. Vision
  - 2. Hearing
  - 3. Taste and Smell
  - 4. Strength, Coordination, and Reaction Time
- B. The Brain in Late Adulthood
- C. Other Physical Changes
- D. Reserve Capacity

IV. **Health in Old Age**

- A. Health Care and Health Problems
  - 1. Medical Conditions
  - 2. Dental Health
- B. Influences on Health and Fitness
  - 1. Exercise and Diet
- C. Mental and Behavioral Disorders
  - 1. Reversible Mental Health Problems
    - a. Depression
    - b. Overmedication

2. Irreversible Mental Problems
   a. Alzheimer's disease
      (1) Causes of Alzheimer's disease
      (2) Symptoms and diagnosis
      (3) Treatment
   b. Other irreversible conditions

INTELLECTUAL DEVELOPMENT

V. Aspects of Intellectual Development

A. Does Intelligence Decline in Late Adulthood?
   1. Two Views of Intelligence
      a. Fluid and crystallized intelligence: Which is more important?
      b. Fluid and crystallized intelligence: How are they tested?
         (1) Sequential testing
         (2) Helping older people improve their intellectual performance
   2. A New View: Mechanics and Pragmatics of Intelligence
B. How Does Memory Change in Late Adulthood?
   1. The Three Memory Systems
      a. Sensory memory
      b. Short-term (or working) memory
      c. Long-term memory
   2. Why Does Memory Decline?
      a. Biological hypotheses
      b. Processing hypotheses
      c. Contextual considerations
      d. Memory training

VI. Lifelong Learning: Adult Education in Late Life

VII. Work and Retirement

A. Why People Retire
B. How People Feel about Retirement
C. Making the Most of Retirement
   1. Planning Ahead
   2. Using Leisure Time Well

KEY TERMS

ageism (page 526)

Alzheimer's disease (541)

dementia (540)

dual-process model (547)

free radicals (533)

gerontology (526)

life expectancy (531)

long-term memory (547)

mechanics of intelligence (547)

plasticity (546)

pragmatics of intelligence (547)

primary aging (534)

programmed-aging theory (533)

reserve capacity (537)

secondary aging (534)

selective optimization with compensation (547)

senescence (530)

sensory memory (547)

short-term memory (547)

terminal drop (545)

wear-and-tear theory (533)

LEARNING OBJECTIVES

After finishing Chapter 16, you should be able to:

1. Describe common attitudes toward old age and the elderly. (p. 526)

2. Identify various categories of elderly people. (pp. 526-528)

3. Explain several specific steps that an older people can take in order to make the most of their later years. (p. 529)

4. Define *senescence* and explain why changes in life expectancy in this century have focused attention on it. (p. 530)

5. Describe current trends in life expectancy. (p. 531)

6. List the major causes of death among older people. (pp. 531-532)

7. Describe the differences in life expectancy attributable to race. (p. 532)

8. Describe the differences in life expectancy attributable to gender. (pp. 532-533)

9. Summarize the main points of the *programmed-aging theory*. (p. 533)

10. Summarize the main points of the *wear-and-tear theory* of aging. (p. 533)

11. Distinguish between *primary aging* and *secondary aging*. (p. 534)

12. Describe the changes in vision associated with old age. (p. 534)

13. Describe the changes in hearing associated with old age. (pp. 534-535)

14. Describe the changes in taste and smell associated with old age. (p. 535)

15. Describe the changes in strength, coordination, and reaction time associated with old age. (pp. 535-536)

16. Describe the physical changes to the skin and bones that are associated with old age. (p. 537)

17. Define *reserve capacity* and explain its relevance to aging. (p. 537)

18. Describe the general health of older people, and list the health problems that commonly affect older people. (pp. 537-539)

19. List and describe the factors that influence health and fitness among the elderly. (pp. 539-540)

20. List and describe some of the reversible mental health problems that afflict older people. (pp. 540-541)

21. Discuss the causes, symptoms, and treatment of *Alzheimer's* disease. (pp. 541-543)

22. Describe some techniques for measuring changes in intellectual functioning. (pp. 543-544)

23. List some physical and psychological factors that can influence older adults' performance on intelligence tests, and how older people continue to learn. (pp. 545-546)

24. Discuss the *dual-process model* of intellectual functioning, which helps explain how some aspects of intelligence seem to increase with age. (p. 547)

25. Describe differences between young people and old people in *sensory*, *short-term*, and *long-term memory*. (pp. 547-548)

26. Summarize the various theories that seek to explain these differences. (pp. 548-550)

27. Discuss the importance of continued mental activity and explain how learning and memory are interrelated. (pp. 550-551)

28. Describe the effect of work and retirement on the older person. (pp. 551-552)

29. List and describe some of the things that can be done to insure a fulfilling retirement. (pp. 552-553)

SUPPLEMENTAL READING

From the south of France to the hills of Cameroon, people are grappling with the meaning of work and whether they can ever afford to retire. This article by Susan Champlin Taylor, with reporting by Mary Blume (France), Mbalaka Robert Bonsasa (Zaire), Prakash Chandra (India), Alison Lester (Japan), and Azah Tebe (Cameroon), is reprinted with permission from the October-November 1993 edition of *Modern Maturity*.

The End of Retirement

Susan Champlin Taylor

In the grassy highlands of Bamenda, Cameroon, Peter Mba Muyu Tebe reaches into his small black bag and pulls out a fistful of polished brass medals. These are his rewards for loyal service to the Ministry of Agriculture, where he's worked for 35 years, driving into the hinterlands to demonstrate farming techniques and equipment. He reaches into the bag again and his hand emerges holding a necklace with a star-shaped pendant, a gift from "the President of the Republic himself." He nods in a small gesture of self-praise.

After all these years, Muyu Tebe looks forward to his retirement three years down the road. He has it all mapped out: "Rest, a lot of travel, and pleasure in a Swiss city on a Mediterranean beach." Oh, yes, and caring for his late father's three elderly wives, educating his 15 children by his own three wives, running two large plantain and coffee plantations in his native village 20 miles away, overseeing the houses he rents out in Bamenda, heading the PTA, championing school reforms, and working with the Credit Unions, Farmers' Cooperative, and the Pipe-borne Water Project.

It should be a very relaxing retirement, indeed.

Muyu Tebe is riding the wave of the future: what you might call the end of retirement as we know it. The world's over-60 population numbered nearly 500 million in 1991; by 2020 it is expected that figure will surge to a full billion older people. This startling shift in demographics leads many experts to predict huge financial and cultural problems down the road--unless we rethink our notions of work and retirement.

The crisis mentality that attends these population figures rests on old assumptions: that the "retired" are dependent, sucking up nations' scarce resources and giving nothing in return; that they have no vital role in, and make no valuable contribution to, their societies.

"You will always have the older old--the fourth age--and yes, more of these people will be dependent," says Julia de Alvarez, one of the Dominican Republic's deputy ambassadors to the United Nations. "But there is no reason to discard a person just because he or she turns 60."

Rather than seeing seniors as an economic burden, adds Mukunda Rao, an international consultant on social-development issues, it's crucial to view them as an untapped resource, not only for themselves, but for the broader society. "Today," he says, "industrialized societies with their outmoded ideas about retirement are wasting their precious resources."

When it originated in the 1800s, the idea of "retirement" was actually intended in part to do the opposite--to avoid wasting resources, human and financial. Forcing (or strongly encouraging) retirement phased out older, more expensive workers and brought in younger, cheaper ones.

In 1889, Germany's "Iron Chancellor," Otto von Bismarck, instituted the first pensions on a national scale. He set an initial eligibility age of 70, later changed to 65. Bismarck was not entirely the altruist this would make him seem (life expectancy then was about 45.) Other countries have adopted different age limits, but the arbitrary nature of retirement ages today--when life expectancy has increased significantly--renders them not only meaningless but wasteful in the extreme. Over the years, the age of retirement has come to symbolize an end to productivity, even when there is no physical or mental reason for it.

"I think this idea of old age linked to retirement, with a sudden dropping-off from the workforce, is an unfortunate product of the industrial revolution," Rao says. "It needs to be rethought." For one thing, in developed countries the need to make room for younger workers will no longer exist; in fact, quite the opposite: The "birth dearth" that followed the baby boom means that fewer young workers will be entering the workforce. Older workers may well become hot commodities. Secondly, we simply can't afford to maintain retirement and pension plans as they've traditionally existed. Finally, the outdated notion of retirement as a withdrawal into some utopian idyll does not play in a rapidly changing world.

Industrialized nations with expansive social-welfare systems are already feeling the cash crunch. Realizing that their systems will prove far too expensive in the future, these countries (primarily in Europe) are having to think about scaling them back--though politically acceptable ways of doing so are hard to come by. In an effort to reduce the cost of public retirement benefits, several countries, including the United States, have started by raising the eligibility age; more draconian measures may be down the road.

The potential costs of health care are also frightening countries with socialized medicine. As a small first step many European countries are leaning more heavily on volunteers, families and creative problem-solving; e.g., Sweden's use of rural mail carriers to look in on the isolated elderly people on their routes.

While money woes are cutting into industrialized nations' ability to care for the old, the globalization of culture and communications is undermining the traditional support networks of developing countries.

"You sit in a remote village in India and you can watch CNN," says Rao. "Is that a good thing or a bad thing? On the one hand, you get instant news; on the other you get MTV. It projects different values. From a young person's perspective, what comes from outside--especially from the West--is always better."

With so many outside influences, young people's respect for tradition and for older generations decreases. Peter Mba Muyu Tebe is a well-respected assistant in Bamenda's ministry of Agriculture. Yet at home he is alarmed by the cultural gap growing between himself and his 15 children. His boys refuse to attend the traditional ceremonies in which elders pay respect to their ancestors, and they will not dress traditionally. "They always want to be in three-piece suits, while the girls are not ashamed to wear trousers like men," Muyu Tebe laments. "Worst of all, they talk of boyfriends or girlfriends and quite often shamelessly kiss before my very eyes. What an abomination books and TV have brought into our culture."

In families where reverence for the elderly remains strong, it is geographic, rather than cultural, separation that may determine whether the younger generations can care for the older. Says Julia de Alvarez, "Years ago, people didn't migrate that much. Now you have young people migrating from developing countries to the already-developed ones, or from rural areas to the cities, where they may have small apartments and can't take care of the elderly. It's not that they don't want to; they're just not in a position to do it."

In Tokyo, housewife Sumiko Yoshida is in the midst of changing cultural expectations. "Today's children are focusing almost entirely on education and getting into good schools, whereas they used to spend time with their grandparents learning about the old days and learning to care about them," she says. "I can see already on the train that young children are happy to sit while old people remain standing." Yoshida herself helps her brother and widowed sister care for their blind 92-year-old mother, yet she does not expect her own 25-year-old daughter, Kyoko, to look after her and her husband in their old age. Though Yoshida's husband used to say he wanted Kyoko "close enough so that the soup doesn't get cold," he is changing his mind, and the couple already discuss plans to move into a new retirement home two blocks from their house.

Similar cultural upheavals are forcing many nations to rethink the whole idea of retirement. In so doing, developing and developed nations can learn from each other. "Industrial countries are moving away from the concept of retirement for economic reasons, but it never really operated in developing countries at all," says Sandeep Chawla, Ph.D., co-author with Marvin Kaiser, Ph.D., of a U.N. study on the implications of population aging in the Dominican Republic, Chile, Sri Lanka and Thailand.

Christine Fry, Ph.D., professor of anthropology at Loyola University of Chicago, notes that in Botswana, among the !Kung Bushmen and Herero of the Kalahari Desert--as in many traditional societies--the notion of retirement is nonexistent. One works until one is no longer physically able. "There's also no retirement in Hong Kong," Fry adds. "People start out having steady work, then get laid off or fired; they may not be able to find another full-time job, so it turns part-time. Then they just gradually withdraw from the workforce."

If people want to remain economically productive and have no physical limitations, however, why not make full use of their skills to benefit society? Julia de Alvarez, for example, helped set up a program in the Dominican Republic in which 12 teachers were brought out of retirement to run a preschool program in the rural mountain area near the Haitian border.

"Without exception these teachers say they feel 'reborn,'" says De Alvarez. "This has added joy to their existence, as well as being economically good for them."

Working after "retirement" for spiritual and economic reward is also a goal of microenterprises--small businesses--run by older people. Such endeavors can provide one alternative for developing nations that can't afford large-scale social-welfare programs for their senior populations. "Microenterprises allow people to be engaged and productive while contributing to their own economic security," says Marvin Kaiser.

Economics isn't everything, however. Focus exclusively on older people working for pay and you miss the many other kinds of contributions they make: to their families, their communities and their cultures.

"Ironically, we measure productivity solely in terms of cash," says Christine Fry. "That means you're not productive, which doesn't make much sense."

In many places where generations live together, older people play vital roles such as cooking, cleaning or providing childcare. When living in Kiev, Ukraine, Igor Persidsky, M.D., his wife, Lena Krushniruk, and their four-year-old daughter, Marina, shared what Persidsky calls "an informal support network" with their 75-year-old neighbor, Maria Skripnik. "She looked after Marina when we were busy after work," says

Persidsky. "And when Maria needed medical attention, I was happy to provide it. Neither of us would ever take money from the other." A standard economic measure would consider Maria Skripnik unproductive. But to Persidsky, the dollar value of her services was, in fact, substantial.

Seemingly invisible contributions like housework and childcare can no longer be ignored, says Charlotte Nusberg, outgoing secretary-general of the international Federation on Ageing: "If you define economic productivity to include unpaid support activities for family and friends, and volunteer activities, then most older people certainly are productive"--even when they're allegedly "retired."

Consider retiree Gian Singh. On a sultry afternoon in the sprawling New Delhi suburb of Janak Puri, he sits in the shade of a neem tree in a local park playing a game of sweep, sipping a Campa-Cola, and joking with his retired friends. The genial, bearded Sikh is enjoying himself; he is not, however, just killing time. After he retired from government service four years ago at age 58, Singh and his friends formed an informal social club that--besides playing cards--takes on local problems.

"For example," Singh explains, "if there is an inflated electricity or telephone bill, we meet the officials concerned. This way we have solved a number of our day-to-day problems." Though club members receive no money for their efforts, Singh says he is "rather happier than when I was in government service and used to go to an office every day." In fact, he adds, outsiders who don't belong to the club "envy our lot."

Similar volunteer efforts--both informal and organized--will be critical in the future, says Mark Gorman, development director of London-based HelpAge International, a multinational coalition of service organizations for the elderly. "Many of our member organizations run different versions of good neighbor programs that show how older people are going to cope in the absence of government support. Basically, it's going to have to be self-help."

In the Mediterranean island nations of Malta, volunteers run an eldercare version of Neighborhood Watch: They look out for each other and quickly spot signs of trouble. If an elderly neighbor fails to show up for church, for example, a volunteer goes out to check on the person.

"These are not high-cost programs at all," says Gorman, "and they're an effective way to maintain people in their own communities and homes so they don't end up institutionalized."

This notion of self-reliance strikes a responsive chord with Mukunda Rao. Government, community and family have vital roles to play in aging issues, Rao says, but the individual is the final key component. "Older people have to develop some real understanding of their own resources. They need to assess their skills and knowledge and adapt themselves to different types of work and employment patterns," he says. "And they need to reassess their own attitudes. Sometimes they look to the past and say, 'This is what was valid before.' They need to see things as they are today."

Armed with this consciousness, Rao says, "Older people need to make their case known--to make known their importance to national development itself."

In this way the alleged "problem" of an aging population becomes its own answer. As Julia de Alvarez says, "Every time I go to talk to policy-makers, they say, 'Here she comes again with a problem.' I tell them, 'I'm not bringing a problem--I'm bringing a solution.'"

Questions:

How do the attitudes reported in this article compare to American ideas about retirement, work, and aging?

How would the extension of work life beyond the traditional age of retirement affect the work force?

SELF TESTS

Multiple-Choice

Circle the letter of the response which best completes or answers each of the following statements and questions.

1. Ageism refers to
   a. reverence and respect for elderly people
   b. prejudice or discrimination based on age
   c. belief that elderly people are especially wise
   d. scientific study of the aging processes

2. The study of the aged and the aging processes is called
   a. ageism
   b. ageology
   c. gerontology
   d. portiology

3. Which of the following statements is true?
   a. People 85 years old and older are the fastest-growing age group in the United States.
   b. The elderly are generally poorly coordinated, feel tired most of the time, and are prone to infections.
   c. The elderly tend to become isolated from their families as they become self-pitying and cranky.
   d. The elderly have little or no interest in or desire for sexual relationships.

4. Which of the following statements is most accurate?
   a. Financial need is one aspect of aging where there are no gender differences.
   b. Older men are more likely to be poor than older women; the major reason for their impoverishment being the death of their wives.
   c. Older women are more likely to be affluent than older men; the major reason being that they are the beneficiaries of their deceased husbands' life insurance policies.
   d. Older women are more likely to be poor than older men; the major reason being the death of their husbands.

5. Which of the following statements is most accurate?
   a. Because old age is the period during which deaths most frequently occur, the elderly are the smallest age group.
   b. Long life expectancy, high birth rates at the turn of the century, and immigration have all caused an increase in the size of the older population.
   c. The size of the elderly population has begun to decline and will continue to do so for several decades.
   d. The size of the elderly population has been stable for decades and is expected to remain so.

6. The health problems of older women are likely to be ________________ while the health problems of older men are generally ________________ .
   a. short-term and fatal; long-term and chronic
   b. long-term and chronic; short-term and fatal
   c. short-term and chronic; long-term and fatal
   d. long-term and fatal; short-term and chronic

7. The majority of people over the age of 85 live
   a. in their own home
   b. in a home of one of their children
   c. in a nursing home
   d. in a hospital

8. Compared to the today's "old-old," future groups of the "oldest old" are likely to be
   a. less healthy and worse off financially
   b. less educated and in greater need of financial assistance
   c. better educated, healthier, and better off financially
   d. in poorer health, although better off financially

9. The branch of medicine concerned with aging is called
   a. gerontology
   b. geriometry
   c. geriatrics
   d. gerontography

10. Which of the following is true about aging?
    a. Most old people are poorly coordinated.
    b. Most old people are isolated from others.
    c. Most old people easily fall prey to infections.
    d. All of these statements are myths.

11. The period of the life span marked by declines in bodily functioning is known as
    a. burnout
    b. climacteric
    c. menopause
    d. senescence

12. Life expectancy, which has been rising, is now expected to
    a. remain the same
    b. begin to decline
    c. stabilize
    d. continue rising

13. The life expectancy in the United States in 1991 was about ________ years.
    a. 76
    b. 80
    c. 68
    d. 83

14. By far, the biggest killer of people over age 65 is
    a. cancer
    b. accidents
    c. heart disease
    d. respiratory illnesses

15. On average white Americans live ____________ than non-white Americans, and women live ________________ than men.
    a. shorter; longer
    b. longer; longer
    c. longer; shorter
    d. shorter; shorter

16. Which theory of aging holds that human bodies age in accordance with a normal developmental pattern built into each organism?
    a. primary-aging
    b. secondary-aging
    c. wear-and-tear
    d. programmed aging

17. Which theory holds that aging is a result of continuous use and of accumulated "insults" to the body?
    a. primary-aging
    b. secondary-aging
    c. wear-and-tear
    d. programmed-aging

18. Research revealing the harmful effects of free radicals is most consistent with which aging theory?
    a. primary-aging
    b. secondary-aging
    c. wear-and-tear
    d. programmed-aging

19. The gradual process of bodily deterioration that begins early in life and continues inexorably through the years is known as
    a. primary-aging
    b. secondary-aging
    c. wear-and-tear
    d. programmed-aging

20. Aging due to disease, abuse, and disuse--factors often under our own control--is known as
    a. primary-aging
    b. secondary-aging
    c. wear-and-tear
    d. programmed-aging

21. Which of the following statements about older people's senses is most accurate?
    a. Farsightedness that begins in middle age will continue to worsen during old age, eventually resulting in functional blindness.
    b. Elderly people, whose other senses have deteriorated, rely more on their sense of smell, which actually improves with age.
    c. Because they generally have more body fat than younger people, the elderly are less sensitive to extremes of temperature.
    d. Hearing loss is very common in old age, with about 3 of 10 people over 65 and half of those over 75 being hearing-impaired.

22. The practical difference between the programmed-aging theory and the wear-and-tear theory is
    a. minimal; the differences are mainly of theoretical interest to scientists who study aging
    b. non-existent; whether programmed-aging or the wear-and-tear theory is correct has almost no practical implications for people's lives or for how we think about aging
    c. that if programmed-aging is correct, there is little we can do to alter the aging process; but if wear-and-tear is correct, we may be able to live longer by eliminating stressors
    d. that if the wear-and-tear theory is correct, there is little we can do to alter the aging process; but if programmed-aging is correct, we may be able to live longer by eliminating stressors

23. What causes the general "slowing down" of older people?
    a. environmental deprivation, depression, and neurological changes
    b. illness, disease, and injury
    c. years of exposure to environmental toxins and pollutants
    d. all of the above

24. Changes to the brains of older people are
    a. consistent and significant, resulting in gradual loss of neurological function
    b. not always destructive, in fact some changes, such as the growth of dendrites, seem to compensate for other factors
    c. the cause of the general decline in most intellectual, emotional, and sensory functioning
    d. non-existent, with most scientists agreeing that the brains of older people are no different from the brains of younger people

25. Which of these is not a physical change associated with old age?
    a. Varicose veins are more common.
    b. Women's hair becomes fuller.
    c. Skin becomes paler and splotchy.
    d. Skin loses elasticity.

26. The extra capacity to increase bodily functions in times of stress is called
    a. supplemental resource
    b. backup capacity
    c. backup reserve
    d. reserve capacity

27. Which of these statements about fitness for older people is false?
    a. Regular exercise helps maintain speed and stamina.
    b. Regular exercise can lead to arthritis as joints are aggravated.
    c. Regular exercise improves mental alertness.
    d. Regular exercise can relieve anxiety and depression.

28. Confusion, forgetfulness, and personality changes that are sometimes associated with old age are characteristics of an apparent general intellectual deterioration called
    a. Alzheimer's disease
    b. dementia
    c. senility
    d. senescence

29. Symptoms of depression in older people include
    a. extreme sadness
    b. lack of interest or enjoyment in life
    c. tending to do childish things
    d. both a and b

30. ______________ is a degenerative brain disorder that gradually erodes intelligence, awareness, the ability to control bodily functions, and finally is fatal.
    a. Alzheimer's disease
    b. dementia
    c. senility
    d. senescence

31. Which of these statements about intellectual functioning in old age is most accurate?
    a. Most psychologists agree that general intellectual decline in old age is a myth.
    b. Most psychologists recognize that deterioration of intellectual functioning is a normal part of aging.
    c. Since abilities related to solving novel problems are at the heart of intelligence, and since there is an increase in such abilities in old age, declining intelligence is not a general problem for the elderly.
    d. There is some disagreement among psychologists about the progress of intellectual functioning in old age.

32. The sudden decrease in intellectual performance shortly before death is known as
    a. terminal drop
    b. senile dementia
    c. anticipatory shutdown
    d. death anticipation syndrome

33. Variability in a person's intellectual performance is known as
    a. elasticity
    b. plasticity
    c. cognitive flexibility
    d. situational variability

34. Content-free architecture of information processing and problem solving refers to the ________________ of intelligence.
    a. synergistics
    b. mechanics
    c. pragmatics
    d. dynamics

35. Practical thinking, application of accumulated knowledge and skills, specialized expertise, professional productivity, and wisdom are known as the ____________________ of intelligence.
    a. synergistics
    b. mechanics
    c. pragmatics
    d. dynamics

36. When a person looks up a telephone number, closes the directory, and then dials, the number is stored in __________ memory, which is relatively unaffected by age.
    a. sensory
    b. working
    c. short-term
    d. long-term

37. With regard to memory in old age, which of the following statements is accurate?
    a. Long-term memory for recent events deteriorates with old age.
    b. Memory for events far in the past declines with old age.
    c. Visual sensory memory deteriorates with advancing age.
    d. Short-term memory is most affected by old age.

38. Older people seem to learn new skills and information best when
    a. the instruction is repeated frequently during a brief period
    b. the material is presented in concentrated form in a relatively short time period
    c. there are few intervals between presentations
    d. the materials and methods take into account the physiological, psychological, and intellectual changes they are encountering

39. Retirement
    a. has little effect on physical health, but it sometimes affects mental health
    b. usually causes a gradual deterioration in physical health
    c. usually results in a general improvement in physical health
    d. usually causes an overall improvement in mental and emotional health

40. Two key elements in helping people find retirement more fulfilling are
    a. continuing to work as late as possible and avoiding structure during retirement
    b. retiring early while one's health is still good and avoiding contact with retired people as long as possible
    c. delaying thinking about retirement as long as possible and avoiding contact with retired people
    d. planning for retirement early and using time productively during retirement

Completion

Supply the term or terms needed to complete each of the following statements.

1. Prejudice or discrimination based on age, which is usually directed against older persons, is known as ________________ .

2. ________________ is the study of aging and the aging process.

3. The period of the life span known as ________________ is marked by changes in physical functioning associated with aging.

4. ____________________ refers to the number of years that a person is expected to live based on statistical data.

5. On the average, white Americans live ____________ than black Americans, and women live ____________ than men.

6. The idea that there is an inherent pattern to the aging process and that this pattern is only slightly modifiable is consistent with the ________________ theory.

7. The idea that aging is a result of deterioration of the body as a result of continuous use is consistent with the ____________________ theory of aging.

8. ________________ is the gradual, inevitable process of bodily deterioration that begins early in life and continues through the years.

9. ________________ is the result of disease, abuse, and disuse and is to some extent avoidable and under people's control.

10. The farsightedness that affects most people in middle age _________ at about age 60.

11. Older people can do most of the things that younger people do, but they do them more _______________.

12. The ability of the body to put forth more effort than usual during times of stress is known as the ________________ .

13. People who _____________ tend to live longer.

14. The general term for the apparent intellectual deterioration associated with old age, characterized by confusion, forgetfulness, and personality changes, is ___________ .

15. From 2 to 10 percent of people over 65 are victims of ______________, a degenerative brain disorder that affects intelligence, awareness, and the ability to control bodily functions.

16. Schaie and Baltes maintain that some intellectual abilities, mostly _________ abilities, either hold their own or increase in later life.

17. The poor showings of older people in cross-sectional studies of intelligence may be due to _______________, a sudden decrease in intellectual functioning shortly before death.

18. The variability or modifiability of a person's performance is called _____________ .

19. ______________ of intelligence consist of content-free areas of information processing and problem solving.

20. ______________ of intelligence includes such areas as practical thinking and the application of accumulated knowledge and skills.

21. Pragmatic intelligence can help older people maintain their intellectual functioning through ______________________.

22. Images in _________________ memory fade very quickly unless they are transferred to short-term memory.

23. One memory study showed that older people had trouble _____________ items, but they did just as well as younger people in _____________ items.

24. Motivation, intelligence, learning habits, degree of familiarity with test items, and type of task are all ________________ factors, which may account for individual differences in memory.

25. Older people can learn new skills, but they learn better when the instruction takes into account the ____________, ______________, and ______________ changes they may be going through.

26. Most people leave their jobs _____________________ the retirement age their employers set.

27. The proportion of older women who work has ____________ from 1950 to 1990.

28. The most satisfied retirees tend to be _______________ people who are using their skills in part-time paid or volunteer work.

29. Retirement has little effect on ___________ health but it sometimes affects ___________ health.

30. Two key elements for a fulfilling retirement are ______________ before retirement and good use of _______ during retirement.

ANSWERS FOR SELF-TESTS — CHAPTER 16

Multiple-Choice

		Page				Page	
1.	b	526	factual	21.	d	534	conceptual
2.	c	526	factual	22.	c	535	conceptual
3.	a	528	factual	23.	a	535	factual
4.	d	528	conceptual	24.	b	537	conceptual
5.	b	528	conceptual	25.	b	537	factual
6.	b	529	conceptual	26.	d	537	factual
7.	a	529	conceptual	27.	b	540	factual
8.	c	529	factual	28.	b	540	factual
9.	c	529	factual	29.	d	541	conceptual
10.	d	529	conceptual	30.	a	541	factual
11.	d	530	factual	31.	d	543	conceptual
12.	d	531	factual	32.	a	545	factual
13.	a	531	factual	33.	b	546	factual
14.	c	531	factual	34.	b	547	conceptual
15.	b	532	factual	35.	c	547	conceptual
16.	c	533	conceptual	36.	c	547	conceptual
17.	c	533	conceptual	37.	a	547	conceptual
18.	c	533	conceptual	38.	d	551	conceptual
19.	a	534	conceptual	39.	a	552	factual
20.	b	534	conceptual	40.	d	552-553	factual

Completion

		Page			Page
1.	ageism	526	17.	terminal drop	545
2.	gerontology	526	18.	plasticity	546
3.	senescence	530	19.	mechanics	547
4.	life expectancy	531	20.	pragmatics	547
5.	longer; longer	532	21.	selective optimization with compensation	547
6.	programmed aging	533	22.	sensory	547
7.	wear-and-tear	533	23.	recalling; recognizing	549
8.	primary aging	534	24.	contextual	550
9.	secondary aging	534	25.	physiological; psychological; intellectual	551
10.	stabilizes	534	26.	at or before	551
11.	slowly	535	27.	decreased	551
12.	reserve capacity	537	28.	physically fit	552
13.	exercise	539	29.	physical; mental	552
14.	dementia	540	30.	preparation; time	552
15.	Alzheimer's disease	541			
16.	crystallized	543			

CHAPTER 17

Personality and Social Development in Late Adulthood

INTRODUCTION

How people adapt to aging depends, to a large extent, on their personalities and on how they have adapted to situations throughout life. They can experience the last stage of life positively and may even experience it as a time of growth and fulfillment.

- Chapter 17 begins with an examination of two theories of psychological development in late adulthood: Erikson's eighth crisis, integrity versus despair, and Peck's three crises of late adulthood.

- The chapter then describes the results of several research studies pertaining to emotional health and the stability of the personality in late adulthood.

- Several approaches to successful aging are discussed, including activity theory and disengagement theory.

- The relationship between personality and patterns of aging are discussed, and four major personality types, with associated patterns of aging are described.

- The chapter examines several social issues related to aging, such as changes in income, choices of living arrangements (including nursing homes), and the shocking problem of abuse of the elderly.

- A discussion of personal relationships in late life is provided, including such topics as: marriage and marital happiness, divorce, surviving a spouse's death, remarriage, sexual relationships, relationships with siblings, and friendships.

- The chapter concludes with an exploration of relationships with adult children, with a discussion of childlessness, and with the benefits of grandparenthood.

CHAPTER OUTLINE

I. **Theory and Research on Personality Development**

   A. Erik Erikson: Crisis 8--Integrity versus Despair
   B. Robert Peck: Three Adjustments of Late Adulthood
   C. George Vaillant: Factors in Emotional Health
   D. Research on Stability and Change in Personality
   E. "Approaches to Successful Aging"
      1. Disengagement Theory
      2. Activity Theory
      3. Personal Definitions of Aging Successfully
   F. Personality and Patterns of Aging

II. **Social Issues Related to Aging**

   A. Income
   B. Living Arrangements
      1. Living Independently
      2. Living in Institutions
         a. Who lives in nursing homes?
         b. What makes a good nursing home?
         c. Problems in nursing homes
   C. Abuse of the Elderly

III. **Personal Relationships in Late Life**

   A. Marriage
      1. Marital Happiness
      2. Strengths and Strains in Late-Life Marriage
   B. Being Single Again: Divorce and Widowhood
   C. Remarriage
   D. Single Life: The "Never Marrieds"
   E. Sexual Relationships
   F. Relationships with Siblings
   G. Friendships
   H. Relationships with Adult Children
      1. How Parents Help Children
      2. How Children Help Parents
   I. Childlessness
   J. Grandparenthood and Great-Grandparenthood

KEY TERMS

activity theory (page 562)

elder abuse (570)

disengagement theory (562)

integrity versus despair (558)

LEARNING OBJECTIVES

After finishing Chapter 17, you should be able to:

1. Explain Erikson's eighth crisis--*integrity versus despair*--and the virtue that results from its successful resolution. (pp. 558-559)

2. Describe the three psychological adjustments of late adulthood according to Peck.

   a. broader self-definition versus preoccupation with work roles (p. 559)

   b. transcendence of the body versus preoccupation with the body (pp. 559-560)

   c. transcendence of the ego versus preoccupation with the ego (p. 560)

3. Describe some of the factors that have been found to be associated with emotional health in late adulthood. (pp. 560-561)

4. List and discuss some of the research findings on stability and change in personality in late adulthood. (p. 561)

5. Summarize the main ideas of the following two theories of successful aging:
   a. *disengagement theory* (p. 562)

   b. *activity theory* (pp. 562-563)

6. Describe the four major personality types found in elderly people.
   a. integrated (p. 564)

   b. armor-defended (p. 564)

   c. passive dependent (pp. 564-566)

   d. unintegrated (p. 566)

7. Explain how income affects the way people adjust to aging. (p. 566)

8. Discuss the relationship between one's living arrangements and the way one adjusts to aging. (pp. 566-570)

9. Describe each of the following independent living arrangements.

   Retirement and life-care communities (p. 569)

   Sharing a house (p. 569)

   Group homes (p. 569)

   Accessory housing (p. 569)

10. Describe those elderly who live in nursing homes. (pp. 569-570)

11. Describe the characteristics of a good nursing home. (p. 570)

12. List and discuss some problems sometimes found in nursing homes. (p. 570)

13. Discuss the problem of abuse of the elderly. (pp. 570-572)

14. Describe some research findings about marital happiness in long-term marriages. (pp. 572-573)

15. Discuss some of the strengths and strains in late-life marriage. (p. 573)

16. Discuss the issue of divorce among the elderly. (p. 574)

17. Discuss remarriage in late adulthood. (p. 574)

18. Explain how being single and never married is related to growing old. (pp. 574-575)

19. Describe how sexual relationships develop in old age. (pp. 575-576)

20. Explain the significance and quality of relationships between elderly people and the following:

    a. siblings (p. 576)

    b. friends (pp. 576-577)

    c. adult children (pp. 577-578)

21. Describe what life is like for the elderly who are childless. (pp. 578-580)

22. Discuss how the elderly adapt in roles as grandparents and great-grandparents. (pp. 580-581)

SUPPLEMENTAL READING

This article by Bill Hewitt (with Gabrielle Saveri in Rome, Margaret Wright and Ellin Stein in London, and Nancy Matsumoto in Los Angeles) describes how science is enabling women to give birth after menopause, raising the troubling question, "How old is too old?." This article is reprinted with permission from the January 24, 1994 issue of *People*.

Turning Back The Clock

Bill Hewitt

It's one thing when life imitates art. When it begins to imitate the supermarket tabloids, even the most jaded can't help but take notice. So it was when the London papers heralded the news that a prosperous 59-year-old businesswoman identified only as Jennifer F. had given birth on Christmas Day--to twins, no less.

Last spring in Rome, using sperm from Jennifer's 45-year-old fiancé (who became her husband in November), Dr. Severino Antinori, a reproductive specialist, fertilized four eggs donated by a young Italian woman and implanted them in Jennifer's uterus, which he had earlier regenerated from the effects of menopause with hormone therapy. Hailed as one of the oldest women ever to give birth, Jennifer was described by one friend as being "ecstatically happy."

Most other people seemed more shocked than delighted. Few had dreamed that postmenopausal women could be capable of giving birth. Yet in recent years, without much fanfare, scores of women old enough to be grandmothers have done just that--most of them in Europe but a growing number in the U.S. as well. And if there is anything miraculous to the procedure, it is its relative simplicity. In essence, Antinori, 48, and other scientists have discovered that once the uterus is reconditioned with hormone treatments and donor eggs are found, doctors can use much the same in vitro fertilization methods they do for younger women who experience difficulty getting pregnant. Given the opportunity to help Jennifer and others, asked Antinori, who has helped facilitate 54 births in women over 50, "Who am I to play God and say that she should not have a chance?"

More and more, however, the bundles of joy are coming wrapped in controversy, especially in Britain, where the Jennifer F. case has unleashed a fierce debate. Some medical ethicists argue that the prospect of women giving birth in their 50's and 60's raises a host of disturbing questions. "I don't believe any woman has an inalienable right to have a child. I am 73 and the thought of having a 14-year old around appalls me," says Dame Mary Donaldson, former chairwoman of the British fertilization and embryology licensing authority. Adds Dr. Richard Marrs, director of the Center for Assisted Reproductive Medicine in Santa Monica: "Are we going to have children who are orphans at the age of 12 because their parents die of old age?"

Other experts contend that disqualifying women on the basis of age alone creates a double standard. In the wake of the controversy created by Jennifer's twins, Prof. Robert Edwards, one of the pioneers of IVF, complained, "If a man of 60 fathers a baby, then we buy him a drink and toast his health at the pub. But it is totally different with a woman of the same age. It's unfair."

And what of the women themselves? How have they fared in this brave old world? By and large, they seem delighted with their choice. For more than 20 years, Liliana Cantadori and her husband, Orlando, of Modena, Italy, had been trying to have a child. At the time of their marriage, in 1972, Liliana was already 41, 10 years older than her husband. After two miscarriages and repeated fertility treatments, they had all but given up hope of a baby. Then, in the early '80s, with the growing success of IVF, the Cantadoris once again went searching for a miracle. By this time Liliana was in her early 50s and had to lie about her age; the doctors would not consider helping any woman over 50. She was able to fool her doctors, in part because she had been taking hormones on her own for years and had not passed through menopause. There was also the issue of money. Liliana, who worked as a midwife in a hospital, says that she and her husband, a hospital porter, scrimped and saved and took out loans to pay for the treatments, which eventually cost $300,000.

In 1986 she turned up at Antinori's clinic in Rome; she was 55 but told people she was 45. After two years of trying, without success, she traveled to Bologna to consult with yet another specialist, Prof. Carlo Flamigni, telling him that she was 47. After three tries at IVF she got pregnant using donated eggs and her husband's sperm. "I knew the risks, and I knew that the baby could die, that I could die, that we both could die," she said. "But I did it anyway."

The pregnancy went smoothly until the seventh month, when Cantadori came down with severe hypertension (dangerously high blood pressure) and swelling and had to enter the hospital until she delivered. Nevertheless, on July 27, 1992, Andrea was born in excellent health at 6 lbs. 6 ozs.--thereby earning Liliana a place in the *Guiness Book of Records* as the oldest-ever birth mother. The cesarean section, however, took a severe toll on Liliana, who didn't admit to an angry Flamigni that she was 61 until after she got pregnant. "I thought I would die," she recalled. "They had trouble waking me up. If in pregnancy a 30-year-old loses her strength, imagine a 60-year-old."

These days those memories have largely faded. Now 18 months old, Andrea is doing well. "We give him the best steak," said Liliana. "He doesn't lack anything." On Jan. 1 she began receiving her pension, which provides a helpful supplement to Orlando's salary. Liliana has few regrets about her decision. In fact, there are rumors in the Italian press that she is trying to get pregnant again. She admits that she would like another child, but as to whether she is actually trying she will say only, "It's a secret." Likewise, for American country singer Jonie Mosby Mitchell the pleasures of late motherhood far outweigh the drawbacks. In March 1992 Mitchell, now 54, gave birth to a son, Morgan, using donor eggs from a 30-year-old woman, a procedure that cost a total of $20,000. "I feel wonderful," says Mitchell, whose husband Donnie, 47, supplied the sperm. "I probably feel better now than I did when I was younger, working in smoky bars."

Which is not to say that motherhood gets any easier after 50. Up each day at 5 a.m., Mitchell does chores in the morning before dropping Morgan off at day care. Then she puts in a half day of work at the country music club she and her ex-husband, Johnny Mosby, run in Ventura, California. Picking up Morgan in the afternoon, she heads home to prepare dinner. By 8:30 p.m. she's in bed and ready to start the cycle all over again. In contrast to most other older moms, Mitchell already had four children from her marriage to Mosby, which ended in 1977. But she and Donnie--who have an adopted daughter, Sydney, age 5--were considering adopting another child when they learned about IVF. "When you give birth, you have more control over the situation," says Mitchell.

"You're not dealing with attorneys or worrying about getting a call and losing the baby." Mitchell says that most people she meets, once they get over the initial shock of mistaking her for Morgan's grandmother, express nothing but support. "Women will go, 'Hey, Jonie, right on!'" she says. "I have not heard one negative comment."

Indeed, as Mitchell sees it, about the only static has come from her own family. She says her 29-year-old daughter, Lindy, was taken aback by the pregnancy. "She wasn't that wild about it, I'll admit," says Mitchell. If nothing else, Jonie thinks, she may have unintentionally stolen the spotlight when she had Morgan only 2 1/2 months after Lindy gave birth to her own daughter, Natalie. Since then, Lindy and her mother have learned a new way of bonding and are now sharing baby-sitting duties.

Given the profound jolt to the family structure that comes with late-life pregnancies, it is hardly surprising that relatives can be some of the sternest critics. As Jennifer F.'s brother told London *Daily Mail*, "I think she has gone stark raving mad. She's going to be drawing child benefits at the same time she draws her old-age pension." Her decision to have a baby so late in life, he added, was essentially selfish. "She's spent her whole life making money and now suddenly she's found that she's been making it for no purpose," he said. "She thinks children will provide a purpose. [But] no child deserves to be born to such an old mother. I honestly don't think about the future."

But one friend of Jennifer's was more sympathetic. "She had everything--a great job, a $900,000 house and a loving partner," the friend told the *Daily Express*. "The one thing she didn't have was children. She thought she had missed the boat."

In truth, the motivation of some of the older mothers can at times seem questionable, if quite understandable. One of

Dr. Antinori's most celebrated current cases in Italy involves a farmer's wife named Rosanna Della Corte, who will turn 63 next month. She is now three months pregnant and thus a candidate to become the oldest woman ever to give birth. Della Corte began dreaming of having a baby after her only child, Riccardo, was killed in a motor-scooter accident in July 1990 at the age of 17. The fact that Rosanna is still mourning Riccardo, to whom she gave birth when she was 42, has led some critics to suggest that she is merely trying to re-create her lost offspring. (Before she decided to become pregnant, she and her husband, Mauro, first tried unsuccessfully to adopt.)

Rosanna, who was implanted with a donated egg fertilized by Mauro, 65, doesn't deny wanting to replace their lost son. "If I still had Riccardo I never would have done it," she told the *Times* of London. "I would so like to have another boy. I would so like to see the likeness of Riccardo again, but I will accept the child just as it comes." For his part, Antinori argues that a team of psychologists cleared Della Corte for his treatment. As for her ability to nurture her son into adulthood, he points out that her parents lived into their 90's. "If she stays in good condition," he says, "she'll live another 30 years."

Antinori's efforts have brought him considerable attention, not all of it flattering. Some critics have questioned whether he is more interested in fame than in his patients. One woman, who wishes to remain anonymous, says that four years ago, at the age of 36, she gave birth to triplets thanks to Antinori's treatment. According to the woman, who is a municipal employee, she agreed to do some promotional work for Antinori in return for his waiving part of her bill. She says she had no idea that a photographer would be present in the delivery room or that photographs of her newborns would be sold to a string of newspapers and magazines. "He thinks he is a personality and that's all that matters," says the woman. "I would be afraid to send someone to him." Antinori staunchly denies that he is after publicity--or money. "My family is rich," says the doctor, who has two teenage daughters with his wife, Caterina, 43, a biologist. "I already had a Ferrari at 20 years of age."

All the same, Antinori, who originally trained to be a veterinarian before going into gynecology, has displayed a gift for stirring up controversy. He once said that he had been present at the 1978 birth of Louise Brown, the world's first test-tube baby--a claim denied by the medical team that delivered the child. Last year he disclosed that he had been asked to treat Jane Fonda, now 56, who had recently married Ted Turner. Both Fonda and Turner promptly declared that wasn't so.

As the debate has grown over the propriety of impregnating older woman, so too have calls for government-imposed age limits. In response, Antinori--whose fertility clinic in Rome is located a quarter mile from that staunch foe of IVF, the Vatican--vigorously defends the rights of researchers to pursue their efforts unfettered by regulation. Even so, he does say that he personally considers 63 or 64 the outer limit. "The only important consideration," he says, "is the individual decision by the doctors and the couple."

In the end, of course, the symbolic importance of later-life pregnancies as a way to level the biological playing field will probably always be far greater than the number of woman actually seeking the treatment. Yet, for those few older woman who do choose the option, the rewards of nurturing can seem as real as they are intangible, much as they do for younger couples. Two years ago, one of Antinori's patients, Giuseppina Maganuco, now 56, managed to have a baby after 20 years of trying. She sees her daughter, Anna Maria, as a godsend. "I don't care what people think," she says. "My house has been reborn." Mention the future--or the chance she will die while her daughter is still young--and she quickly changes the subject to the present. "I have wanted a baby all my life," she says. "All the love we can give, we are giving. I will give all I can until I die, and then after...I don't know."

<u>Questions</u>:

What are some of the social issues that parenthood in old-age raises?

How does parenthood in old-age alter our concept of old-age?

SELF TESTS

Multiple-Choice

Circle the letter of the response which best completes or answers each of the following statements and questions.

1. The virtue resulting from successful resolution of Erikson's last crisis of personality development is
   a. will
   b. wisdom
   c. generativity
   d. care

2. According to Erikson, during the last developmental stage, people who do not gain a sense of order and meaning from their lives will experience
   a. bereavement
   b. overwhelming despair
   c. paranoia
   d. schizophrenia

3. Which of the following statements is most consistent with Erikson's view of late adulthood?
   a. While integrity must outweigh it, some despair is inevitable as people mourn their own misfortunes and lost chances as well as general human transience.
   b. Despair is best avoided by completely avoiding thoughts of one's own impending death.
   c. Integrity is achieved by careful scrutiny of one's life, with serious consideration of what could have been done better and what was done wrong.
   d. The healthiest development is attained from using the remaining years to try to make up for the mistakes and poor choices of the past.

4. According to Robert Peck, people need to redefine their worth as human beings, beyond their work roles, through a process of
   a. transcendence of integrity
   b. focusing on the past life of work
   c. broader self-definition
   d. consolidation of physical abilities

5. Peck suggests that in dealing with the physical decline which accompanies aging, a person should
   a. find compensatory satisfactions
   b. develop a focus on relationships
   c. concentrate on improving muscular coordination and strength
   d. both a and b

6. According to Peck, the most difficult task older people face is
   a. adapting to the prospect of death
   b. cultivating mental and social powers
   c. living alone
   d. living in institutions

7. Peck feels that it is possible for people to feel positive about their own death through
   a. children they have raised
   b. the way they have lived and their personal relationships
   c. contributions they have made to their culture
   d. all of the above

8. Some older people, instead of achieving self-transcendence, become preoccupied with
   a. intimate relationships
   b. ambition
   c. meeting their own needs
   d. accomplishments

9. The longitudinal study of George Vaillant found that
   a. the best adjusted 65-year-olds were scholarly, analytic, or creative
   b. a happy marriage, a successful career, and a childhood free of major problems were all unimportant in predicting good adjustment late in life
   c. good adjustment in later life depended on the same factors linked to adjustment earlier, like spontaneity and making friends easily
   d. earlier traits linked to good adjustment, such as organization, stability, and dependability, were not important in predicting late life adjustment

10. Studies on the stability of personality in old age have concluded that
    a. personality is fundamentally stable, and therefore further development of the personality in old age is highly unlikely
    b. personality is basically fluid, with fundamental change in most aspects of personality being highly likely in old age
    c. some aspects of personality were stable throughout old age, while others were changeable, suggesting that personality development in old age is possible
    d. the measurement of personality traits is so difficult that it is impossible to assess the stability of such traits in old age

11. The theory that sees aging as a process of mutual withdrawal is called
    a. activity theory
    b. wear-and-tear theory
    c. programmed-aging theory
    d. disengagement theory

12. The more active older people remain, the better they age, is the basis for
    a. activity theory
    b. wear-and-tear theory
    c. programmed-aging theory
    d. disengagement theory

13. Disengagement theory suggests that
    a. people voluntarily want to cut down on activities and commitments
    b. the older a person gets, the more active he or she becomes
    c. our culture encourages people to stay involved in work and work-related associations
    d. none of the above

14. The activity theory of aging suggests that
    a. the earlier people retire, the happier they are
    b. roles are a major source of satisfaction in life
    c. the happiest people are those involved in structured activities
    d. the less active people are, the more successfully they age

15. Research comparisons of disengagement theory and activity theory
    a. have produced findings generally consistent with disengagement theory
    b. have produced findings generally consistent with activity theory
    c. has not shown that either of these models is more accurate than the other
    d. have not been conducted

16. Studies comparing middle-aged and older people found that the older respondents
    a. expressed unhappiness with family problems
    b. indicated that they would change nothing in their lives except their health
    c. were eager to accomplish more in terms of schooling or occupation
    d. emphasized continuous growth as important

17. One classic study identified four major personality types associated with aging. The largest group of people, who were functioning well with high levels of satisfaction, had a pattern of life called
   a. integrated
   b. armor-defended
   c. passive-dependent
   d. unintegrated

18. The personality type of people who were achievement-oriented, striving, and tightly controlled is called
   a. integrated
   b. armor-defended
   c. passive-dependent
   d. unintegrated

19. People who sought comfort from others or who were apathetic were classified as
   a. integrated
   b. armor-defended
   c. passive-dependent
   d. unintegrated

20. Disorganized people, with gross defects in psychological functioning, poor control over their emotions, and deteriorated thought processes possessed a style called
   a. integrated
   b. armor-defended
   c. passive-dependent
   d. unintegrated

21. One of the major findings about older adults' income is that
   a. those who live alone are often more financially secure
   b. for most people, pensions and IRAs are the single largest source of income
   c. many people face poverty for the first time in old age
   d. old age is the time when people have the highest income

22. Which of the following statements about poverty and older people is most accurate?
   a. A wife's death is a major financial risk factor for her widower.
   b. Most women are better off financially following the death of a husband.
   c. Single people are at higher risk of poverty than married people.
   d. Married couples rarely become impoverished after retirement.

23. The majority of elderly people
   a. live in institutions
   b. live with spouses, children, or other relatives
   c. are widowed men
   d. are eager to give up their independence and prefer to live with their children

24. Living arrangements available for the elderly include
   a. group homes and retirement communities
   b. cooperatives, shared housing, and "granny" flats
   c. independent living and nursing homes
   d. all of the above

25. The single most important factor keeping people out of nursing homes is being
   a. in poor health
   b. mentally incapacitated
   c. poor
   d. married

26. The best quality nursing home care is provided by
   a. larger, non-profit facilities with a high ratio of nurses to nursing aides
   b. small, family style facilities with lay staff
   c. state or local government operated facilities with licensed or certified staff
   d. private facilities operated for profit and licensed by the government

27. Elder abuse, the neglect or physical or psychological abuse of a dependent older person, is most likely to occur
    a. to elderly people living with a spouse or child
    b. to elderly people living in a nursing home
    c. to elderly people living alone
    d. to minority elderly people or to those who are poor

28. The primary source of emotional support for the elderly is
    a. friends and coworkers
    b. family
    c. both a and b
    d. neither a nor b

29. It has been reported that there is greater marital satisfaction in late adulthood because
    a. people are at a stage when they can enjoy life in general
    b. the decision to divorce usually comes in the earlier years of a marriage
    c. there are fewer strains on a marriage at this time
    d. both a and b

30. Success of marriages in late life is enhanced by
    a. the couple's ability to adjust to the personality changes of middle age
    b. one partner being increasingly dependent on the other
    c. the changing roles of husbands and wives as they get older
    d. the deteriorating health of one partner

31. What is the most common reason older men give for deciding to remarry?
    a. They are forced to by circumstances beyond their control.
    b. They want better housing.
    c. They want more money.
    d. They want companionship and relief from loneliness.

32. Compared to the typical person of their age, older never-married people tend to be
    a. less independent
    b. not satisfied with their lives
    c. less lonely
    d. more affected by aging

33. Sexuality in old age is
    a. related to the consistency of sexual activity over the years
    b. characterized by greater physical intensity
    c. marked by increased sexual tension
    d. more frequent than at younger ages

34. Research suggests that siblings
    a. become less involved with each other as they grow older
    b. have the same kind of relationships in old age that they had in middle age
    c. tend to see each other less often than they did in middle age
    d. view relationships with each other as less important than they did earlier

35. Among older people, which of the following are especially important in maintaining family relationships?
    a. brothers and sisters equally
    b. brothers
    c. sisters
    d. children and grandchildren more than brothers and sisters

36. Which of the following statements about older people's relationships with friends is most accurate?
    a. Spending time with friends results in greater satisfaction with life.
    b. Friends are a powerful source of immediate enjoyment.
    c. Older men tend to value friendships more than older women do.
    d. Friends provide more reliable emotional support than do family members.

37. Older people's relationships with their children
 a. become more distant than at any other time
 b. grow closer when the older person's health is poor
 c. become more actively parental when their adult children need help
 d. is of decreasing importance to both the parents and the children

38. Children's relationships with elderly parents are typically characterized by
 a. resentment of the demands that their parents place on them
 b. indifference toward the needs of their parents
 c. conflict as their aging parents' needs increase
 d. conscious recognition of their obligation to their parents

39. Older people without children generally are
 a. lonelier than older people with children
 b. more negative about their lives than older people with children
 c. not different from older people with children
 d. more afraid of death than older people with children

40. The longing to transcend mortality by investing oneself in the lives of future generations is most often reflected in
 a. grandparenthood
 b. charitable and philanthropic donations
 c. remarriage
 d. relationships with siblings

Completion

Supply the term or terms needed to complete each of the following statements.

1. Erikson's eighth crisis in personality development is ________________ versus ________________.

2. The virtue of Erikson's eighth stage is ________________.

3. Peck's first crisis in late adulthood is broader self-definition versus ________________.

4. The need to overcome concerns about one's physical condition and to find compensating satisfactions is what Peck calls ________________ versus ________________.

5. Disengagement theory holds that disengagement is ________________, ________________, and ________________.

6. ________________ theory holds that the more active older people remain, the better they age.

7. The happiest elderly people are the ones involved in ____________ activities; whereas ____________ activities actually had a negative effect.

8. Of the four major personality types mentioned in terms of their relationship to aging, the ____________ people were functioning well, with a high level of satisfaction.

9. Of the four major personality types mentioned in terms of their relationship to aging, the ____________ people either sought comfort from others or were apathetic.

10. Of the four major personality types mentioned in terms of their relationship to aging, the ______________ people had low activity levels and low life satisfaction.

11. ________________ is the largest source of income for older people in the U.S.

12. ______________ older people live in poverty today than in the past few decades.

13. _______ percent of older people live in the community, and about ______ percent live in institutions.

14. Independent housing units created by remodeling a home or set up on the property of a home are called ____________________________________.

15. The single most important factor keeping people out of institutional living arrangements is being _______________ .

16. It is estimated that many of the people who go into nursing homes _____________ nursing care but have no better alternative.

17. An essential element in good nursing home care is the opportunity for residents to ____.

18. The neglect or abuse of dependent older people is known as _______________ .

19. The success of a marriage in late life may depend on the couple's ability to adjust to the personality changes of ____________________________________.

20. Marital problems in later life most often arise in situations where the husband is retired and the wife is ____________________ .

21. ______________ in late life is rare; if a couple are going to take this step, they usually do it at an earlier stage.

22. In a survey asking why they had decided to remarry, men tended to mention _______ and ____.

23. In a survey asking why they had decided to remarry, women tended to mention ______________________________ or ______________________________.

24. Research by Masters and Johnson concluded that people who have ________________ during their younger years are likely to remain sexually active in later life.

25. _____________ relationships are the longest-lasting ties in most people's lives.

26. Although ____________________________ provide more reliable emotional support, older people enjoy more the time they spend with _________________.

27. When older people need help, they usually turn first to ______________________.

28. Adult children help their aged parents in many ways, sometimes just by their _____ .

29. Studies show that grandparents play a _________________ role in family dynamics.

30. ______________________________ tend to have closer, warmer relationships with grandchildren than ______________________________ do.

ANSWERS FOR SELF-TESTS — CHAPTER 17

Multiple-Choice

		Page	
1.	b	559	factual
2.	b	559	conceptual
3.	b	559	factual
4.	c	559	conceptual
5.	d	559	conceptual
6.	a	560	factual
7.	d	560	factual
8.	c	560	conceptual
9.	b	560	conceptual
10.	c	561	conceptual
11.	d	562	factual
12.	a	562	factual
13.	a	562	conceptual
14.	b	562	conceptual
15.	c	562	conceptual
16.	b	563	conceptual
17.	a	564	factual
18.	b	564	factual
19.	c	564	factual
20.	d	566	factual
21.	c	566	conceptual
22.	d	566	conceptual
23.	b	566	factual
24.	d	569	factual
25.	d	569	factual
26.	a	570	conceptual
27.	a	570	factual
28.	b	572	factual
29.	d	572	conceptual
30.	a	573	conceptual
31.	d	574	factual
32.	c	574	conceptual
33.	a	575	factual
34.	b	576	conceptual
35.	c	576	factual
36.	b	577	conceptual
37.	c	577	factual
38.	d	578	conceptual
39.	c	579	factual
40.	a	581	conceptual

Completion

		Page
1.	integrity; despair	558
2.	wisdom	559
3.	workrole preoccupation	559
4.	body transcendence; body preoccupation	560
5.	normal, universal, necessary	562
6.	activity	562
7.	informal; formal	562
8.	integrated	564
9.	passive-dependent	564
10.	unintegrated	566
11.	social security	566
12.	fewer	566
13.	95%; 5%	569
14.	accessory housing	569
15.	married	569
16.	do not need	569
17.	make decisions	570
18.	elder abuse	570
19.	middle age	573
20.	still working	573
21.	divorce	574
22.	companionship; relief from loneliness	574
23.	their feelings for their husbands; their husbands' personal qualities	574
24.	active sexual lives	575
25.	sibling	576
26.	family members; friends	576
27.	their children	577
28.	existence	578
29.	limited but important	580
30.	grandmothers; grandfathers	581

CHAPTER 18

Death and Bereavement

INTRODUCTION

Chapter 18, the final chapter of the text, examines the final chapter of life--death and bereavement.

- The chapter begins with a discussion of three aspects of death: biological, social, and psychological.

- Attitudes, at different ages, toward death and dying are discussed, as are the idea of confronting one's own death and dealing with bereavement, mourning, and grief.

- Coping with the death of a spouse is discussed, as are various aspects of living as a widow or widower.

- Several important controversial issues related to death and dying are examined, namely, euthanasia and suicide.

- Finally, the chapter concludes with an examination of finding a purpose in life and death, which includes a discussion of the meaning of death.

CHAPTER OUTLINE

I. Three Aspects of Death

II. Facing Death

A. Attitudes toward Death and Dying across the Life Span
   1. Childhood
   2. Adolescence
   3. Young Adulthood
   4. Middle Adulthood
   5. Late Adulthood
B. Confronting One's Own Death
   1. Changes Preceding Death
      a. Personality changes
      b. Near-death experiences
   2. "Stages of Dying": Elisabeth Kübler-Ross
C. Bereavement, Mourning, and Grief
   1. A Multicultural Perspective on Mourning
   2. Forms of Grief
      a. Anticipatory grief
      b. "Grief work": A three-phase pattern
      c. Other patterns of grieving
   3. How Children Cope with Bereavement
   4. Helping People Deal with Dying and Bereavement
      a. Implications of research
      b. Grief therapy
      c. Hospices
      d. Support groups and services
      e. Death education
         (1) Goals of death education
         (2) Teaching children about death
D. Widowhood: Surviving a Spouse
   1. Adjusting to the Death of a Spouse
   2. Living as a Widow or Widower

III. Controversial Issues of Death and Dying

A. Euthanasia and the Right to Die
B. Suicide
   1. Patterns of Suicide
      a. Suicide among children
      b. Suicide among adolescents
      c. Suicide among adults
   2. Preventing Suicide
      a. What society can do
      b. What family and friends can do
         (1) Warning signs of suicide
         (2) Actions that might avert suicide

IV. Finding a Purpose in Life and Death

A. The Meaning of Death
B. Reviewing a Life

KEY TERMS

active euthanasia (page 603)

anticipatory grief (596)

bereavement (593)

death education (600)

grief (593)

grief therapy (599)

hospice care (599)

life review (611)

living will (605)

medical durable power of attorney (609)

mourning (593)

near-death experience (592)

passive euthanasia (604)

thanatology (588)

LEARNING OBJECTIVES

After finishing Chapter 18, you should be able to:

1. Define *thanatology*. (p. 588)

2. Describe recent developments in the field of *thanatology*. (p. 588)

3. List and define three aspects of death. (p. 589)

4. Describe young children's attitudes toward death. (pp. 589-590)

5. Describe adolescents' attitudes toward death. (p. 590)

6. Describe how attitudes toward death develop from early to late adulthood. (pp. 590-592)

7. Discuss attitudes of people of different ages as they confront the approach of their own death. (pp. 592-593)

8. Identify some intellectual and personality changes which people often undergo shortly before death. (pp. 592-593)

9. Describe the results of studies of *near-death experiences*. (p. 593)

10. Explain Kübler-Ross's five stages of coming to terms with death. (p. 593)

    denial

    anger

    bargaining

    depression

    acceptance

11. Compare and contrast the concepts of *bereavement*, *mourning*, and *grief*. (p. 593)

12. Describe how *mourning* attitudes and practices vary in different cultures. (pp. 594-596)

13. Describe the various forms of *grief*. (pp. 596-598)

14. Describe the three phases that characterize the pattern of "grief work." (p. 597)

15. Summarize the five common beliefs about loss and the findings that these beliefs may not be valid. (pp. 597-598)

16. Describe the special aspects of mourning associated with grieving and mourning by children. (pp. 598-599)

17. Explain how the following are ways of helping people deal with dying and *bereavement*:

    grief therapy (p. 599)

    hospice (pp. 599-600)

    support groups and services (p. 600)

    death education (pp. 600)

18. Discuss the problem of adjusting to the death of a spouse. (pp. 601-602)

19. Describe living as a widow or widower. (p. 602-603)

20. Discuss the following controversial issues regarding death and dying.

    euthanasia and the right to die (pp. 603-605)

    suicide (p. 605)

21. Differentiate between *active euthanasia* and *passive euthanasia*. (p. 603-605)

22. Outline the common provisions of a *"living will."* (p. 605)

23. Describe patterns of suicide among different age groups. (pp. 605-608)

24. Describe some actions that can be taken to help prevent suicide. (pp. 608-610)

25. Discuss the challenge of finding a purpose in life and death and factors which most influence attitudes. (pp. 610-611)

26. Discuss the *life review* and its benefits. (pp. 611-612)

SUPPLEMENTAL READING

The loss of a child is the most devastating thing that can happen to parents; grieving together can help a couple through the worst moments. This article by Diane Cole, the author of *After Great Pain: A New Life Emerges*, is reprinted with permission from the March 1994 issue of *Parents* magazine, Gruner + Jahr USA Publishing.

When A Child Dies

Diane Cole

"Peter was born the day after Mother's Day in 1990, and that Father's Day was just a wonderful celebration with my husband, Phil, and our other kids, Hannah and Andrew," recalls Ruth Skopek, of Bowie, Maryland.

"But the next day when I picked him up, it was like a movie in slow motion. He was cold and stiff, and his face looked like a mask with a ring of purple."

Terrified, she ran to the phone and dialed 911. "I heard this scream going off in my head even while I was giving Peter CPR. Then I realized it was like breathing into a brick wall because his tongue was cold."

Every parent's nightmare had happened to Ruth. Peter Skopek had died of sudden infant death syndrome at the age of 5 weeks.

The death of a child inevitably brings parents feelings of shock, rage, devastation, and despair. And because children are in a very real sense a part of ourselves as well as our future, "The loss of a child is the most significant, most long-lasting of all griefs," according to Catherine M. Sanders, Ph.D., a psychologist specializing in bereavement issues, and the author of *How to Survive the Loss of a Child* (Prima Publishing).

It is a loss that defies expectations and betrays belief in a safe and orderly world, not only for the parents but also for friends and family members who may wish to be helpful and yet who feel paralyzed by their own anguish and fear. The journey through grief is never easy, but knowing more about what helps and what does not can help everyone ease the pain.

And though it may not seem possible at the time, life will go on--although differently. Thus, two and a half years after Peter's death, Ruth Skopek puts her life in perspective this way: "We've had another little boy--not a replacement, because you can never replace a child--but a natural extension of our family. And though I never thought I'd be able to feel this, my life is really good again. But I am the mother of four children raising three children, and that will always hurt."

Ruth's acknowledgement of grief as a fact of life is natural, notwithstanding the conventional wisdom (or perhaps just wishful thinking) that tells us to "climb back in the saddle" and without a backward glance. But do you ever "get over" the loss of a child? How could you, psychologists and parents alike ask, if "getting over" a loss means forgetting the child you raised?

The Urgent Need to Remember the Child

"Some bereaved parents think they have to forget--that that's what they are supposed to do," says Irene Pollin, a Washington, D.C. area psychiatric social worker who established a foundation in memory of her daughter, who died at 16. "They have a very hard time because what you really want to do is hold on to the spirit of the child."

"Now, this doesn't mean that you're neurotic or holding on to grief," adds Pollin. "It just means that you're holding on to both the memory and a very special relationship."

"Many people will say to bereaved parents, "Don't dwell on it; get on with your life!" affirms Ronald J. Knapp, Ph.D., professor of sociology at Clemson University, in South Carolina. "But remembering--the desire never, ever, to forget the child--is what gives a sense of meaning to these parents' lives. And getting on with life means finding one that will incorporate the memory of the child in some meaningful way." That is why, for many bereaved parents, *not* talking about the child can be the most hurtful blow of all.

The first Christmas after their son Kyle's death at 7 months from spinal muscular atrophy (a form of muscular dystrophy), Lee and Stuart M., of central New Jersey, felt disheartened when family members did not acknowledge Kyle in the traditional predinner holiday grace. "They said they didn't want to make us sad by remembering," Lee says. "But we didn't want to sweep Kyle's name or memory under the rug."

"Later, we all sat down and had a long, hard but ultimately wonderful discussion that cleared the air. Now, at Christmas and Thanksgiving, the blessing includes Kyle and other people who are no longer with us." And there will be a Christmas stocking hung for Kyle this year and every year, right beside the one for Lee and Stuart's new infant daughter.

In order to remember, many bereaved parents find it helpful to write memoirs or journals, make scrapbooks, or compile a videotape that they will always have. In a similar vein, many also donate, help raise money, or volunteer on behalf of a scholarship, charity, research fund, or other organization that in some way pays tribute to their child's memory while also helping someone else.

The parents' urgent need to remember--and talk about--their child is also why support groups, private counseling, and just talking informally to other bereaved parents can be the most effective sources of help and comfort.

"I remember the first person I spoke to about volunteering at Mothers Against Drunk Driving (MADD), hearing about her daughter's death, and suddenly feeling, 'I'm talking to someone who actually understands what I feel'," recalls Denise McDonald, victim-services coordinator of MADD-Illinois, whose 19-year-old son, Sean, died in a car crash in 1986. "It was comforting to me because I could see that she was still functioning, still alive, and I thought that maybe I could survive this horror, too. Now, one of the things I do in my job is to tell grieving parents, 'You are not crazy; this is a normal reaction to something that is crazy'."

Getting through the First Weeks and Months

By listening to one another, bereaved parents can also reinforce the lesson that there is no single "right" way to mourn and that the stages of grief come at a different pace for everyone. For most, however, the first few weeks and months seem like an unending nightmare. Indeed, Linda N. Edelstein, Ph.D., a psychologist in Evanston, Illinois, found that for mothers, the first year after a child's death lacks all meaning, so much so that some of the women she interviewed for a study that she did on maternal grieving flirted with thoughts of suicide.

Even more universal are ever present thoughts of the dead child. For Ruth Skopek, for instance, the first few months came and went in blankness: "All I wanted to talk about or could think about--the only thing that was real--was the loss."

Gradually the pain lessens, although Edelstein says that, "up to six years afterward, the mothers were still coping. It didn't end--it changed."

"It does get better," Denise McDonald concurs. "I don't think of Sean every single minute of every single day. But there are still days that are bad. Grief is not an event. It is a process that can take your whole life."

"You simply cannot put a time limit on grief," echoes Karen Kemp, a teacher's aide in New York City whose 7-year-old daughter, Bethany, died in a car accident in 1991. "It bugs me when people say that things will be better after the first year, because there's nothing magical about reaching that first anniversary. In a way, for me, the pain was worse the second year because I'd gone through a whole year without hearing my child's voice."

Eventually, though, the acute, torrential storm of grief comes to resemble a cloud hovering overhead--a feeling that Ronald Knapp calls "shadow grief." "Shadow grief is like a common cold that you just cannot shake," he says. "It's a dull, background ache that you can't get rid of. It lifts its head and looks you in the eye on birthdays, death days, all the times that children are supposed to be present in our lives."

There are as many ways to mourn as there are people who have suffered a loss.

Months and years later, strong feelings can be triggered without warning. For instance, watching parents drop off their children on the first day of school more than a year after her daughter died, Karen found herself so overwhelmed that she nearly fainted.

"The first feelings of not being able to take her to school were so painful that I literally had to sit down because I thought I was going to pass out," she recalls. "It had been more than a year since Bethany died, and I just wasn't prepared for those emotions. Later, though, I was also able to feel grateful for having had the opportunity to enjoy the years I had with Bethany."

Because we all grieve differently, however close marriage may be, husband and wife will also mourn in his or her own way--a disparity that can lead to additional misunderstandings and tension at an already difficult, painful time.

The bereaved mothers that psychologist Linda Edelstein spoke to said that they benefitted from having friends who rallied around them; their husbands, however, had fewer people to turn to. This difference stemmed from the men's feelings that they had to seem strong at the office; to do otherwise would not have seemed manly. Yet, a bereaved mother who needs to talk may misinterpret her quieter husband's stoicism for a lack of feeling, and vice versa.

"Our griefs are very personal," says Lee M. of the ways in which she and her husband, Stuart, have mourned for Kyle. "I think Stuart grieved more for the son that he wouldn't have, and afterward he would get very sad when he saw a little blonde 2- or 3- or 4-year-old. But because I knew from the time of Kyle's diagnosis that his life would be very short, I never imagined his growing to that age, and that image did not trouble me as much.

"Instead, as the primary caretaker, I grieved more for the physical nurturing that I longed for. I did not feel whole anymore," Lee continues. "At first there wasn't any reason to get up in the morning because there wasn't any diapering or holding or feeding. My arms and my life both felt very empty."

Support Groups Help

For Lee and Stuart, support groups and family counseling helped ease these differences--and helped them soothe each other--both during Kyle's illness and after his death. "Stuart and I were never at odds with each other. We were able to support each other, and we made it a priority to allow ourselves to grieve," Lee remembers.

Ruth Skopek also found support groups helpful in understanding differences between her own grief and her husband's. "I was at home, taking care of the children, and suddenly the responsibility of parenthood really weighed heavily on me. "If something happens again to a child in my care," I thought, "I don't know if I'll be able to handle that," she says.

"But Phil, having gone back to work, did not have that particular feeling, and I found myself getting angry at him because he was able to escape these emotions," Ruth continues. "But because the support group had warned us in advance that spouses can feel differently, we were prepared and knew that emotions can come out that don't have to do with your *spouse* but with your own grief bottled up inside."

Unbottling those feelings also can help the deceased child's surviving siblings, psychologist Catherine Sanders emphasizes. "When the children learn that it's okay to talk about their feelings, they can feel that their emotions are okay too. Instead of feeling isolated, they will see that their parents are there to help them work things through."

Seeking Comfort through Religious Faith

For many, religious faith also offers solace and support. Ronald Knapp estimates that about 70 percent of bereaved parents seek comfort in faith. "We are devout Catholics, and when Peter died, I saw how much our faith did come through," Ruth Skopek says. "Believing in God doesn't mean terrible things won't happen, but it can help you through whatever does happen in life."

Many parents, like Karen Kemp, also hope to meet their children again in the afterlife. "Bethany is alive in heaven," she says, "and I have no doubt whatsoever that she is waiting for us."

But how much comfort is received from religious faith may depend on your beliefs beforehand, observes Linda Edelstein, who has found that those holding prior religious beliefs are more likely to find comfort through faith, while those who are not already religious rarely become so.

And so, perhaps most of all, a child's death challenges--and changes--a parent's perspective on life itself. "The death of a child results in a changed value system and lifestyle," says Knapp. "It makes them more tolerant and compassionate toward people who have had difficulties in life." Many parents devalue wealth, status, and materialistic views of success in favor of family and community, as well as of social or spiritual concerns, commitments, and responsibilities.

"After a shock like this, you look at people and wonder, 'Why are you so materialistic?'" says Lee M. "At work my husband would hear friends complain about their kids and wonder why they didn't realize how much they have!"

Karen Kemp adds, "Since this happened, I can't stand petty things. When I hear people gossiping, for instance, I just walk away."

Work, too, may come to seem mechanical and without meaning. "When Kyle died, I didn't want to go back to work, I wanted to be a mother," Lee recalls. Similarly, Denise McDonald says, "After Sean's death, I felt that everything in life was stupid, frivolous, without meaning."

But volunteer work--or paid work that reaches out to others in a meaningful way--can often help transform personal grief into a sense of new purpose and remembrance. Denise explains: "My volunteer work for MADD was the only thing that had meaning for me, but I couldn't afford to do only volunteer work. So when a paying job at MADD as victim-services director became available, I called and said, 'You have to hire me for this job'--and they did! I think that MADD saved my life by hiring me. Because anything I can do to alleviate someone else's pain is worthwhile."

How Friends and Family Can Really Help

Each bereaved parent will seek and find solace in his or her own way, but friends and family members can provide important and timely help by remembering--and by simply listening.

"Some of the things people say make you angry," Denise says, "because they minimize the pain with things like 'He's in a better place' and 'It's God's will,' or 'I know how you feel.' *Nobody* knows what I feel. No two people can feel precisely the same way."

Perhaps that is why the best thing to do is simply to say "I'm sorry" or to offer an embrace. Then let your friend know that you care by keeping in touch. Offer practical assistance such as cooking a meal, doing the grocery shopping, helping around the house, baby-sitting for the other children, or coaxing your friend outside to enjoy a sunny afternoon. Writing is another thoughtful expression. Ann Pleshette Murphy, editor-in-chief of *Parents*, remembers how much it helped her to receive letters after her baby died, no matter how simple the correspondence.

Karen Kemp remembers the wonderful outlet she found when friends got her and her husband out on the tennis court one day. "At the time, I felt so angry and sad that if you just looked at me the wrong way, I would cry. But when I started playing tennis, I was just hitting those balls and hitting them, and that exercise was a tremendous way of channeling what I felt."

Colleagues at work can provide similar support by noting--not ignoring--what happened. Karen felt a sense of "overwhelming support and comfort" just from seeing the many co-workers come to Bethany's memorial service. She was further touched to learn that so many teachers at Bethany's school had made donations in her memory and that the PTA had set up a Bethany Kemp Memorial Fund to purchase special-education equipment.

Keeping in touch as time passes--inviting the bereaved parents to spend time with your own family, for example--may also be perceived with gratitude, but do be sensitive to the different moods of grief. If the parents have lost their only child, it may be too painful at first for them to spend time with your children. Later, however, seeing their children's friends grow may create a special bond. Denise McDonald, for instance, has felt a sense of healing by maintaining friendships with her son's friends. "In some ways it is bittersweet to see them growing and to wonder what Sean would look like and what he'd be doing," she says, "and yet it touches me that they think of him and remember him."

"They make me think about a friend of mine whose daughter used to put a purple flower--scilla--in her hair. The first spring after her daughter's death, my friend just wanted to stomp that flower out whenever she saw it, because it lived and her daughter didn't," Denise continues. "But now my friend loves to see that purple flower each spring because she can still see it in her daughter's hair and that gives her joy."
But it took time for Denise's friend, and it takes time for everyone. The challenge is to find ways to remember; to remain connected to a relationship that will never die; and, regarding that we cope, to discover a way to go on, in mutual support and hope.

Questions:

How do peoples' responses to the death of a parent or older person differ from their responses to the death of a spouse or child?

Do you think that the phases of normal grief described in the textbook would be the same for the death of a child as for the death of an older person? Why?

SELF TESTS

Multiple-Choice

Circle the letter of the response which best completes or answers each of the following statements and questions.

1. The study of death and dying is known as
   a. thanatology
   b. mortology
   c. mortuary science
   d. deathology

2. Generally, death is most accurately defined, in biological terms, as cessation of
   a. heart activity
   b. brain activity
   c. bodily processes
   d. blood flow

3. Social aspects of death most properly include
   a. saying goodbye to friends before dying
   b. paying all debts before dying
   c. funeral and mourning rituals
   d. severance of all social contacts in preparation for death

4. The psychological aspects of death involve the
   a. rituals and customs that we use to help cope with the death of a loved one
   b. way people feel about their own death and that of those close to them
   c. termination of the three personality components; the id, ego, and superego
   d. failure to respond to any psychological processes such as conditioning

5. Children below about age 5 often believe that death is
   a. universal
   b. functional
   c. permanent
   d. reversible

6. Somewhere between the ages of 5 and 7, children's understanding of death begins to include the idea that death is
   a. irreversible and universal and that dead people are non-functional
   b. just physical and that the soul endures beyond physical death
   c. an event that is marked in all cultures with certain customs and rituals
   d. something that doesn't happen only to old people

7. Adolescents are generally concerned, not with how <u>long</u> they will live but rather with
   a. how long their <u>parents</u> will live
   b. <u>how</u> they will live
   c. how much fun they can have <u>before</u> they die
   d. how long their <u>friends</u> will live

8. Adolescents who are in mourning often feel more comfortable grieving with
   a. outsiders, whom they are less likely to know well
   b. family from "out of town," who are both close and distant
   c. strangers, whose opinions about their behavior can easily be dismissed
   d. their peers than with adults, around whom they feel embarrassed

9. The period of life when feelings about imminent death are likely to be strongest is
   a. childhood
   b. adolescence
   c. young adulthood
   d. middle adulthood

10. The age at which most people really know, deep inside, that they are going to die is
    a. childhood
    b. adolescence
    c. young adulthood
    d. middle adulthood

11. Compared to middle-aged people, older people are
    a. more anxious about death
    b. less anxious about death
    c. more likely to avoid thinking about death
    d. no different in their feelings toward death

12. Which of the following statements about attitudes toward death in late adulthood is most accurate?
    a. Older people, realizing and accepting their own mortality, tend to be less anxious about death than other age groups.
    b. Older people, realizing that death is drawing closer, become more fearful and anxious about death.
    c. Older people who feel that their lives have been full and meaningful are less able to accept the prospect of death.
    d. Older people, having lost many friends to death and losing their physical vigor, resent younger, healthier people.

13. Research has shown that, compared with people who were not near death, people within a year of death tended to
    a. score higher on cognitive tests
    b. be less introspective
    c. be more aggressive
    d. be less docile

14. People whose lives are stable, and who are close to death are
    a. likely to exhibit a special fear of death
    b. become preoccupied with death
    c. both show special fear of death and become preoccupied with death
    d. not likely to show special fear of death nor preoccupation with it

15. A feeling of well being, a new clarity of thinking, a sense of being out of one's body, and visions of bright lights are all characteristic of
    a. the effects of drugs used to ease the pain of dying
    b. a healthy acceptance of the inevitability of one's own death
    c. near-death experiences
    d. hallucinations resulting from the denial of imminent death

16. The person credited with having sparked the current interest in the psychology of death and dying is
    a. Jean Piaget
    b. Elizabeth Kübler-Ross
    c. Erik Erikson
    d. Lawrence Kohlberg

17. A dying person who says, "Why me?" is probably in which stage of dying?
    a. anger
    b. bargaining
    c. acceptance
    d. denial

18. A dying person whose first thought is, "This can't be happening to me," is probably in which stage of dying?
    a. anger
    b. bargaining
    c. acceptance
    d. denial

19. A dying person who prays, "If I can just see my son get married . . ." is probably in which stage of dying?
    a. anger
    b. bargaining
    c. acceptance
    d. denial

20. Mark is dying and says, "My time is very close now, and it's all right." Mark is probably in which stage of dying?
    a. anger
    b. bargaining
    c. acceptance
    d. denial

21. Behavior associated with death, such as an Irish wake or the Jewish shiva, is called
    a. mourning
    b. acceptance
    c. bereavement
    d. grief

22. The objective fact of loss is called
    a. mourning
    b. acceptance
    c. bereavement
    d. grief

23. The emotional response of a person experiencing loss is called
    a. mourning
    b. acceptance
    c. bereavement
    d. grief

24. Cross-cultural comparisons of grief and mourning indicate that
    a. there is no "best" way to cope with death
    b. grieving is best accomplished by breaking emotional ties to the deceased
    c. survivors should "get on with living" as soon as possible
    d. remembering the dead beyond a few days excessively prolongs mourning

25. Mourning before the actual death of a person is known as
    a. anticipatory grief
    b. pre-mourning
    c. premature grief
    d. impulsive mourning

26. The initial phase of grief, which may take several weeks, is called
    a. preoccupation
    b. summative
    c. shock and disbelief
    d. resolution

27. The phase of grieving during which one cannot yet accept the death, is called
    a. preoccupation
    b. summative
    c. shock and disbelief
    d. resolution

28. The stage when the bereaved resumes interest in everyday activities is called
    a. preoccupation
    b. summative
    c. shock and disbelief
    d. resolution

29. Research which studied reactions to a major loss, such as the death of a loved one, have shown that
    a. many common assumptions and beliefs about loss are surprisingly accurate
    b. many common assumptions and beliefs about loss are more myth than fact
    c. despite apparent cultural differences in mourning rituals, the underlying psychological reactions to loss are universal
    d. all people react to a major loss in similar ways but may express that reaction differently depending on the cultural context in which they live

30. In helping children cope with the death of someone close, it is best to
   a. avoid terms that emphasize the finality of death
   b. use terms like "death" and "die" to help them realize that death is final
   c. describe the deceased as "sleeping" or "resting" to ease the pain of their loss
   d. avoid discussing it to prevent them from becoming preoccupied with death

31. To help people face death better and to help make dying and bereavement more humane, several movements such as ____________________ have arisen.
   a. euthanasia suicide societies
   b. "death with dignity" organizations
   c. doctor assisted suicide programs
   d. hospice, grief therapy, and death education programs

32. The social, financial, and medical hardships that follow the death of a spouse
   a. are usually severe for women but barely noticeable for men survivors
   b. are usually severe for men but barely noticeable for women survivors
   c. often affect both men and women whose spouse has died
   d. affect only a small minority of men and women whose spouse has died

33. Killing a terminally ill person at his or her own request, or to end suffering, is called
   a. anticipatory grief
   b. euthanasia
   c. mercicide
   d. morbid grief

34. When an action is taken deliberately with the purpose of shortening a life it is called
   a. active euthanasia
   b. passive euthanasia
   c. deliberate assisted suicide
   d. inactive assisted suicide

35. Mercy killing as the result of withholding treatment that may extend life is called
   a. active euthanasia
   b. passive euthanasia
   c. deliberate assisted suicide
   d. inactive assisted suicide

36. A person's wishes regarding the use or non-use of life-sustaining treatment is often spelled out in a document called a
   a. medical release
   b. termination of treatment order
   c. death wish
   d. living will

37. Children diagnosed as suicidal had which of these traits?
   a. were more likely to cry after being hurt
   b. seemed less depressed
   c. were more aggressive
   d. all of the above

38. Adolescents who have attempted suicide tend to be
   a. unlikely to have a history of emotional illness or depression
   b. impulsive, have poor control, and have a low tolerance for frustration
   c. from stable, supportive, and financially secure families
   d. clinically no different from non-suicidal adolescents

39. Talking to someone about their suicidal thoughts is generally thought to be
   a. a mistake that could reinforce the validity of those thoughts
   b. wrong in that it could put ideas into an unstable person's mind
   c. a helpful way to bring feelings into the open
   d. a contributing factor in people following through on suicidal ideas

40. Reminiscence that enables a person to see the significance of his or her life is called
    a. preparatory morbidity
    b. anticipatory grief
    c. life review
    d. living will

Completion

Supply the term or terms needed to complete each of the following statements.

1. The study of death and dying is called ____________________.

2. Though legal definitions vary, in general, ____________ death is considered the cessation of bodily processes.

3. It is usually around the ages of 5 to 7 that children come to understand that death is __________--that a dead person, animal, or flower cannot come to life again.

4. At about 5 to 7, children realize that death is ___________ (all living things inevitably die), and that a dead person or thing is _______________ (all life functions end at death).

5. Of the different age groups, __________________tend to have highly "romantic" ideas about death.

6. It is in _______________ that most people really know, deep inside themselves, that they are indeed going to die.

7. _________________ changes often begin to take place even before physiological signs indicate that a person is dying.

8. _________________ often include a feeling of well-being, a new clarity of thinking, a sense of being out of one's body, and visions of bright lights.

9. ____________________ is the person widely credited with having inspired the current interest in the psychology of death and dying.

10. The five steps in coming to terms with dying, as proposed by Elisabeth Kübler-Ross, are ___________(refusal to accept the reality of what is happening), anger, bargaining for extra time, depression, and ultimate acceptance.

11. ________________ refers to the behavior of the bereaved and the community after a death.

12. The objective fact of loss is called ____________ .

13. When the family and friends of a person who has been ill for a long time prepare themselves for the loss before the person dies, they are said to be experiencing ________________________________.

14. ____________________________ with the memory of the person who has died is the second phase of grief work.

15. In normal grief, the initial phase, when survivors often feel lost, dazed and confused, is ____________________________.

16. The final phase of grief, ______________________________, has arrived when the bereaved person resumes interest in everyday activities.

17. A program to help the bereaved cope with their losses is called ____.

18. The ________________ movement began in response to a need for warm, personal patient- and family-centered care for the terminally ill.

19. ______________________________ refers to programs aimed at various age levels and groups to teach people about dying and grief and to help them deal with these issues in their personal and professional lives.

20. If for no other reason than that they live longer, widowhood is a burden that _______ are far likelier to carry than __________.

21. The people who adjust best to widowhood are those who keep busy, develop new roles, or become more deeply involved in _____________.

22. Many controversial issues of death and dying have arisen because of _____________________________ advances such as antibiotics and wonder drugs, respirators, and organ transplants.

23. Injecting a terminally ill person with a fatal dose of a drug to end his or her suffering is an example of ______________________________________.

24. Withholding treatment that might extend a person's life, such as medication, life-support systems, or feeding tubes, is known as __________________.

25. A person's wishes regarding the termination of life extending treatment can be spelled out in a document called a ___________________________.

26. Despite evidence which shows that suicide is increasing, statistics probably ______________________________ the number of suicides.

27. One of the warning signs of suicide is ___________ from family or friends.

28. According to Elisabeth Kübler-Ross, ____________________ is the key to personal growth and to the development of human potential.

29. Older people's natural tendency to talk about the people, events, and feelings of previous years is an important part of the ____________________ process.

30. Of the various types of reminiscences identified by researchers, those classified as ____________________________ help people to accept their pasts as worthwhile, resolve past conflicts, and reconcile the discrepancy between what they considered ideal and what really occurred.

ANSWERS FOR SELF-TESTS — CHPATER 18

Multiple-Choice

		Page				Page	
1.	a	588	factual	21.	a	593	factual
2.	c	589	factual	22.	c	593	factual
3.	c	589	factual	23.	d	593	factual
4.	b	589	factual	24.	a	596	conceptual
5.	d	590	conceptual	25.	a	596	factual
6.	a	590	conceptual	26.	c	597	conceptual
7.	b	590	conceptual	27.	a	597	conceptual
8.	d	590	conceptual	28.	d	597	conceptual
9.	c	591	factual	29.	b	597	conceptual
10.	d	591	factual	30.	b	598	conceptual
11.	b	591	conceptual	31.	d	599	factual
12.	a	591	conceptual	32.	c	601-602	conceptual
13.	b	592	conceptual	33.	b	603	factual
14.	d	592	conceptual	34.	a	603	factual
15.	c	592	factual	35.	b	604	factual
16.	b	593	factual	36.	d	605	factual
17.	a	593	conceptual	37.	c	606	factual
18.	d	593	conceptual	38.	b	607	factual
19.	b	593	conceptual	39.	c	610	conceptual
20.	c	593	conceptual	40.	c	611	factual

Completion

		Page			Page
1.	thanatology	588	16.	resolution	597
2.	biological	589	17.	grief therapy	599
3.	irreversible	590	18.	hospice	599
4.	universal; nonfunctional	590	19.	death education	600
5.	adolescents	590	20.	women; men	601
6.	middle age	591	21.	activities	602
7.	psychological	592	22.	technological	603
8.	near-death experiences	592	23.	active euthanasia	603
9.	Elisabeth Kübler-Ross	593	24.	passive euthanasia	604
10.	denial	593	25.	living will	605
11.	mourning	593	26.	understate	605
12.	bereavement	593	27.	withdrawal	610
13.	anticipatory grief	596	28.	awareness of death	610
14.	preoccupation	597	29.	life-review	611
15.	shock and disbelief	597	30.	integrative	611